The White Racial Frame

In this book Joe Feagin extends the systemic racism framework in previous Routledge books by developing an innovative concept, the white racial frame. Now four centuries old, this white racial frame encompasses not only the stereotyping, bigotry, and racist ideology emphasized in other theories of "race," but also the visual images, array of emotions, sounds of accented language, interlinking interpretations and narratives, and inclinations to discriminate that are still central to the frame's everyday operations. Deeply imbedded in American minds and institutions, this white racial frame has for centuries functioned as a broad worldview, one essential to the routine legitimation, scripting, and maintenance of systemic racism in the United States. Here Feagin examines how and why this white racial frame emerged in North America, how and why it has evolved socially over time, which racial groups are framed within it, how it has operated in the past and in the present for both white Americans and Americans of color, and how the latter have long responded with strategies of resistance that include enduring counter-frames.

In this new edition, Feagin has included much new interview material and other data from recent research studies on framing issues related to white, black, Latino, and Asian Americans, and on society generally. The book also includes a new discussion of the impact of the white frame on popular culture, including on movies, video games, and television programs as well as a discussion of the white racial frame's significant impacts on public policymaking on immigration, the environment, health care, and crime and imprisonment issues.

Joe R. Feagin is Ella C. McFadden Professor at Texas A&M University. Feagin has done much research on racism and sexism issues for forty-nine years and has served as the Scholar-in-Residence at the U.S. Commission on Civil Rights. He has written fifty-nine scholarly books and more than 200 scholarly articles in his research areas, and one of his books (*Ghetto Revolts*) was nominated for a Pulitzer Prize. His recent books include *Systemic Racism* (Routledge 2006) and *White Party, White Government* (Routledge 2012). He is the 2006 recipient of a Harvard alumni association's lifetime achievement award and was the 1999–2000 president of the American Sociological Association.

The White Racial Frame

Centuries of Racial Framing and Counter-Framing

Second Edition
Joe R. Feagin

 Routledge
Taylor & Francis Group

NEW YORK AND LONDON

Second edition first published 2013
by Routledge
711 Third Avenue, New York, NY 10017

Simultaneously published in the UK
by Routledge
2 Park Square, Milton Park, Abingdon, Oxon OX14 4RN

Routledge is an imprint of the Taylor & Francis Group, an informa business

First edition published by Routledge 2009

Library of Congress Cataloging in Publication Data
Feagin, Joe R.
  The white racial frame : centuries of racial framing and counter-
framing / Joe R. Feagin. — 2nd ed.
    p. cm.
  Includes bibliographical references and index.
  1. United States—Race relations. 2. Race discrimination—United States.
  3. African-Americans—United States—Social conditions. 4. African-
  Americans—United States—Public opinion. 5. Whites—United
  States—Attitudes. I. Title.
  E184.A1F395 2013
  305.800973—dc23

                                                        2012031133

ISBN: 978-0-415-65761-7 (hbk)
ISBN: 978-0-415-63522-6 (pbk)
ISBN: 978-0-203-07682-8 (ebk)

Typeset in Minion
by RefineCatch Limited, Bungay, Suffolk
Printed and bound by CPI Group (UK) Ltd, Croydon, CR0 4YY

Contents

Preface

In November 2008, more than two centuries after this country's founding, Senator Barack Obama became the first American of color to win the U.S. presidency. He won nearly 53 percent of the national vote, compared to about 46 percent for his white opponent, Senator John McCain. Since Obama's election, the increase in emphasis on the United States being post-racial has been dramatic, especially among whites and in the mainstream media.

Like many media outlets, the national business newspaper the *Wall Street Journal*, framed Barack Obama's election as a great tribute to how democratic and non-racist the United States now is:

> A man of mixed race has now reached the pinnacle of U.S. power only two generations since the end of Jim Crow. This is a tribute to American opportunity, and it is something that has never happened in another Western democracy—notwithstanding European condescension about "racist" America.[1]

After the assertion of moral superiority over Europe, this white-framed editorial added: "One promise of his victory is that perhaps we can put to rest the myth of racism as a barrier to achievement in this splendid country. Mr. Obama has a special obligation to help do so."[2]

Writing from a common white viewpoint, this editorial writer called on President-elect Obama to lead an effort to kill the supposed "myth of racism." But did this important election really signal a major decline in U.S. racism? Even the election itself was revealing on this score. While it was not as close as the two previous presidential elections, it was close enough that a shift of just 4 percent or so of the total voters from Obama to McCain would have given McCain a presidential victory. Significantly, one recent social science study examined the many racially charged Internet searches by people for the word "nigger" for most of the 200 U.S. media markets in 2008, and compared those searches (as a proxy for anti-black prejudice) to an area's votes for Obama. The researcher suggests from these data on racially charged searches that candidate Obama likely lost a significant percentage of 2008 white voters because he was black.[3] Indeed, if it had only been up to white voters in 2008, Senator McCain would have become the 44th U.S. president, for he won an estimated 55 percent of the white vote nationally, and a substantial majority of white voters in thirty-two of the fifty states. In contrast, more than two thirds of voters of color voted for Senator Obama.[4]

The United States came out of the 2008 presidential election as still quite racially polarized. Researchers have shown that about half of all the presidential votes cast in 2008 were in counties where Senator Obama or Senator McCain won by at least 20 percent of the total vote. The percentage of voters residing in these very polarized "landslide" counties grew substantially from 27 percent in 1976 to 48 percent in 2008. Even more striking was the racial polarization. Those counties where candidate McCain won with a landslide margin of 20 percent or more were overwhelmingly white, with the black and Latino voting age population averaging only a sixth of those counties' populations. Where Obama won a county, in contrast, the black and Latino population averaged about 43 percent of the voting age population. Paralleling this voter polarization, moreover, was the continuing and extensive residential and school segregation that is revealed in much research on U.S. towns and cities.[5] Even with the election of the first African American president in 2008, the harsh realities of institutional racism in major sectors of U.S. society have remained quite evident to the present day.

Today, those who do this significant research and analysis of U.S. racial patterns frequently make use of a disease metaphor, such as the idea that racism is a "cancer" in the "body" of society. In a recent search for phrases like "racism is a cancer" or the "cancer of racism" in published research papers and popular articles, I found thousands of uses of this strong metaphor. The commonplace idea is that racism is an unhealthy social condition, one stemming from pathogenic conditions in an otherwise healthy societal body. Yet, this view is inadequate. Our society was built from the beginning with racial oppression as a central part of its societal structure. In this sense, there never was a "healthy" societal body that the cancer of racism could invade.

A better metaphor is that of white-imposed racism as an important part of the structural "foundation" of the U.S. "house." Racial oppression was not added later on in the development of this society, but was the foundation of the original colonial and U.S. social systems, and it still remains as a U.S. foundation. This structural-foundation metaphor relates much better to the historical and contemporary reality of this country. I have searched hundreds of relevant scholarly papers and many Internet websites for phrases like "racial foundation of the United States," the "country's racial foundation," and the "nation's racial foundation," and not one such phrase appeared other than my own. In light of the historical and contemporary data assessed throughout this book, this structural-foundation metaphor captures the realities of this country's racism, past and present, better than a disease metaphor.

This societal reality is significantly different from that of other leading industrialized countries in the West. Countries like Great Britain and France were central to centuries of European colonialism, including the Atlantic slave trade and slave plantations in the Americas, but their early and later growth as nations was not built directly on an internal labor force of enslaved Africans or on local lands stolen by recent conquests of indigenous people.

Knowing North American racial history is important for making sense out of the current realities of this society. For many years, I have been researching this history in an attempt to analyze accurately the major impacts on U.S. culture and institutions of this country's foundation in systemic racism. The United States is a country with systemic racial oppression—centuries of genocide, about 246 years of slavery, and about ninety years of Jim Crow, altogether most of our history.

In this book I am especially influenced by the long tradition of black countersystem analysis—such as that of Frederick Douglass, W. E. B. Du Bois, Kwame Ture, Derrick Bell, and Angela Davis—that has regularly highlighted the institutional and systemic character of racial oppression over these centuries. Following in this tradition, and drawing on others critically analyzing societal oppression, we will examine here numerous lasting legacies of past racial oppression in our contemporary patterns of racism. We will assess the evidence of systemic racism in the colonial and U.S. economic, legal, and political systems, to the present day. As in the past, *systemic racism* today includes:

1. the complex array of recurring exploitative, discriminatory, and other oppressive white practices targeting Americans of color;
2. the institutionalized economic and other social resource inequalities along racial lines (the racial hierarchy); and

3. the dominant white racial frame that was generated to rationalize and insure white privilege and dominance over Americans of color.

Systemic here means that the oppressive racist realities have from the early decades been well institutionalized and manifested in all of this society's major parts. Break a three-dimensional hologram into separate parts and shine a laser through any one, and you can project the whole three-dimensional image again from that part. Much like this hologram, major parts of this society—such as the economy, politics, education, religion, and the family—reflect in numerous ways the fundamental reality of systemic racism.

In this book I focus mainly on systemic racism's harsh reality as it operates in and through what I call the *white racial frame*—the dominant racial frame that has long legitimated, rationalized, and shaped racial oppression and inequality in this country. This white racial frame is a centuries-old worldview that has constantly involved a racial construction of societal reality by white Americans. I explain this frame in detail in the next chapter, but let us consider a brief example of it in everyday use. In a recent research study of black pilots with major airlines, one senior pilot noted well how the white racial frame plays out in his life:

> At the hotel, I can be standing there waiting for the van to take us to the airport and [white] passengers have come up and dropped their bags at my feet on more than one occasion. I was flying with a black captain and we were waiting in the lobby, in full uniform, and a white guy walked up to him and said, "Can you get my cab for me?" The captain looked at him and said, "The only thing we know how to do is fly airplanes." The man said, "I understand that, but can you get my cab for me?" He just couldn't get it through his mind that he was talking to a pilot.[6]

In this recent incident a white man actively reveals his racially stereotyped framing of black men. He does not "see" the uniforms of these black pilots or the possibility that they are indeed major airline pilots, but rather only observes them as *black men*. Even after being corrected, the white man does not "get it." This racial framing is firmly fixed in his mind.

Throughout this book I discuss many aspects of the white racial framing of numerous important U.S. groups, including not only white Americans and African Americans, but also Latinos, Native Americans, and Asian Americans. My analysis of the framing and experiences of these groups will be integrated into various chapters, but I pay more attention to the framing and experiences of African Americans. In addition to spatial limits in this short book, a main reason for this emphasis is that social science research shows that most whites have a much more developed and detailed racial framing of black Americans than they do of other Americans of color. The contemporary Native American, Latino, and Asian American subframes of the dominant white frame are, as we will see, quite important and very damaging, but seem on the whole less fully developed than the black subframe of the dominant white frame. After centuries of continuing white oppression of African Americans in most regions, and centuries of racial framing rationalizing that oppression, African Americans today remain very central to the dominant white racial frame. Whites have made this to be so.

For the period of North American development from the seventeenth century to the present, I track in this book the character, persistence, impact, and evolution of this well-developed white racial framing. I accent its holistic and gestalt character. As I will show, this omnipresent white frame encompasses much more than verbal-cognitive elements, such as racial stereotyping and ideology, concepts emphasized by many analysts. Considered more comprehensively, the white racial frame includes a broad and persisting *set of racial stereotypes, prejudices, ideologies, interlinked interpretations and narratives, and visual images*. It also includes *racialized emotions* and *racialized reactions to language accents* and *imbeds inclinations to discriminate*. This white racial frame, like most social frames, operates to assist people in defining, interpreting, conforming to, and acting in their everyday social worlds.

Today, as in the past, this dominant racial frame is taught in many different ways to people young and old—at home, in schools, on public playgrounds, in the media, in workplace settings, in courts, and in politicians' speeches and corporate decisions. This frame rationalizes and structures the racial interactions, inequalities, and other racial patterns in an array of societal settings. It routinely operates in both the micro (interpersonal) and macro (institutional) areas of society.

In my view the best social science is interpretive, searching for complex webs of meanings connecting individuals and their groups and larger institutions, and thoroughly empirical, bringing relevant data to bear on important societal questions. Here I use a broad interpretive approach that examines complexities of interpersonal and intergroup meanings and relationships in our racialized institutions and that brings much empirical data, historical and contemporary, to bear on critical questions about how this society works in its everyday racialized operations.

Overview of Revisions and the Chapters

Responding to students and other readers, I have added throughout this edition numerous revisions and updates to the chapters. I have included much new interview material and other data on framing issues related to white, black, Latino, and Asian Americans, and on society generally, from recent research studies.

Throughout the book I have clarified and expanded important points about the white racial frame, counter-frames, and home-culture frames, and I have added additional analysis of related concepts such as white character structure and collective memory in regard to U.S. racial history.

In Chapter 6 I have added an extensive new discussion of the impact of the white frame on popular culture, including on movies, video games, and television programs.

In Chapter 7 I have added a major new discussion of the white racial frame's significant impacts on public policymaking on immigration, the environment, health care, and crime and imprisonment issues.

In the concluding Chapter 9 I have also added a substantial new discussion of contemporary anti-racist groups and their often successful educational and other activist strategies.

Here is a brief overview. Chapter 1 explains why we need a new social science perspective that goes beyond conventional approaches accenting traditional non-systemic concepts such as prejudice, stereotyping, and discrimination by bigots. I assess the Eurocentric and white-centered perspectives of classical and contemporary social scientists, and then explain the concept of the white racial frame and its dimensions. After assessing the importance of white groups in perpetuating the frame, I examine the concepts of home-culture frames and counter-frames, those developed by Americans of color to cope with the dominant white frame.

Chapter 2 examines the development of this country's system of racial oppression, including its racial hierarchy and racialized capital, over centuries of European colonialism, land theft, and African American enslavement. I assess this history of material oppression and unjust enrichment for Europeans and European Americans, especially as it has been supported by, and integrated into, this country's major legal and political institutions.

Chapter 3 assesses the rationalization and legitimation of this North American exploitation and oppression in the emerging white racial frame, with its pro-white and anti-others subframes. I explore the background of the white frame in "great chain of being" framing and analyze early negative framing of Native Americans and African Americans. Then I highlight the central role of elite whites in generating and maintaining the important elements of the dominant racial frame.

Chapter 4 examines the development of the white racial frame from the late eighteenth century to the twentieth century. I give attention to the early racist framing of white founders and later leaders, racism in popular culture, the white obsession with black Americans, and the extension of the racial frame to other Americans. Later sections assess the role of powerful whites in perpetuating the white frame through the Jim Crow era.

Chapter 5 moves to an examination of the contemporary white racial frame, with attention to new variations and the persistence of old pro-white and anti-others elements. I analyze how the contemporary frame is learned, its colorblind variation and emotions, and its continuing preoccupation with the negative framing of black Americans. I also assess the continuing white racist framing of Native Americans, Latinos, and Asian Americans and provide a conclusion evaluating the impact of some racist framing in the contemporary physical sciences.

Chapter 6 provides numerous examples of the routine implementation of white framing in contemporary white actions, including in backstage settings such as racist parties and in frontstage interactions with Americans of color. I examine important cases of pro-white and anti-others racial framing in popular culture, especially in video gaming and movies and television programs. I conclude with an examination of the impact of whites' racist framing and actions on Americans of color.

Chapter 7 examines the impact and operation of the white racial frame in important U.S. institutions, including legal, political, and economic institutions in the past and present. I evaluate the impact of the white frame on contemporary public policymaking in regard to immigration, the environment, health care, and criminal justice, as well as for U.S. foreign policy. I also examine other global impacts of the white frame.

Chapter 8 assesses in detail the counter-frames and home-culture frames developed and implemented over the centuries by African Americans, Native Americans, Latinos, and Asian Americans to cope with and resist the messages and impacts of the white racial frame.

Chapter 9 reviews pressures and possibilities for moving beyond systemic racism and its white frame to a truly democratic and egalitarian society. I give significant attention to racial change issues—deframing and reframing away from the white frame, teaching whites to listen to people of color, education on dissent, and how anti-racist groups have sometimes been successful in working for change. Concluding sections examine the need for reparations for those suffering from the impact of centuries of racial oppression, the societal costs from persisting oppression, and the societal benefits likely to result from major changes in the social justice direction.

Acknowledgments

I am greatly indebted to many colleagues, students, and others who over recent years have helped me sort out and document the general and specific research issues raised in this book. I cannot name them all, but among them are Jennifer Mueller, Ruth Thompson-Miller, Leslie Houts Picca, Kristen Lavelle, Hilario Molina, Todd Couch, Glenn Bracey, Sean Elias, Reuben May, Clarence Munford, Ben Carrington, Chris Chambers, Shari Valentine, Rosalind Chou, Herbert Perkins, Margery Otto, Carolyn Pegg, Tim Johnson, Bundy Trinz, Zinobia Bennefield, Pat Bell, Yanick St. Jean, Sean Chaplin, Brittany Slatton, Nick Lalone, and Dan Rigney. I am especially indebted to the late Melvin Sikes, Hernán Vera, Jessie Daniels, Maria Chávez-Pringle, Wendy Moore, Adia Harvey Wingfield, Bernice Barnett, Louwanda Evans, Nestor Rodriguez, and Terrence Fitzgerald for extensive discussions, data sources, and suggestions on racism issues raised in this book over some years. I would also like to thank the reviewers for Routledge for comments on improving this edition: David Brunsma, University of Missouri; Maria Chávez-Pringle, Pacific Lutheran University; Elizabeth Higginbotham, University of Delaware; Emily Noelle Ignacio, University of Washington; Anita Kalunta-Crumpton, Texas Southern University; David Leonard, Washington State University; Wendy Leo Moore, Texas A&M University; and Charles Quist-Adade, Kwantlen Polytechnic University.

This book is dedicated to Americans of all backgrounds, especially Americans of color, who have sacrificed greatly to move this country in the direction of the old but still unfulfilled ideals of liberty and justice for all.

The White Racial Frame

The better we know our racial past, the better we know our racial present. The United States is a fairly young country, just over 400 years old if we date its beginning from Jamestown's settlement. For much of this history, extreme racial oppression in the form of slavery and legal segregation was our foundational reality. The first successful English colony was founded at Jamestown in 1607, and in 1619 the first Africans were purchased there by English colonists from a Dutch-flagged slave ship. It was exactly 350 years from 1619 to 1969, the year the last major civil rights law went into effect officially ending legal segregation. Few people realize that for most of our history we were a country grounded in, and greatly shaped by, extensive slavery and legal segregation.

In terms of time and space, we are today not far from our famous "founding fathers." There have been just three long human lifetimes since the 1776 Declaration of Independence was proclaimed, a document principally authored by the prominent slaveholder Thomas Jefferson. We are just two long human lifetimes from the 13th amendment (1865) to the U.S. Constitution that ended two-plus centuries of human slavery. And we are only one human lifetime from the era when segregationist mobs brutally lynched African Americans and other Americans of color, and when many whites, including Supreme Court justices and Senators, were members of the Ku Klux Klan, the world's oldest violence-oriented white supremacist group. For a bit more than four decades, we have been an officially "free" country without large-scale legal discrimination. Certainly, that is not enough time for this country to eradicate the great and deep structural impacts of three and a half centuries of extreme racial oppression that preceded the current era. Much social science analysis of major aspects of this society today reveals the continuing impact and great significance of the *systemic racism* created by these centuries of extreme oppression.

Let us consider briefly some spatial impacts. In its geographical patterns the twenty-first century United States demonstrates the impact of this oppressive past. Even a brief study of the demographic map reveals that a substantial majority of African Americans today live in just fifteen of the fifty U.S. states—and very disproportionately in southern and border states. In these states, as elsewhere, the majority of these "old stock" Americans reside in relatively segregated areas of towns and cities. In many cities there are still the infamous railroad tracks, as well as major highways, that divide them into communities of mostly whites and communities of mostly people of color. Why is this segregated residential pattern still the reality in what is termed an "advanced democracy"? The answer lies in centuries of slavery, legal segregation, and contemporary racial discrimination that have set firmly in place and maintained this country's important geographical contours.

In a great many cases, these racially segregated areas and geographical dividing lines are not recent creations, but have been shaped by white decisionmakers' actions over a long period of time. Consider too that these distinctive areal patterns signal much more than information about our geographical realities, for they have many serious consequences for much that goes on in society. We can see this clearly, to take one example, in the racially polarized voting patterns for the landmark 2008 election noted in the Preface.

Well into this twenty-first century, racial segregation and separation along the color line are very much a major part of our psychic geography. Racial separation affects the ways in which white Americans view society, especially on racial matters. The evidence of white denial and ignorance of the reality of U.S. racism is substantial. For example, one national survey of 779 whites found that 61 percent viewed the average black person as having health care access at least equal to that of the average white person. Yet, research data show whites are far more likely to have good health insurance and to get adequate medical care than black Americans. About half the white respondents felt that black Americans had a level of education similar to or better than that of whites. Half the white respondents felt that, on average, whites and blacks are about as well off in the jobs they hold. Once again, the research data show that neither view is accurate. When the results of several such questions were combined, 70 percent of whites were found to hold one or more erroneous beliefs about important white-black differentials in life conditions. Only one in five whites evaluated the current societal situation accurately on a question about how much discrimination African Americans faced. The majority of whites are willfully ignorant or misinformed when it comes to understanding the difficult life conditions that African Americans and other Americans of color face today. Interestingly, in another survey white respondents were asked if they "often have sympathy for blacks" and again if they "often feel admiration for blacks." Only 5 percent of whites said yes to both questions.[1]

One goal of this book is to examine why so many whites believe what is in fact not true about important racial realities. In insisting on apparently sincere fictions about life conditions of African Americans and other Americans of color, a great many whites exhibit serious collective denial in believing what is demonstrably untrue. The principal reason for these strong racialized views is the *white racial frame*. As I noted in the Preface, this dominant frame is an overarching white worldview that encompasses a *broad and persisting set of racial stereotypes, prejudices, ideologies, images, interpretations and narratives, emotions, and reactions to language accents, as well as racialized inclinations to discriminate.* For centuries now, it has been a dominant and foundational frame from which a substantial majority of white Americans—as well as many others accepting or seeking to conform to white norms and perspectives—view our still highly racialized society.

Mainstream Social Science: The Need for a New Paradigm

Traditional social science and other mainstream academic and popular analysis has mostly portrayed U.S. racism as mainly a matter of racial "prejudice," "bias," and "stereotyping"—of racial attitudes directed at outgroups that indicate an ethnocentric view of the world and incline individuals to take part in bigotry-generated discrimination. Much recent research on racial matters continues to emphasize the prejudice and bias terminology and approach in assessing what are often termed racial "disparities," a common term for inequalities. These concepts, although certainly useful, are far from sufficient to assess and explain the foundational and systemic racism of the United States. We need more powerful concepts like *systemic racism* and *the white racial frame* that enable us to move beyond the limitations of conventional scientific approaches. Traditional approaches do not capture or explain the deep structural realities of this society's racial oppression in the past or present.

The dominant paradigm of an established science makes it hard for scientists to move in a major new direction in thinking or research. Most scientists stay mostly inside the dominant paradigmatic "box" because of concern for their careers or accepted scientific constraints. One important barrier to developing new social science paradigms is that new views of society are regularly screened for conformity to preferences of elite decision-makers in academia or in society generally. This vetting and validation process is implemented by research-granting agencies, faculty advisors in academic programs, promotion reviews, and media or other public criticism of scholars who significantly deviate.[2]

Today, most mainstream social science analysis of racial matters is undertaken and accepted because it more or less conforms to the preferences of most elite decisionmakers. For this reason, many racial realities of this society have rarely or never been intensively researched by social scientists. Ironically, U.S. social scientists who research societies overseas often accent the importance of uncovering hidden empirical realities and concealing myths of those societies, yet are frequently reluctant to do similar in-depth research on and analysis of their home society.[3]

Since the full emergence of the social sciences in the United States in the late nineteenth and early twentieth centuries, mainstream social scientists have periodically developed influential theories and concepts designed to interpret racial and ethnic "relations" in this society. These mostly white mainstream analysts have historically included such prominent scholars as Robert E. Park, Gunnar Myrdal, and Milton Gordon. These influential scholars and their colleagues have usually had difficulty in viewing U.S. society from any but a white, albeit often liberal, racial framing. Moreover, over more recent decades the analytical perspectives and much conceptual terminology of mainstream researchers like Park, Myrdal, and Gordon, though periodically elaborated and revised, have continued to significantly influence the way that a majority of social scientists and other researchers have viewed and researched important racial issues.[4]

Certainly, the mainstream "race relations" theories and concepts have provided handy interpretive tools for understanding numerous aspects of racial oppression, but they also have significant limitations and carry hidden assumptions that frequently trap analysts into a limited under-standing of racial inequalities and patterns. Included among these are traditional concepts such as bigotry, bias, prejudice, stereotype, race, eth-nicity, assimilation, and bigotry-generated discrimination. These concepts have been widely used, and are frequently valuable, but do not provide the essential array of conceptual tools necessary to make sense out of a highly racialized society like the United States.

These conventional analytical concepts tend to be used in decontextual-ized and non-systemic ways. Even a quick look at today's social science journals or textbooks reveals the frequency and limitations of these com-monplace concepts. Many analysts who use them tend to view racial inequality as just one of numerous "social problems." Social problems text-books dealing with racial issues often have a section on something like the

U.S. "race problem," as do other textbooks such as those used in law school courses on Constitution and racial issues. This "problem" view is similar to the cancer view of racism, in that the problem is considered to be an abnormality in an otherwise healthy system.[5] Such an approach typically views the race problem as not foundational to society, but as temporary and gradually disappearing as a result perhaps of increasing modernity. Thus, one common approach in conventional analyses is to view historical or contemporary acts of discrimination as determined by individual bias or concern for views of bigoted others. This bigot-causes-discrimination view is, like other mainstream views, generally oriented to individual or small-group processes and does not substantially examine the deep structural foundation in which such acts of discrimination are imbedded.[6]

Classical Social Scientists: Trapped in the Eurocentric Context

The habit of not thinking realistically and deeply about a country's undergirding racial structure extends well beyond U.S. social scientists, past or present, to numerous prominent figures in the long tradition of Western social science. Consider the still influential intellectual giants of the Western tradition such as Max Weber, Karl Marx, Emile Durkheim, and Sigmund Freud. They loom large in much contemporary Western social science. Three were of Jewish background and were personally familiar with European anti-Semitism. Several gave some attention to that anti-Semitism, yet they provided brief or no analytical attention to the systems of racial oppression that operated conspicuously within Western countries' growing imperial and colonial spheres during their lifetimes. Not one assessed in significant depth the extreme racialized oppression that played out in front of them as a central aspect of European imperialism and colonialism. Even Karl Marx, a critic of class oppression who knew Western history, never offered a sustained analysis of the highly racialized character of the colonizing adventures overseas by Western governments and capitalistic enterprises. The widespread omission of a serious and sustained analysis of Western racial expansion and oppression, and the consequent racialized social structures, is striking given how fundamental these processes and structures have been to the prosperity and global dominance of major Western countries, now for centuries.

Historically, these influential social science analysts have been European or European American. These analysts have generally prized European civilization over that of other continents, and characteristically viewed Western racial matters from an educated version of the dominant white frame, which I explain fully in the next section. For the most part, these theorists and analysts have been handicapped by the fact that they typically have thought out of the dominant racial framing that most European

Americans and Europeans at all class levels have used now for several centuries.

Take the example of Max Weber, who died in the early twentieth century but has had a great impact on Western social science ever since. Like other social scientists of his era, he held to the tenets of blatant biological racism, a view that infected his historical and geopolitical arguments, yet one that almost never gets critically discussed in textbooks and empirical analyses that to this day use his analytical concepts. Weber wrote unreflectively of the "hereditary hysteria" of Asian Indians, of Africans as genetically incapable of factory work, and of Chinese as slow in intelligence and docile, with these traits viewed as shaped by biology. As with most European scientists, central to Weber's work was the idea of Western "rationality," which he viewed as having hereditary grounding. Western capitalism had evolved through the process of "modernization," which Weber and his peers contrasted to the "traditionalism" of "Oriental" civilizations. Weber held to the Eurocentric view that European capitalism was an "intellectual progression, an ascent of human 'rationality,' meaning intellect and ethics" from ancient society to modern society.[7] Beyond Europe, other countries were viewed as to some degree backward. Edward Said has described this as an ideology of Orientalism, a Western-centered framing unable to see beyond Eurocentrism.[8] Since the time of Weber, many Western social scientists assessing European industrialization and capitalism have continued to accent European superiority in modernity.

To take a more recent example, consider the leading U.S. social theorist, Talcott Parsons. Parsons viewed U.S. racism as an anachronism representative of a premodernist mode of thinking and likely to be dissolved with more industrialization and modernization. Even a scholar who probed deeply into Western civilization was unable to see the racialized "water" in which he metaphorically swam, the water of a sophisticated white framing of Western societies.[9] That frame and the racial oppression it aggressively rationalizes have always been much more than a "premodern survival" attached to an otherwise advanced society. The system of white-imposed racism and its rationalizing frame have long been part of U.S. foundational realities, yet not one major white theorist in the U.S. social science canon has substantially analyzed and understood well that major foundation.

Consider too that the idea of Western civilization's modernity, which includes a superior rationality, has long been important in Western analysis, from Max Weber's time to the present. The term "modernity" has functioned as social science shorthand for industrial and technological civilization, for societies shaped by the views that humans should actively transform physical environments, that market economies are best, and that bureaucratized nation-states are necessary for societal well-being.[10] Yet this idea of modernity emerged about the same time as the white framing that, since at least the 1600s, has rationalized racial oppression in North America and elsewhere. The concept of "advanced Western civilization" grew out of the European and European American history of imperialistic subordination of peoples of color and often within the social crucibles of slavery and genocide.

According to many contemporary analysts, modern Western societies supposedly have proceeded well beyond the premodern impulses of group irrationality, superstition, and primitive violence. Yet European enslavement of Africans in North America and European-generated genocides targeting indigenous peoples across the globe, which operated openly until a century or so ago, did *not* result from premodern violent impulses somehow breaking through modernity. Instead, these actions did, and do, constitute the economic and cultural foundations of Western modernity—with its advanced technologies, accent on Western-controlled markets, developed nation-states, and overseas military operations aimed at maintaining Western dominance. Racial oppression and its rationalizing frame have long been central to *modern* Western societies, to the present day.

The White-Centered Perspectives of Contemporary Social Scientists

Today, one observes the continuing reality of a white-centered framing in many scholarly and popular analyses of U.S. society. As with canonical scholars like Max Weber, the language chosen to describe a society demographically or sociologically often reveals a white perspective. For many scholarly and popular analysts in the U.S. and across the globe even the English word "Americans" is routinely used to mean "white Americans." Terms like "American dream" and "American culture" are often used to refer primarily to the customs, values, or preferences of white Americans.

Language evasion or deflection strategies are often used by researchers and other authors to downplay certain racial matters. Many social science and popular analysts phrase analytical sentences about racial issues in the passive tense (e.g., "prejudice has been a problem for African Americans"), or they put vague or general nouns in the subject position of sentences about racial issues ("society discriminates against Latinos"). By such artifices, the whites who do the specific acts of racial oppression are not explicitly positioned as active agents and decisionmakers, and are not named as such in the relevant sentences of an article or book. Of course, authors need a diversity of sentences to maintain readers' interest, and using such passive or general phrasing might be in order to maintain that interest. However, in too many cases such sentences are there to avoid directly asserting that whites, in general or particular, are important decisionmakers and actors in the drama of racial oppression. This nonagentive way of speaking about racial matters is all the more dramatic because some research has shown that U.S. English speakers are generally *more* likely than speakers of languages such Spanish and Japanese to accent the agents of particular events—that is, to speak of specific people *doing* things.[11]

In addition, in many social scientists' and other analysts' writings a good documented discussion of the negative white role in racial matters, such as during the centuries of slavery and Jim Crow segregation, is frequently balanced with positive statements about whites because these analysts apparently feel a need to say something good about whites. An example is paralleling a written section on "bad slaveholders" with another on supposedly "good slaveholders," the latter a contradictory phrase in itself. Take the case of George Washington, perhaps the most famous U.S. founder. Numerous white historians have portrayed him as a superior moral leader and "good" slavemaster in spite of his bloody involvement in extending the brutal slavery system. Washington periodically asserted harshly negative stereotyping of black Americans, had enslaved runaways chased down, had enslaved workers whipped, and had teeth taken from the mouths of those enslaved for his own mouth. Strikingly, one generally savvy historian insists Washington was "not a racist" and that "his unique eminence arises from his sterling personal qualities . . . and from the eerie sense that, in him, some fragment of divine Providence did indeed touch this ground."[12] Similarly, otherwise critical social scientists seem unable to name accurately some of the gendered brutality often directed at black women during the slavery and legal segregation eras as "rape" or "coerced sex." Historian Winthrop Jordan noted that "white men of every social rank slept with Negro women" and that "miscegenation was extensive" in English colonies, but he did not use the words "rape" or "sexual coercion" in his analyses of this violent white male behavior.[13]

Moreover, today many white scholars and other analysts seem puzzled about the constant recurrence of blatantly racist incidents, events, and commentaries in this society. They have often accepted a contemporary racial framing that views U.S. society as "colorblind" or "post-racial" and considers racism to be dead or in significant decline (see Chapter 5). Even white scholars of a liberal inclination regularly underestimate the depth and extensiveness of current racial hostility and discrimination.[14] However, as I will show throughout this book, just because there seem to be fewer overtly racist actions and performances by whites today in public—at least performances viewed as racist by most whites—does not mean that whites' racist thought and action has decreased to a very low level.

The White Racial Frame: Dimensions and Impact

Today, we are in the early stages of developing a major new conceptual paradigm on U.S. racial matters, with an array of conceptual and interpretive tools and a growing number of critical social scientists, critical legal scholars, and others starting to analyze the old "racial relations" paradigm's serious limits.[15] Those working in this contemporary paradigm are attempting to develop a better theory of racial oppression, one that accents this oppression's deep structures, assesses its dimensions and reproductive processes, and demonstrates how both persistence forces and change forces have shaped it over time. For this we need better and agreed-upon analytical and interpretive concepts.

Those working toward a full-fledged structural and systemic racism paradigm have developed new, or extended old, analytical and interpretive concepts, including enhancing concepts from the counter-mainstream historical tradition of scholars and activists of color such as David Walker, Frederick Douglass, W. E. B. Du Bois, Anna Julia Cooper, Ida B. Wells-Barnett, and Oliver Cox in the past (for details, see Chapter 8). Over more recent decades, those working in this structural and systemic racism tradition have been very disproportionately scholars and activists of color, such as Kwame Ture, Rodolfo Acuña, Richard Delgado, Derrick Bell, Angela Davis, and Adrian Piper, to list just a few.

Inspired by this countersystem tradition, I make much use in this book of strong concepts like the white racial frame, the black counter-frame, and institutional and systemic racism. These concepts link well to critical insights that help us build a better social science paradigm that fosters research into the racial foundation of this society. The empirical world of racial experiences is diverse, complex, and saturated with meaning, and these always structured experiences often have no adequate analytical categories in traditional social science.

The central concept of the white racial frame that I develop in this book is one that helps greatly in digging deeply into the operation of racial oppression in this society. What do I mean by "frame"? Several contemporary sciences, especially the cognitive, neurological, and social sciences, have made use of the idea of a perspectival frame that gets imbedded in individual minds (brains), as well as in collective memories and histories, and helps people make sense out of everyday situations. People are "multiframers." They have numerous frames for understanding and interpretation in their minds, and their frames vary in complexity from specific micro-level framing of situations to a broad framing of society.

Cognitive and neurological scientists have used the frame concept to examine minds at work, with significant attention to how mostly unconscious frames shape individuals' socio-political inclinations and actions.

Some social scientists, in contrast, have in recent years used the concept of frame to examine the relatively conscious frames of people in particular social movements. Their concern is with how framed messages aid in getting a particular social movement's members to protest. Other social scientists, especially media researchers, have accented how mass media framing of stories is typically quite conscious. Specific media frames select out limited aspects of an issue in order to make it salient for mass communication, a selectivity usually promoting a narrow reading of that issue. In all these disciplines a frame is form-giving and makes meaningful what otherwise might seem meaningless to the people involved. A particular frame structures the thinking process and shapes what people see, or do not see, in important societal settings.[16]

In examining U.S. racial oppression, I extend these conceptions of societal framing and emphasize the central importance of a broad, long-dominant white racial frame. As I show later, much historical research demonstrates there is in North America and elsewhere a dominant, white-created racial frame that provides an overarching and generally destructive worldview, one extending across white divisions of class, gender, and age. Since its early development in the seventeenth century, this powerful frame has provided the vantage point from which white Americans have constantly viewed North American society. Its centrality in white minds is what makes it a dominant frame throughout the country and, indeed, in much of the Western world and in numerous other areas. Over time, this powerful frame has been elaborated by or imposed on the minds of most Americans, becoming thereby the country's dominant "frame of mind" and "frame of reference" in regard to racial matters.

This white racial frame is broad and complex, as we have seen. Over time white Americans have combined in it a beliefs aspect (racial stereotypes and ideologies), integrating cognitive elements (racial interpretations and narratives), visual and auditory elements (racialized images and language accents), a "feelings" aspect (racialized emotions), and an inclination to action (to discriminate). Moreover, over centuries of operation this dominant white framing has encompassed both a strong positive orientation to whites and whiteness (a pro-white subframe) and a strong negative orientation to racial "others" who are exploited and oppressed (anti-others subframes). Much research shows that this dominant white frame is often negative toward the racial others, that it is full of anti-others subframes. Yet it is much more than that. In the next chapter I show that early in this country's history this overarching racist framing includes a central subframe that assertively accents a positive view of white superiority, virtue, moral goodness, and action. For centuries the white racial framing of ingroup superiority and outgroup inferiority has been, to use Antonio Gramsci's term, *hegemonic*—that is, it has been part of a distinctive way of life that dominates major aspects of society. For most whites, thus, the white racial frame is more than just one significant frame among many; it is one that has routinely defined a way of being, a broad perspective on life, and one that provides the language and interpretations that help structure, normalize, and make sense out of society.

Let us consider a racial event that illustrates several of these important dimensions of the white racial frame. In a journal kept for a college course, Trevor, a white student at a midwestern college, reported on an evening party with other white male students:

> When any two of us are together, no racial comments or jokes are ever made. However, with the full group membership present, anti-Semitic jokes abound, as do racial slurs and vastly derogatory statements. . . . Various jokes concerning stereotypes . . . were also swapped around the gaming table, everything from "How many Hebes fit in a VW beetle?" to "Why did the Jews wander the desert for forty years?" In each case, the punch lines were offensive, even though I'm not Jewish. The answers were "One million (in the ashtray) and four (in the seats)" and "because someone dropped a quarter," respectively. These jokes degraded into a rendition of the song "Yellow," which was re-done to represent the Hiroshima and Nagasaki bombings. It contained lines about the shadows of the people being flash burned into the walls ("and it was all yellow" as the chorus goes in the song).

There is nothing subtle or ambiguous about these performances that frame and target specific groups. Trevor recorded yet more racist performances in this long evening event:

> A member of the group also decided that he has the perfect idea for a Hallmark card. On the cover it would have a few kittens in a basket with ribbons and lace. On the inside it would simply say "You're a nigger." I found that incredibly offensive. Supposedly, when questioned about it, the idea of the card was to make it as offensive as humanly possible in order to make the maximal juxtaposition between warm and ice hearted. After a brief conversation about the cards which dealt with just how wrong they were, a small kitten was drawn on a piece of paper and handed to me with a simple, three-word message on the back. . . . Of course, no group is particularly safe from the group's scathing wit, and the people of Mexico were next to bear the brunt of the jokes. A comment was made about Mexicans driving low-riding cars so they can drive and pick lettuce at the same

time. Comments were made about the influx of illegal aliens from Mexico and how fast they produce offspring.[17]

These white men are well educated and are having great "fun" as part of an extended social gathering, one they reportedly often engage in. Even in this relatively brief journal account we observe that the white racial frame involves a relatively broad framing of society, one that encompasses multiple dimensions. We observe an array of racial stereotypes and images, both explicit and implicit, that mock and signal the inferiority of several groups of color. Even Jewish Americans are included, apparently viewed as people who are not quite authentically white. There is more here than just cognitive stereotypes. The images are vivid, as in the song playing off the "yellow" metaphor. Performances are barbed, emotion-laden, and generally set in a joking format. We observe that the white racial frame prizes whiteness, which is the obvious stance of superiority taken by those doing the racialized performances. Racially framed notions and emotions that they have probably learned from their peers and previous generations have become the basis for extensive racist performances when these white friends gather to socialize.

Note too that the white racial frame structures events and performances, which in turn feed and add to the frame. Several different roles are played by the whites in this one racialized evening. There are the protagonists centrally acting out numerous racialized notions from important subframes within the white racial frame, here in a private "backstage" area where only whites are present. Others who are present agree with the racial performances and seem to act as cheerleading assistants. The recording student apparently acted either as a passive bystander or mild dissenter showing awareness of the moral issues here. No one, however, aggressively dissents and remonstrates strongly with the active protagonists.

In situations like this we see that the socially inherited racial frame is a comprehensive orienting structure, a "tool kit" that whites and others have long used to understand, interpret, and act in social settings. The important aspects of the frame listed above become taken-for-granted "common sense" for those who hold to them, and most holders often use these tools in automatic or half-conscious ways.[18] From the beginning of this country, this white frame has been deeply held and strongly resistant to displacement, and it includes many important "bits"—that is, frame elements such as the stereotyped racial knowledge, racial images and emotions, and racial interpretations in this diary account. These elements are important pieces of cultural information passed along from one person and group to the next. They include elementary elements such as the word-concepts "white," "black," "race," and white-created racist epithets like "nigger"—key words that in daily life regularly activate other elements of the frame. Frame elements are generally grouped into several key subframes within a broad overarching frame, and this broader frame operates as a gestalt, a unified whole that is in significant ways more than the sum of its parts.

This gestalt framing imbeds racist items that are relatively constant, but it also has connections to the ebb and flow of everyday experience that add new items or reshape old items. This dominant frame does not exist apart from everyday experience, and racist practices flowing from it are essential parts of the larger system of racial oppression. Such discriminatory practices are made meaningful to perpetrators by the dominant frame, and these practices show well the intersections of people's material, social, and mental lives.

Central to the dominant racial frame are several "big picture" narratives that connect frame elements into historically oriented stories with morals that are especially important to white Americans. These emotion-laden scenarios include stories about white conquest, superiority, hard work, and achievement. They make powerful use of stereotypes, images, and other elements from the overarching frame. They include rags-to-riches narratives such as that for early English colonists. According to this mythological narrative, most English "settlers" came with little, but drawing on religious faith and hard work they "settled" and made a nearly "vacant" land prosper, against "savage" Indians. This heroic narrative was later extended as whites moved westward and concocted a "winning the West," manifest destiny myth. In that narrative white "settlers" again fought battles against "savage" Indians, with the heroes being rewarded with land and villainous Indians being killed off or isolated on reservations. (The facts, such as the reality that the indigenous peoples were the successful and established settlers of lands that were stolen from them, are often suppressed in these narratives.) Interestingly, these fictional white narratives are still very much with us. Today, in their homes and in schools and the media a great many whites tell themselves and others false and fabricated narratives of how this country was created and founded. Perhaps most importantly, many try to live by the emotion-laden values and fiction-laden interpretations that they claim as meaningful from these common mythological narratives.[19]

From such narratives, as well as from the student diary account, we see that the persisting white racial framing of society is about much more than words. In addition to its many stereotypes and other belief elements, this powerful frame includes deep emotions, visual images, and the accented sounds of spoken language. Powerful emotions, deep negative feelings, about Americans of color frequently shape how whites behave and interact, and in spite of the liberty-and-justice language they may assert. Emotions of the conventional white frame have included racial hatred, racial arrogance, and a sense of racial superiority; greed and other emotions of gratification; and a desire for dominance over others. The emotions of white racism also include fears and anxieties, conscious and unconscious, that whites have long held in regard to Americans of color because of the latter's resistance to oppression. Moreover, for some whites guilt and shame have become central emotions, especially as the venality and immorality of racism have become more obvious to them. Significantly, too, those whites who do move to a substantial anti-racist framing of society and into significant anti-racist action often feel and accent the positive emotions of empathy, compassion, and hope for a better future.

Operating out of the White Frame

Although they live in several U.S. regions and often have different occupations and educations, most whites have revealed in numerous research studies that they often hold broadly similar positive stereotypes, images, and understandings about whites and broadly similar negative stereotypes, images, and understandings of Americans of color.[20] Nonetheless, as I see it, the concept of the white racial frame is an "ideal type," a composite whole with a large array of elements that in everyday practice are drawn on selectively by white individuals acting to impose or maintain racial identity, privilege, and dominance vis-à-vis people of color in recurring interactions. People use what they need from the overarching frame's elements to deal with specific situations. Individuals mostly do not make use of the bits of this dominant frame in exactly the same way. For most people there seems to be an internal hierarchy of racial ideas, narratives, images, and emotions, such that a given person may be more comfortable with some of these elements, especially once they become conscious to the individual, than of other known frame elements. Indeed, racially liberal whites may reject certain elements of the traditional white racial frame while consciously or unconsciously accepting or highlighting yet others. Moreover, over time many people may rework, challenge, or transform the version of the white frame they inherited.

The use of critical frame elements often varies by age, gender, class, and other social variables. The strength and use of white power and privilege is variable across such white subgroups, so the utilization of the framing to rationalize and act in societal situations also varies. In addition, the dominant racial frame regularly overlaps with, and is connected to, other collective frames that are important in viewing and interpreting recurring social worlds. Once a frame is utilized by a person, it often activates related frames or subframes. Frequently, the dominant racial frame activates and relates to class-oriented and patriarchal ways of looking at society. Indeed, from the first century of European colonization, as we will see later, the class and patriarchal frames of oppression have been linked to the white racial frame or nested within it.

By constantly using selected bits of the dominant frame to understand and interpret society, by integrating new items, and by applying its elements such as stereotypes, images, and interpretations in their exploitative and discriminatory actions, whites have for centuries incorporated this interpretive frame in their minds as well as, to varying degrees, the minds of many people of color. Contemporary neurological research shows that strongly held views, such as those of the white frame, are deeply imbedded in the neuronal structure of human brains. Repetition is critical in this process. The dominant racial frame becomes implanted in the neural linkages of a typical brain by the process of constant repetition of its elements— which are heard, observed, or acted upon repeatedly by individuals over years and decades.[21]

Once deeply imbedded in the mind and brain, this frame tends to be lasting and often resistant to change. Activation of it tends to suppress alternative or countering frames. For most whites the dominant frame has become so fundamental that few are able to see it or assess it critically. When important but inconvenient facts are presented that do not fit this dominant frame, whites tend to ignore or reject those facts. For example, for several centuries whites have held to very negative views of black Americans as not nearly as hard-working as white Americans, in spite of great historical evidence to the contrary. Frames as entrenched as the dominant white frame are hard to counter or uproot.

In fact, the white racial frame has become a major part of most whites' character structure, a character structure habitually operated out of, with important individual variations, in everyday life. A concept developed a century ago by psychologist William James, character structure refers to the internalization of historically conditioned understandings from a person's social environment and to the everyday habits developed that reflect such understandings. This habituated character structure is what French sociologist Pierre Bourdieu has more recently termed the "habitus," and a few social scientists, such as Eduardo Bonilla-Silva, have aptly referred to this white character structure as the "white habitus."[22]

Because this white character structure imbeds the white racial framing of society, it regularly generates discriminatory habits that have major structural impacts. From the beginning, the white racial frame has played a central role in regularly structuring society by providing important racialized understandings, images, narratives, emotions, and operational norms that determine a great array of individual and group actions within major societal sectors. This dominant frame is directing, and it is learned at parent's knee, in school, and from the media. Once learned, it guides and rationalizes much discriminatory behavior. Whether it is a white child racially abusing a black child in the schoolyard, or a white adult discriminating against a Latino adult in a job situation, the dominant frame is both activating and activated, and central in creating much social texture in everyday life.

Frame interpretations and other elements do not stand outside daily life and just remain latent in the minds of individuals, but directly shape the everyday scripts whites and others actually act on, such as in acts of discrimination in important social settings. In that way the white racial frame re-creates, maintains, and reinforces the racially stratified patterns and structures of this society. For centuries, the dominant racial frame has protected and shaped society's inegalitarian structure of resources and hierarchy of power. This frame has persisted over centuries because it is constantly validating, and thus validated by, the racially inegalitarian accumulation of many economic, political, and other societal resources.[23]

Collective Memories and Collective Forgetting

Very important to the persistence of the white racial frame are friendship and kinship groups, for in such networks important elements of that frame become common cultural currency. Sociologist Maurice Halbwachs suggested that our personal understandings about society are not just in some nook of our minds to which we alone have access. Instead, our social understandings, and thus important interpretive frames, are regularly reiterated for us by external groups. The groups of which we are part give us the "means to reconstruct" such frames if we "adopt ... their way of thinking." An individual's important understandings, images, knowledge, and framing hang together substantially because they are part of the "totality of thoughts common to a group."[24]

Over time our groups, small and large, become major repositories of congealed group memories and associated social frames. We human beings gain most of our racial frame's understandings, images, and emotions from imbibing and testing those of parents and peers, the media, and written accounts handed down over generations. We do this learning mostly within significant networks of relatives, peers, and friends—as we saw in the example of white college students engaging in racist performances earlier in this chapter. Constant repetition and performance of the frame's racialized information and other bits—together with the relevant intonation and style, nonverbal gestures, and facial expressions—are essential to the successful reproduction of that frame across social networks, geography, and time.[25]

Collective memory is central to these networks. How we interpret and experience our racialized present depends substantially on our knowledge of and interpretations of our racialized past. The collective memory of that racist past not only shapes, but also legitimates, the established racial structure of today's society. Moreover, if major groups in society hold significantly different collective memories of that racist past, they will as a rule have difficulty in sharing understandings of racial experiences in the present. Most groups have important collective memories, but those with the greatest power, principally white Americans in the U.S. case, typically have the greatest control over society-wide institutional memories, including those recorded by the mainstream media and in most history books, organizational histories, laws, textbooks, films, and public monuments.[26]

What the dominant racial framing ignores or suppresses is critical to the continuation of oppression. Collective *forgetting* is as important as collective remembering, especially in regard to the prevailing narratives of this country's developmental history. Historical events may stay in the collective records of memory, or they may be allowed to deteriorate, slowly or rapidly, through the overt choices of the powerful. The latter usually seek to suppress or weaken collective memories of societal oppression, and to construct positive and often fictional memories of that history. White Americans and their acolytes in other groups have long tried to sanitize this country's collective memories and to downplay or eliminate accurate understandings of our extraordinarily racist history. Over nearly four centuries, a critical part of the dominant framing of whites' unjust enrichment at the expense of Americans of color—for example, killing off Native American populations and enslaving and segregating African Americans—has included much collective forgetting and mythmaking in regard to these often bloody historical realities. Significant portions of North American histories about centuries of racial oppression have been allowed to disappear from public consciousness, or to be downplayed and mythologized in scattered societal portrayals.

For example, research by sociologist Kristen Lavelle has dramatized the importance of contemporary white historical memories that sanitize and reinterpret the brutal realities of the Jim Crow segregation that lasted until the 1960s. Lavelle's interviews with older white southerners, all lifetime residents of a southern city important in the 1960s civil rights movement, revealed that most remember Jim Crow segregation as a pleasant era with peace, security, and "good racial relations" between white and black residents. While most acknowledge to some degree the racial inequality of Jim Crow, they do not remember that era for what it really was—one of extensive and brutal racial discrimination and other racial oppression. One older white resident put it thus:

There was a place for blacks, and there was a place for whites. Yes, I can remember goin' in restaurants where they had colored bathrooms . . . and I can remember when . . . we'd go into restaurants, and they were given food out the back because they were black, but they were not mistreated. Back then, that was a way of life. . . . Nobody ever even thought that they were really doin' anything wrong. . . . Black people or white people never felt like that was wrong.

In her white memory and framing, the all-encompassing anti-black discrimination of the Jim Crow era was not really mistreatment, and she also asserted unrealistically that the black residents did not view legal segregation as wrong either. In a joint interview a white husband and wife also remembered Jim Crow segregation as an era of good and unproblematic racial relations, until the civil rights era:

[Husband]: 'Course we didn't go to church with 'em, didn't go to school with 'em—it was segregated there. But [we] didn't have any real problems. Rode the bus all the time, and 'course they sat in the back of the bus. I never saw the bus driver ask one to move. You really didn't see much controversy until World War II . . . .
[Wife]: Oh yes! They didn't cause trouble. I mean, we all got along! . . .
[Husband]: Now it wadn't all roses—every now and then there'd be somebody stir up something. Back in . . . the sixties I guess, when we had most of our race riots here.[27]

Significantly, the older white southerners who were interviewed rarely connected themselves personally to the often extreme Jim Crow oppression. They have developed various excuses to rationalize the racist views and discriminatory actions of themselves, their relatives, and their acquaintances in that era. Like this husband and wife, many viewed the "bad" racial relations as occurring only during the period of civil rights protests that ended legal segregation. They recall the period of local desegregation as a time of danger and victimization *for whites*. As Lavelle notes, "whites' perception, largely imagined, of their own racial victimization . . . is a major ideological and emotional facet of the white racial frame, whereby whites dismiss the historical and contemporary reality of white racism." This perception lets these whites draw on an old and essential element of that frame and "assert themselves, individually and collectively, as racial innocents and 'good' people." Such efforts are about the "myriad active and subtle ways that whites continue to construct themselves positively and construct people of color, especially black Americans, negatively."[28]

Evidently, one key purpose of the contemporary white racial frame in regard to our history is to provide a type of social "shrouding"—that is, to conceal much of the brutality of the racist history, especially perhaps for younger whites and new immigrants. This shrouding involves the hiding of the brutal racist realities of an era and/or the rewriting of its history so that key events are mostly recalled from a white point of view.

Much of this white historical mythology has been absorbed even by Americans who are not white, but who have incorporated in their minds significant elements of the white framing of history. For example, Fareed Zakaria—an immigrant journalist who studied at Harvard and works for a U.S. news-magazine—has written about the historical rise and power of the West, yet with no significant references to the role of European-generated slavery and genocide in that process. He writes like many contemporary white historians: "Contact with the rest of the world stimulated Europe.... Everywhere Europeans went they found goods, markets, and opportunities. By the seventeenth century, Western nations were increasing their influence over every region and culture with which they came in contact." Indeed, most areas of the world became "marked for use by Europeans."[29] In a substantial discussion of these historical issues, Zakaria makes only one fleeting reference to enslavement of Africans and no explicit reference to the genocide directed at indigenous peoples such as Native Americans. For him, as for most historians of the West, modernization is about industrialization, urbanization, education, and wealth, and not centrally about genocide, land theft, slavery, and unjust enrichment of European countries.

When such a momentous and bloody past is suppressed, downplayed, or mythologized by elites and historians, ordinary Americans, especially whites, understandably have difficulty in seeing or assessing accurately the present-day realities of unjust enrichment and impoverishment along racial lines. Moreover, misunderstandings and myths of our highly oppressive past are frequently passed along from one generation to the next, and from one person to the next, by means of recurring and ritualized performances. Commemorative ceremonies on holidays, such as Columbus Day, honoring our history, celebrate and in part help to sanitize a horrific past, thereby shaping contemporary communal memories by accenting the continuity of the present racial status quo with a positively portrayed racial past. Sharing elements of the white racial frame in such ceremonies generally promotes solidarity in the dominant group, and often with other racial groups that accept white dominance.[30]

The Importance of Counter-Frames

While the central concern of this book is developing the concept of the white racial frame and showing how it has developed and operated across the centuries, we need to realize and accent the point that this is not the only important collective frame directed at racial matters. Most people carry several perspectival frames applicable to particular situations in their heads at the same time. As I suggested previously, people are indeed multiframers. In examining the significant and sometimes contested history of the dominant white racial frame, I will deal to some degree with three other important categories of frames in everyday operation: (1) a white-crafted liberty-and-justice frame; (2) the anti-oppression counter-frames of Americans of color; and (3) the traditional home-culture frames that Americans of color have drawn on for their everyday lives and in developing counter-frames.

One of the great ironies of this country's early history is that white Americans' conception of their freedom and of social justice was honed within a slavery system. By the mid- to late eighteenth century, the white colonists had developed what I call the white "liberty-and-justice frame," one that they loudly proclaimed against British officials who were suppressing their liberties. This liberty-and-justice frame is important because most white Americans have, in the past and present, regularly articulated some version of it. We see the importance of this framing in the founding documents of the United States, including the "establish justice" and "secure the blessings of liberty" language of the preamble to the U.S. Constitution.

Since the American Revolution most whites have held in their minds some version of a liberty-and-justice frame, one that is real to them but that is usually treated as rhetorical or hypothetical when it comes to serious threats to the perpetuation of the U.S. system of racism. The liberty-and-justice frame has been routinely trumped by the white racial frame, and has too often been reserved for rhetorical speeches and sermons. Still, over the centuries of this country's existence, modest numbers of whites have taken the liberty-and-justice frame *very* seriously in regard to the racially oppressed situations of Americans of color. We see this in the white abolitionists who, with black abolitionists, protested and fought to bring down the slavery system. Later on, in the 1950s and 1960s, we again see a small group of whites actively allying themselves with black civil rights protesters, whose efforts in the South played a major role in bringing down legal segregation.

In addition to the dominant white racial frame and the white version of the liberty-and-justice frame, there are two groups of perspectival frames that are highly relevant to understanding resistance to systemic racial oppression in North America over the centuries: (1) the anti-oppression counter-frames of Americans of color; and (2) the home-culture frames that Americans of color have drawn on for their everyday lives and to develop effective anti-oppression counter-frames. In opposing the dominant racial frame, Americans of color; have frequently developed a significant counter-frame, an important frame that has helped them to better understand and resist whites' racial oppression. Freedom-oriented resistance frames appear in the earliest period of racial oppression. The early counter-frames of Americans of color, primarily those of Native Americans and African Americans, were initially developed for survival purposes, and over time they have added critical elements that have strengthened their understandings of institutionalized racism and the strategies of everyday resistance to that racism.

The resistance frames have often drawn heavily on elements from the cultural backgrounds of those oppressed. For example, since the first century of their enslavement, African Americans have maintained a home-culture that is a hybrid, with cultural features stemming in part from the African cultural background and in part from their experiences and adaptations in North America. Confronted regularly by extreme oppression and white attempts to eradicate their African cultures, the many African groups among those enslaved became a single African American people with a home-culture that drew substantially on family, spiritual, and moral elements from their African backgrounds. With strong African roots, these African Americans shaped their religion, art, music, and other cultural elements not only for sustaining everyday life but also for understanding white oppression and generating resistance to it.

The resistance counter-frames of Americans of color have also drawn on the ideals or terminology from whites' own liberty-and-justice frame. Indeed, since the early decades of slavery and genocide whites have greatly feared that African Americans and Native Americans would operate out of a liberty-and-justice counter-frame of their own. Thus, whites feared its influence and use in African Americans' revolts against slavery, and such fears even accelerated with the end of slavery—fears that played some role in the emergence and structure of the near-slavery of Jim Crow segregation. Today, as we will see in later chapters, white Americans still fear, and attack, the stronger counter-frames as they are used by many Americans of color. One example of such white fear can be seen in the widespread, fierce, and irrational white reactions during the pathbreaking 2008 presidential election to the strong anti-racist perspective articulated by black leaders such as Dr. Jeremiah Wright, an African American minister who at the time had been President Barack Obama's pastor for several decades.

In Chapter 8, I will examine Dr. Wright's critical perspective on U.S. history as an example of a contemporary counter-frame arising out of the black tradition. I will also explore briefly other important counter-frames, including those of Native Americans, Latinos, and Asian Americans. Historically and in the present, these counter-frames have provided valuable tool kits for oppressed Americans, offering individual and collective tools for countering widespread white hostility and discrimination.

Conclusion

In this chapter I have defined and detailed the useful concept of the white racial frame and suggested its utility in making sense out of racial oppression, mainly in North America. In the next chapters I examine questions about how and why this dominant racial frame and its important elements arose over several centuries. I also ask, how has this frame shaped the past and present structure of society? In these chapters I seek to answer these and related questions and to make the often-hidden white-racist realities of this country more obvious—to take them "out of the closet" so that they can be openly analyzed and, hopefully, redressed or removed.

For centuries, to the present, the dominant racial frame has sharply defined inferior and superior racial groups and authoritatively rationalized and structured the great and continuing racial inequalities of this society. In a whitewashing process, and most especially today, this dominant framing has shoved aside, ignored, or treated as incidental numerous racial issues, including the realities of persisting racial discrimination and racial inequality. By critically analyzing this dominant racial frame's elements and its numerous structuring impacts, we can see more clearly how this country is put together racially—and, perhaps, how it might be able to change in the direction of the liberty-and-justice society long proclaimed in its dominant political rhetoric.

CHAPTER 2

Building the Racist Foundation
Colonialism, Genocide, and Slavery

Why is the white racial frame so deep and so foundational in the United States? The central reason is that this country is built on 350 years of extreme racial oppression. Over its first centuries of operation, this oppression aggressively targeted indigenous peoples for extermination or expulsion, and targeted African Americans with a bloody slavery system. From the 1840s to the 1960s, powerful white capitalists and politicians gradually brought into this preexisting system of extreme racism yet more people of color such as the Chinese and Mexicans in the 1840s and 1850s—frequently to secure low-wage labor for whites' wealth-generating economic enterprises. Not surprisingly, whites have long tried to legitimate and rationalize these extensive and lasting patterns of societal oppression they have created and maintained. Over centuries a large majority of whites, both elites and ordinary whites, have become partisans and defenders of white power and privilege, especially by means of the white racial frame. Playwright Eugene O'Neill once wrote that "There is no present or future, only the past, happening over and over again, now." The better we understand this past of bloody racial oppression, the better we can understand our present racial situation, with its still-dominant racial hierarchy and rationalizing white racial frame.

European Colonialism: Bloody Exploitation

Today, many scholars and popular analysts continue to describe contemporary Western societies with terms like "modern" and "modernity." They emphasize as positive certain characteristics of these modern societies: industrialization and technology, market economies, national governments, and complex bureaucratization. Significantly, however, numerous supposedly positive features of this distinctive modernity have played a major and negative role in the genocide, land theft, and labor theft that accompanied the global expansion and colonialism of European countries beginning in the late 1400s.

Strikingly, colonialism, capitalism, modernity, and global exploitation all have a common genealogy. European colonialism and capitalism were in their early stages of development when they generated the cross-Atlantic slavery system. European colonialism took on its exploitative wealth-generating form in concert with the enslavement of Africans and other indigenous peoples across the growing north and south Atlantic economies. The bloody European theft of land and super-exploitation of enslaved labor were presided over by ever-growing and bureaucratized nation-states, the latter usually described by Western social scientists as signs of the modernization process. From its beginnings, European colonialism relied heavily not only on a growing entrepreneurial bourgeoisie but also on these nation-states, most especially upon their well-equipped military organizations.[1] The political-economic theorist Karl Marx once captured the world-shattering significance of this European colonialism and imperialism in a brief statement in his famous book on Western capitalism:

> The discovery of gold and silver in America, the extirpation, enslavement and entombment in mines of the aboriginal population, the beginning of the conquest and looting of the East Indies, the turning of Africa into a warren for the commercial hunting of black-skins, signaled the rosy dawn of the era of capitalist production. These idyllic proceedings are the chief moments of primitive accumulation. ... [C]apital comes dripping from head to foot from every pore with blood and dirt.[2]

The rise of Western capitalism is rooted in the global seizing of the land, resources, and labor of people of color by violent means. Commercial and industrial capitalism develops over this era because of the expanding Atlantic system of slavery. Marx noted these close connections in an 1846 letter:

> It is slavery which has given value to the [American] colonies, it is the colonies which have created world trade, and world trade is the necessary condition for large-scale machine industry. Consequently, prior to the slave trade, the colonies sent very few products to the Old

World, and did not noticeably change the face of the world. Slavery is therefore an economic category of paramount importance. ... [W]ipe North America off the map and you will get anarchy, the complete decay of trade and modern civilization. But to do away with slavery would be to wipe America off the map.[3]

Clearly, systemic racial oppression—in the form of massive enslavement of African-origin people and extreme oppression of indigenous people—and commercial-industrial capitalism emerged together as part of the *same* political-economic system that took root in European countries and their colonies in North America. In this early period, thus, modern capitalism *was* systemic racism, and systemic racism *was* modern capitalism.

Note too that in the Americas the coercing of the labor of indigenous Americans and Africans by European capitalists and other colonizers meant not only the extraction of "surplus value" from the productive work of these coerced workers, but often the extraction of the "subsistence value" of their work. That is, the (money) value of the work was almost entirely taken by the European and European American capitalists, so much so that many coerced laborers died from not having enough basic food, clothing, or shelter under this highly exploitative colonialism. In the case of North America, the theft of the land, resources, or labor of indigenous peoples and enslaved Africans lasted for centuries.

Significant here is that, for the first time in world history, militaristic colonialism was global in scope and encompassed several continents. From the sixteenth to the nineteenth centuries, European invasions forced a political-economic and demographic reorganization of a large part of the globe at the expense of indigenous peoples. The Spanish nation-state was the first to colonize and plunder on a large scale indigenous societies in the Americas for their land and the resources, but its growing wealth and military apparatus were soon countered by the expansion of competing English, Dutch, and French nation-states and private companies seeking to gain wealth from overseas exploitation. European nation-states and associated private companies, such as English firms operating in the Caribbean and North America, discovered there were huge profits to be made from overseas agricultural plantations using enslaved African labor on indigenous lands. Indeed, by the end of the eighteenth century a huge share of the profits coming into British coffers came from overseas slave plantations producing important agricultural products.[4]

Well-organized nation-state and private bureaucracies in Europe and the emerging colonies were critical to aggressive colonization. In North America the English colonies were often state enterprises created under the auspices of the king or state-fostered enterprises developed by entrepreneurs, plantation owners, or merchants. The first English joint-stock companies were formed by merchants under the auspices of James I of England. Employees of the Southern Company settled Jamestown, Virginia, the English colony that brought in the first African laborers.

A principal objective of this European colonization was to secure land and raw materials and to develop markets. Once land was taken from indigenous societies, the Europeans' search for labor to work that land soon led to the extensive use of the African slave trade. At an early point, the private sector and the state sector collaborated in global exploitation and enslavement, which were rationalized in a Eurocentric racial framing. Racial formation theorists Michael Omi and Howard Winant have expanded our understanding of government actors' role in creating racialized organizations and institutions. Yet, their historical analyses do not go far enough in analyzing how at an early point in time the principal European nation-state actors collaborated with major capitalistic economic actors to generate the imperialism, genocide, and slavery that created the racial underpinning of modern Western countries like the United States.[5]

Social scientist Max Weber famously wrote of the "Protestant ethic and the spirit of capitalism" in assessing the fostering conditions before and around modern capitalism. However, in this great European expansion one sees what might more accurately be termed the "predatory ethic" of Western capitalism. Central to European colonialism and capitalism was a predatory ethic that asserted the right of Europeans to take the land and labor of others by violence. As we will see in Chapter 8, this highly materialistic and greedy approach to encounters with new environments and peoples baffled Native Americans at the time. It has been described by many indigenous Americans as a "despiritualized" worldview, and in their view a despiritualized approach to environments and other beings resulted in the latter's dehumanization and exploitation. European invaders showed little concern for the lives and livelihoods of indigenous peoples during the bloody process of colonial wealth generation. By the nineteenth century, in the United States this predatory ethic was given a rationalizing name, "manifest destiny," which asserted the right of whites to expand wherever they needed to increase their prosperity, no matter the cost to those killed and exploited in the process. Significant too is that this predatory ethic was from the first dressed up in religious language, as something God-ordained.

Significantly, most critical political-economic analysts have generally ignored or downplayed the racist architecture of these long centuries of Western colonialism. Even for these analysts, the dominant white racial frame seems to be a difficult set of blinders to get beyond. Most major groups that were exploited by the early and later European accumulation of wealth in this global colonizing system were non-European, and each was soon denigrated (the word literally means "blackened") in an increasingly developed Eurocentric framing of colonialism and the new colonial societies. European entrepreneurs and colonists carried with them, or soon developed, not only the often-noted realities of Western modernity such as so-called private enterprise and advanced technology, but also other central societal developments ignored or neglected by most historical analysts— systemic racial oppression and a rationalizing racist frame.

The concurrent emergence of European capitalism, colonialism, and racial oppression marked the creation of a *global racial order* with European-origin people at the top, one that has ever since regularly shaped not only individual societies but also world patterns of trade, finance, employment, politics, and communications.

White Prosperity: Native American Lands and African American Labor

As most schoolchildren know, the first task the European colonists under-took in North America was to "settle the land." This is the euphemistic phrase European Americans have long used for the theft of Native American land—which regularly required bloody wars, often genocidal wars, because Native Americans usually had some resources to resist. Once the land had been stolen, the need for labor to work large sections of the land soon exceeded the supply of white agricultural workers. Enslaved African Americans became a group that was internally central, as essential labor, to the prospering of the North American colonies. By the eighteenth century, the slavery-centered society directly involved a large proportion of white Americans in all major social classes. These included economically success-ful slaveholders in southern and northern states, the owners of slave-trading enterprises (often in the North), associated bankers and insurance brokers (often in the North), and leading southern and northern politicians who supported slave plantations and the Atlantic slave trade.

In addition, a large number of ordinary whites in all colonies, northern and southern, worked in occupations linked directly or indirectly to the slavery system. These included white-collar clerks and other white employ-ees working for various slave-related enterprises, overseers on slave farms and plantations, sailors on slave ships, slave-catchers who chased runaways, small farmers who grew agricultural products needed on slave plantations, lumber workers who cut timber for slave ships, fishers who traded fish meal to North American and Caribbean plantations, local and federal govern-ment workers policing enslaved runaways and other workers processing the slave-produced products destined for export, and small farmers and urban entrepreneurs who rented their enslaved workers for temporary profit.[6] A great many whites benefited economically in one way or another from the slavery-centered economic complex—which encompassed the slave trade, commercial trade with slave farms and plantations, international trade in slave-produced products, and the array of slavery supporting occupations across the country and, indeed, across the Atlantic. Over two centuries most whites gained significant material and/or symbolic benefits from the racialized system of African American slavery, and often from continuing anti-Indian oppression.

The word "exploit," in the sense of taking advantage of others for personal gain, appears in the English language in the 1840s during a peak period of African American enslavement. For centuries, as pioneering historians like Edmund Morgan have made clear, this African American enslavement was a major foundation for this country—for its economy, politics, and other societal institutions. If there had been no African American enslavement, there probably would not have been the huge North American wealth generation—and possibly no modern wealth-generating British and America capitalism on the massive scale that developed over these centuries. Enslaved workers cultivating tobacco, rice, sugar, cotton, and other major crops generated very large amounts of economic capital, much of which circulated throughout the European and North American banking and other economic institutions. This white-controlled capital in turn generated much spin-off prosperity, including important industrial breakthroughs. Enslaved black Americans created much of the surplus capital (wealth) of this country for its first two centuries, indeed for half this country's lifetime. Their labor provided some of the wealth that the white colonists used to fight a successful war against Britain. As Morgan has put it, white Americans "bought their independence with slave labor."[7] Without the substantial enslavement of African Americans, thus, there quite possibly would not have been a United States and U.S. Constitution—at least not in the late eighteenth century.

Creating a Racial Hierarchy: Racial Capital and Frame Assumptions

As the colonies expanded over the seventeenth century, European American officials, assisted by ordinary colonists, institutionalized a social hierarchy, with group positions arranged in ladder-like levels and with significant socioeconomic benefits and social privileges associated with the white level at the top, and none attached to the bottom level, which was initially reserved for Africans and Indians. These societal benefits and privileges were soon a type of *racial capital* reserved for European Americans. From the seventeenth century to the present, whites have gained much racial capital from this country's hierarchical system of racial oppression.

This important racial capital has encompassed not only economic and other material capital, such as greater income and wealth, but also substantial social status, social networking, and symbolic capital. Symbolic capital comes from shared assumptions, understandings, and inclinations to interact in certain ways, and much of it is unrecognized and taken for granted. From the beginning symbolic capital has been a central part of whites' racial framing of society, for it operates to link white acquaintances and strangers. Examples of these shared assumptions and understandings can be seen, today or in the past, in the relatively easy ways in which even white strangers relate to each other, as compared to the tensions and other difficulties whites often have in relating to people, strangers or acquaintances, who are not white. Part of this process is what I call "frame assumption"— that is, the assumption that other whites share one's own racialized framing of the everyday social world. Perceiving and accenting white skin privilege in everyday interactions is very important for the operation of the long-dominant U.S. racial hierarchy.

This hierarchy has persisted as the heart of systemic racism to the present. It involves recurring racial discrimination and exploitation and an alienating racist relationship—at a lower level, the racially oppressed, and, at a much higher level, racial oppressors. These socially separated and alienated groups have different interests. The former seeks to overthrow the racial hierarchy, while the latter seeks to maintain it. The interests of the white racial group have included not only a concrete interest in labor and other social exploitation of Americans of color during the slavery and Jim Crow segregation eras, but also a concrete interest later on, in our contemporary era, in maintaining the racial power and significant privileges commonly inherited from white ancestors. Everyday interactions have thus long involved the calculation of particular racial-group interests.

Legalizing Oppression: The U.S. Constitution

One reason that the bloody realities of slavery, and later the near-slavery of Jim Crow segregation, have shaped this society so fundamentally is because from the first decades they were imbedded in important private and public bureaucracies, and were legitimated under this country's overtly racist legal system. The early systematic oppression of Native Americans and African Americans was made possible by the increasing power of various bureaucratic organizations, both private companies and government agencies of European nation-states. Large-scale killings and attacks on Native Americans would have been possible without military and other state bureaucratic organizations, but recurring wars on Indians and a large-scale system of African enslavement were not. Then, as in recent times, extensive societal oppression requires complex organizations and organizational agents carrying out dominant group goals.

The bureaucratization of oppression was accompanied by a strong accent on written records. Walter Ong has shown how a heavy accent on the written word and literacy is a societal development that generally represents a different way of viewing society—a viewpoint that commonly emphasizes abstractions, distancing of people from one another, and a new kind of dogmatic authority. The written word "distances the writer of a thought from the receiver" of that thought.[8] In contrast, the substantially *oral* worlds of the invaded indigenous peoples had vivid and accessible collective memories and orientations, which tended to make people more sensitive to and responsive to those around them. Institutionalization of written rules and records in colonial America, and later the United States, helped to assist the white elite and populace in operating effectively to dominate the new country—by means of a growing number of powerful political, legal, and economic organizations. It reinforced the type of distancing decisionmaking that went along with the private and government bureaucracies that organized the systemic exploitation directed at Native and African Americans.

Central to the legitimation and organization of North American slavery was the colonial legal system. As Charles Mills has pointed out, this society began with a generalized "racial contract" in which people's duties and rights were distributed on a racially unequal basis. From the beginning, the legal system was written and institutionalized. For centuries now, this extensive institutionalization has involved many powerful white judges and other white officials, thereby solidifying well white power and privilege. The principal foundation of this country's legal system is the U.S. Constitution. In 1787, at Philadelphia, fifty-five white men met and created a constitution for what most have viewed as the "first democratic nation." These founders were of white men of European background and mostly well off. Some 40 percent were or had been slaveowners, and many others profited as merchants, shippers, lawyers, or bankers from economic connections to the slavery system.[9]

In the preamble to the Constitution these white founders cite "We the People," but this phrase did not include those enslaved, then a fifth of the population. These founders clearly viewed the new United States from an aggressive white racial perspective. At least seven sections of the new Constitution protected the already old system of racialized enslavement: (1) Article 1, Section 2 counts an enslaved person as only three-fifths of a white person; (2) Article 1, Sections 2 and 9 apportion taxes using the three-fifths formula; (3) Article 1, Section 8 gives Congress authority to suppress slave insurrections; (4) Article 1, Section 9 prevents abolishing the slave trade before 1808; (5) Article 1, Sections 9 and 10 exempt slave-made goods from export duties; (6) Article 4, Section 2 requires the return of fugitive slaves; and (7) Article 4, Section 4 stipulates that the federal government must help states put down domestic violence, a provision that the framers included in part to deal with slave uprisings.[10] As we observe in these provisions, enslaved African Americans were frequently on the minds of the framers, who referred to African American enslavement numerous times at the Constitutional convention and generally with euphemistic language in the final Constitution. Their constitutional debates revealed that most generally viewed those enslaved as property as less than fully human. At this point in time, the white racial frame and the slavery system it rationalized were more than a century old and were aggressively enhanced and imbedded in the new and inegalitarian U.S. political institutions.

Numerous other provisions of the Constitution besides those listed above helped to institutionalize slavery. One surprising example is the provision for a required federal population census. While some type of census would have been necessary to apportion the new U.S. House, requiring a U.S. census as part of the Constitution was an idea pressed by southern slaveholders seeking to insure that the South's growing white and black populations would be counted for the purpose of increased white representation. In this way southern elites would soon be able to counter the North's demographic dominance. Leading northern delegates, however, opposed the provision for a regular census that was put in the Constitution, in part because the North then dominated in population and would have a majority in Congress. Soon after the U.S. government was created, in 1790 the Secretary of State used federal marshals to do a federal census of the country, which counted 3.9 million inhabitants. About one-fifth were African Americans who were not citizens and had no political representation under the Constitution.[11]

Federal population counts buttressed the Constitution's infamous three-fifths clause (termed the "federal ratio"), which counted three-fifths of enslaved African Americans for the purpose of expanding white political representation in the growing southern slave states. With their large enslaved populations in mind, the representatives of southern slaveholders at the Constitutional convention operated out of a strong white master frame and insisted on carefully counting those enslaved. They thereby got many extra white representatives in the new U.S. Congress—and thus extra votes in the undemocratic "electoral college" that has chosen the U.S. president ever since.

Thomas Jefferson would not have become the third U.S. president without the extra votes he got in the electoral college because of the white electors who were there only because of the three-fifths counting of enslaved black Americans in southern states. Also, without these extra white members of Congress provided to southern whites by the three-fifths clause, numerous actions of Congress and presidents in the slavery era would likely have had different results. Slavery would have been banned in the new state of Missouri, the slaveholding President Andrew Jackson would have failed to pass his extreme 1830 Indian Removal Act, and the Kansas-Nebraska bill allowing residents to choose slavery in these midwestern areas would not have become law. The United States, thus, became a quite different country than it might have been because of seven long decades of substantial slaveholders' control of U.S. political institutions.[12]

In addition, operating out of a strong white framing, these elite founders instituted a U.S. Senate, an anti-democratic political institution designed, as the slaveholding architect of the U.S. Constitution James Madison put it, "to protect the people against the transient impressions into which they themselves might be led." As a result, until the early twentieth century U.S. Senators were even elected by state legislators, *not* directly by ordinary voters, and they have always served staggered six-year terms so they can serve longer than members of the more democratic U.S. House. This oligarchical U.S. Senate was critical to the protection of the racialized interests of white slaveholders and segregationists for most of U.S. history, from the 1790s to the 1970s. Southern Senators frequently articulated aggressive versions of the white racist frame for the general public and the other Senators; and, using anti-democratic Senate rules, they were able to block every significant piece of anti-slavery legislation before the Civil War and every significant piece of civil rights legislation between the 1870s and the 1964 Civil Rights Act.[13]

Another undemocratic invention of the white framers is the U.S. Supreme Court. Intentionally created as an unelected body with little democratic overview, over time the Court has gained great unsupervised power, much of it legislative: "No other tribunal on earth rivals it. No other [major] government reserves the last word for the judiciary to pronounce."[14] Consider the membership of the Supreme Court over its history. For long periods a majority of Supreme Court justices were southern slaveholders or segregationists. As of 2012, a total of just 112 people, 108 men and 4 women, have ever served as powerful Supreme Court justices. More than 97 percent have been white, and 93 percent have been white men. Given this extremely biased demographic reality, the dominance of a strong male-oriented (patriarchal) version of the white racial frame in many U.S. court decisions and in much U.S. law, now over more than two centuries, is certainly unsurprising.

That dominant frame has long been central in decisions of the high court. From the 1790s to the 1930s, with rare exceptions, the Supreme Court played a central and overt role in the maintenance of racial slavery and Jim Crow segregation for African Americans, as well as in the oppression of other Americans of color. In this long era, the high court majority usually rejected accounts of oppression and pleas for redress provided by African Americans in regard to slavery, segregation, and other racial oppression. The all-white-male justices in that era periodically made it clear that African Americans did not have any legitimate voice in U.S. social and legal affairs. In the infamous 1856 *Dred Scott v. Sandford* decision the Court's slaveholding majority ruled that black Americans were, in the words of the white chief justice, "beings of an inferior order, and altogether unfit to associate with the white race, either in social or political relations; and so far inferior that they had no rights which the white man was bound to respect."[15] A strong racist framing of black inferiority and white superiority was openly articulated by many Supreme Court and other federal judges for the next century, indeed into the 1950s and 1960s.

Another slavery-shaped feature of the U.S. Constitution and of numerous later congressional actions and judicial decisions is the heavy accent on "state's rights," which emphasis has from the beginning been used to protect racial oppression—first slavery, then legal segregation, and now some contemporary racial discrimination. For centuries now, whites in many areas have pressed for strong white-controlled local and state governments, and a relatively weak federal ability to intervene in certain local government matters, often including civil rights matters such as segregation ordinances and restrictions on the voting rights of residents of color.

The colonial and U.S. slavery system was a direct contradiction of the white liberty-and-justice frame in numerous ways, not the least of which was that major slaveholders would not allow majorities of people to have substantial power over their economic and political concerns, especially within southern and border states. Once the colonies had banded together in a federal union, these slaveholders, as Robin Einhorn has shown, came to understand that truly democratic governments at the local level could be a serious threat to their power and to slavery. For that reason, the slaveholding elite usually took control over state and local governments where there were numerous enslaved Americans. The states' rights and other anti-federal-government rhetoric that has long pervaded this country's legal and political debates is historically rooted in the interests of whites during the slavery and Jim Crow eras—and not just in idealistic conceptions of liberty.[16] While there are other sources of contemporary anti-government rhetoric, a major early source was the fear of white slaveholders and their segregationist descendants in more recent decades that federal agencies might interfere with their "freedom" to dominate Americans of color.

Using the great power given to them by the three-fifths clause and other provisions of the Constitution, southern slaveholding interests effectively used the federal government to support their major political-economic interests until 1860. In 1850, thus, Congress passed a Fugitive Slave Law, which slaveholders won only because of the federal ratio. Under this law, a federal marshal could command any citizen to "aid and assist" in apprehending enslaved African American runaways. Such a provision for a federal "posse comitatus" was another support for what white southerners framed in their minds as a white slaveholding republic. From 1850 to 1865 such laws were used to force all white citizens, however they felt, to support the slavery system.[17]

The "founding fathers" created a U.S. origins narrative that was (and still is) substantially mythological, a story in which a mostly anti-democratic, often slaveholding, group of elite white men were said to be heroes championing ideals of equality and democracy for a new United States. These elite leaders created an imagined community, that is, a heralded "democratic" society in which all Americans supposedly shared comradeship. However, contrary to this mythology, the U.S. Constitution did not create a democracy where most adult Americans had the right to participate substantially and freely in political institutions. Native Americans and African Americans, constituting at least a fifth of the population, were excluded. As Vincent Harding has put it, the U.S. constitutional convention was "more like a poorly attended dress rehearsal, with most of the rightful and necessary performers and creators *barred from the stage*."[18]

From the beginning, the democratic rhetoric was usually more about public relations and the interests of the white elite than about creating actual democratic institutions. The new U.S. society was highly inegalitarian, with extreme inequality across the color line. The new United States was mostly led by white men who were overt white supremacists. It was a society that had no sense of shared comradeship among its white, black, and Native American residents. In 1843 no less a figure than former president and then member of Congress John Quincy Adams asserted in a congressional speech that the United States had *never* been a democracy because it had long been effectively controlled by a few thousand slaveholders.[19] In this era U.S. political institutions were often openly pro-slavery, and an overtly white supremacist framing and dominance was asserted by many white leaders through these institutions until the ending of Jim Crow segregation in the 1960s.

Local Enforcement of Systemic Racism

Operating under the undemocratic Constitution, and under white-framed congressional and presidential actions flowing from it, white elites in slaveholding states enforced and extended the slavery system using local and state governments and private institutions. Harriet Beecher Stowe, the white abolitionist famous for her anti-slavery novel *Uncle Tom's Cabin*, put together a nonfiction book with much evidence to support the accounts of brutal enslavement in her novel. In that second book she provides many examples showing the role of southern white judges, ministers, and newspaper publishers in protecting and extending black enslavement. As one historian has noted, "Slavery brutalized, made insensitive to the suffering of others not only the masses but judges and magistrates, legislators, professors of religion, preachers of Christianity, persons of property and members of the highest strata."[20]

In her nonfiction book Stowe reprints many slaveholders' advertisements for enslaved runaways, in which references to scars and disabilities reveal how physically abused they were. These advertisements signal how well organized the slave-catching system was across many states. Stowe concludes from extensive research that the "legal power of the master amounts to an absolute despotism over body and soul; and that there is no protection for the slave's life and limb, his family relations, his conscience, nay, more his eternal interests, but the character of the master."[21] North American slavery, especially in the South, was a type of "totalitarian" social system, one that controlled all major aspects of the lives of African Americans (and some Native Americans) who were enslaved. Stowe is also critical of racism in New England. The official abolition of slavery there did not remove the "most baneful feature of the system—that which makes American worse than Roman slavery—the prejudice of caste and color."[22] Indeed, New England whites created the first Jim Crow laws and customs that excluded "free" African Americans from schools, juries, and voting.

In numerous northern areas whites tried to drive out black residents by means of settlement and tax laws or by violently destroying their homes and businesses. In northern newspapers, as in southern newspapers, there was a recurring framing of black Americans as alien, lazy, or dangerous—stereotyped images that rationalized and facilitated the segregation or enslavement of black Americans. In northern and western areas, as in the South, most whites also held to the idea of the United States being a "white republic." In the 1850s even the still greatly celebrated U.S. "poet of democracy," Walt Whitman, asked this rhetorical question aggressively from the white racial frame: "Is not America for Whites?"[23]

Conclusion: The Persistence of Racial Oppression

A striking feature of systemic racism in the United States is how long it has persisted with a strikingly inegalitarian hierarchy firmly in place. A useful concept here is that of the *social reproduction* of racial hierarchy. The perpetuation of this hierarchical system has required a constant reproducing of major inegalitarian institutions and their discriminatory arrangements and processes. For systemic racism to persist across so many generations, white individuals and small groups have had to participate actively in the ongoing collective and discriminatory reproduction of the family, community, legal, political, economic, educational, and religious institutions that undergird this inegalitarian system.

Substantial inequalities between white Americans and Americans of color have been routinely reproduced over the generations in these areas both by individual actions and by institutional forces. Most white Americans are not aware that a majority of white families today are relatively affluent because of many large-scale federal assistance programs and giveaways— such as the 246 million acres of land given away almost exclusively to white families under federal homestead laws from the 1860s to the 1930s or the mostly white, large-scale public support programs, such as federal housing and college assistance programs, provided in the decades immediately after World War II. Such unjust enrichment for whites has long meant unjust impoverish-ment for Americans of color. Over centuries, thus the social relations of exploitation have created much income, wealth, social status, political power and privilege, and other racial capital for whites, which have in turn pro-vided much racial capital for their many white descendants, indeed to the present day.

The deep structure of racial oppression and inequality has been relatively stable over time because its evolution has gradually ruled out other options as important societal choice points pass by. Still, the development of this deep racialized structure has not been inevitable, but has been generated to a substantial degree by elite white choices at key points in time, choice points that have shaped the internal arrangement of its institutional parts and the patterned activities of the actors that constantly reinforce that arrangement. Our racist system exists because of the recurring actions of a great array of human actors, but especially those of powerful white decisionmakers. One revealing bias in many mainstream social science and humanities analyses of North American history is that, while they sometimes depict ordinary whites as prejudiced, they rarely discuss critically and in detail the framing and actions of elite white actors that have greatly shaped and maintained this country's system of racial oppression.

The constant reinforcing decisions of these elite whites and their assistants have perpetuated and maintained the deep structure of U.S. racism through many reciprocal linkages and social feedback loops. The longer a system is in operation, the more ways its actors, especially its controlling decisionmakers, develop connecting relationships among themselves within major institutions, share important socioeconomic resources, and become skilled at maintaining an inegalitarian system. Even if obvious political barriers to significant change in the system of racial oppression can be overcome, there will likely still be the major problem of the interwoven relationships and greatly unequal resources of powerful whites—which have for centuries been constantly regenerated by deep and inegalitarian societal processes.[24]

In a society's history early social choice points are often the most important. In the case of systemic racism in North America, to cite a major example, the choice by elite whites to go with African American enslavement to create economic development and much white wealth has had large-scale impacts on society ever since. The elite choice not to go with free labor, and the elite and rank-and-file whites' choices to kill off or drive out indigenous Americans, have had profound longterm consequences for the racial structure of society. Moreover, when the foundational reality of slavery could have been abandoned, around the time of the 1787 founding of the United States, most powerful white men decided to go with the political and economic choice of expanding the enslavement of the large-scale slavery system rather than to abandon it—often, in part, to increase their own families' wealth.

Once these critical societal choices are made, the system of oppression has a strong inertial force keeping it in place. The first law of physical motion, the famous law of "inertia," asserts that an object at rest will continue at rest, or an object in motion will continue moving in one direction, until an unbalancing counter-force is exerted on it. Applying this idea to the social realm, one observes a very strong tendency for racial oppression's major exploitative mechanisms, resource inequalities, norms, and buttressing attitudes to remain substantially in force and mostly unchanged until a major unbalancing force significantly challenges that oppression. Thus, the everyday operation of racial oppression, its routine and roughly stable equilibrium, is only occasionally disrupted in a significant and lasting way. The racist U.S. system does sometimes change a bit in order to meet important external shifts and environmental pressures, on occasion significantly, but so far without altering much of its deep racist structure. Media-reported societal turbulence over racial matters can periodically make it seem like there is more societal change than there really is, and thus hide the still powerful and enduring realities of systemic racism.

Reacting to social turbulence, those whites in power prefer to make ad hoc modifications, rather than to significantly change the deep racial structure. For example, when U.S. slavery was finally abolished in the 1860s—in part because of great pressure from black and white abolitionists and much everyday resistance from those enslaved—elite white decisionmakers chose to keep as much of the old oppressive system in place as possible by moving to the near-slavery of Jim Crow segregation, rather than to just abandon the racial oppression. When our system of racism does finally change somewhat, a "law of social inertia" seems to operate that keeps the society more like it was in the past than like the "dramatically changed" society that many often celebrate.

CHAPTER **3**

Creating a White Racial Frame
The First Century

As European colonizers spread out across the Atlantic world, in their minds and practices they usually positioned themselves socially and mentally higher than other peoples with whom they came into contact. They saw themselves as exceptional, as "charged with a special spiritual and political destiny" whose task was to build a "New World" as a societal model for all Christians.[1] After developing an extensive colonial system involving land and labor theft across the Atlantic basin, the colonizers worked hard to rationalize, explain, and structure in their minds and writings how it was that they, as "good and virtuous" Christians, could create such a violent and bloody system of human exploitation and subordination.

Rationalizing the destruction of indigenous peoples and enslavement of Africans in North America apparently seemed essential to the European colonizers. Because of the scale of their genocidal and enslaving actions over the next centuries, their rationalizing and interpretive framing needed to be strong and comprehensive. Their written histories are useful for understanding this framing. In their writings, colonialism and imperialism are rationalized by proto-racial thinking that from the beginning inclined the Spanish, English, and other European colonizers to dehumanize the "others" that they killed and enslaved as physically and culturally inferior. Their early framing soon became systematically racialized as a distinctive white racial frame because these Europeans seemed to need that type of framing to rationalize and interpret for themselves and others their extensive land and labor theft from indigenous peoples and their labor theft from Africans.

Central Elements of the Frame: The Great Chain of Being

Recall that European colonialism and oppression in North America brought a social stigmatization of those oppressed. Interestingly, the Europeans' early framing of the latter used the image-schema of an up-down ladder with its hierarchy of superior and inferior human groups. (An image-schema is an image feature of a mental frame that provides understandings of experience.)[2] In their early framing, European colonists drew on an older European image-schema, a hierarchical pattern called the "great chain of being" that dates back to ancient Greece. This is a hierarchical conception of the "structure of the world which, through the Middle Ages and down to the late eighteenth century, many philosophers, most men of science, and, indeed, most educated men, were to accept without question." In this conception of the universe there is an "infinite number of links ranging in hierarchical order from the meagerest kind of existence, which barely escapes nonexistence, through 'every possible' grade up to ... the highest possible kind of creature."[3]

Long before the colonial era, Europeans had put human beings at the top of creation because of reasoning abilities. The higher up the chain of being, the more valued and human a group is, and the lower down, the less valued and human. Christians were firmly above non-Christians, aristocrats above ordinary people, and men above women. A folk theory of a natural order is mapped onto a moral order. Persisting social inequalities are viewed as natural and legitimate.

Prior to its use in framing non-European peoples, the great-chain-of-being frame was an integral part of European patriarchal thinking that placed men above women in the human hierarchy. When they imposed their colonial rule on indigenous and African-origin peoples in North America, English colonizers already held in their minds a patriarchal frame and frequently used its family imagery in conceptualizing new overseas communities as legitimately under the control of European American "patriarchs."[4]

Europeans and European Americans extended understandings from the old great chain of being model to prescribe and defend societal hierarchies in which they were dominant and in which non-Europeans were subordinated. Seeking to rationalize what they were doing, the European Christians leading the colonization of the Americas and Africa framed newly conquered non-Europeans as being in the *bottom* levels of this great chain of being, with Europeans and their colonial descendants at the top. European men led colonial efforts and created a legitimating societal frame that was highly gendered. European colonialism involved a labor system with a division of labor and social status in which European American men were at the top, European American women well below, and indigenous people and African Americans were at the bottom. For centuries following North American colonization, European missionaries, government officials, and soldiers imposed Western views and hierarchical structures across the globe. The European male conquerors were "superior," "powerful," and "manly," while the subordinated peoples, male and female, were "inferior," "weak," and "childlike." Indeed, in this great-chain thinking we already see the close relationships, the intersections, between racial and gender framing by European and European American men.[5]

Early Racial Framing of Native Americans and African Americans

Scholars have debated whether the earliest European colonizers' views of Native Americans and African Americans were actually "racial" in a contemporary sense. Some argue that using the idea of "race" here reads back into past history contemporary racial ideas and that early colonists identified themselves mainly in terms of national identity and religion.[6]

Yet other analysts have shown from historical data like that presented later in this chapter that the main elements of the modern racial frame did exist in the earliest English American perspectives on Native Americans, Africans, and African Americans. Among the important ingredients of this frame are: (1) the recurring use of certain physical characteristics, such as skin color and facial features, to differentiate social groups; (2) the constant linking of physical characteristics to cultural characteristics; and (3) the regular use of physical and linked cultural distinctions to differentiate socially "superior" and "inferior" groups in a social hierarchy. These frame features are found in the earliest colonial thought among the European colonizers, as can be seen in their early tracts, laws, and sermons. Once these distinctions of superior and inferior group membership were in place, they served to justify concentrating an array of material and other resources in the hands of the supposedly superior group. The operation of this distinctive frame is clearly to be seen in the everyday thinking and practices of European Americans that actively biologized and dehumanized Native Americans and African Americans.

To prevent confusion, thus, I will refer to this rationalizing and interpretive European frame in the early seventeenth century as racial, though some readers may prefer to consider it to be proto-racial until the last decades of the seventeenth century, when the dominant European American frame was even more explicitly racialized.[7]

In the first decades of the colonizing invasions, the distinctive European framing of Native Americans and African Americans was already being developed. Each outgroup that was central to capital accumulation in Europe's colonizing expansion was denigrated. Almost immediately, the

English American colonists made great use of physical and biological markers in defining and oppressing "Indians" and "Negroes," both labels they borrowed from the Spanish language of earlier invaders of the Americas. Those subordinated were colorized and biologized, with skin color and other physical features negatively characterized and connected to their low position at the bottom levels of the great chain of being. These views were, from the beginning, much more than verbal-cognitive, for they involved very strong negative images and emotions. The colonists put European Americans as fully human beings at the top of that great-chain-of-being hierarchy, with African Americans and Native Americans as less than fully human at the bottom. Religious-cultural and physical-biological interpretations coexisted, although religion got more emphasis at the early stage and the biological/physical aspect got more attention and was explicitly named as a matter of "race" by the late 1600s. The major defining dimensions of the European American racial frame were already in place by the early decades of the 1600s, albeit dimensions that became ever more systematized over the next century.[8]

Negative biologically oriented thinking about the oppressed others and negative culturally oriented thinking about them have been closely linked from at least the early 1600s. From the beginning, European Americans have merged cultural and physical aspects of groups in their minds, both for themselves and for outgroups they have routinely subordinated.

Early Framing of Indigenous Peoples

Conceptions of the "others" encountered and used in the European colonial expansion varied with their utility for European colonizers. In colonial conquests in Central and South America, early Spanish conquerors defined and viewed indigenous peoples as inferior "Indians" and "natural slaves, as subhuman beasts of burden."[9] Columbus recorded details about the lives of indigenous peoples of the Caribbean, as he and his men proceeded to subordinate, enslave, and kill them in the thousands. Over centuries of colonization of the Caribbean, Central America, South America, and North America, the Spanish sought indigenous peoples' lands and labor and brought genocidal wars, enslavement, and European diseases that killed tens of millions of indigenous inhabitants.

In North America, later English colonizers and their descendants were much less interested in using Indians as enslaved laborers, although they did enslave some for a time. English colonists were mainly interested in stealing land. Prior to arrival, the English colonizers knew little about "Indians," except what they had gained from Spanish writings. The Spanish influence can be seen in the Spanish-derived English words "Indian" and "Negro" (black).[10] In addition, these English umbrella-type words, "Indian" and "Negro," indicate that European colonists often saw few differences among the many indigenous American groups and the many African groups they encountered. They lumped these culturally diverse groups together into umbrella categories. Such categorizing suggests that a prototypical visual image and associated set of racialized stereotypes had already become part of early European American framing of those oppressed.

Significantly, most English colonists early defined indigenous Americans as the uncivilized enemy, and wars with the Native Americans who resisted invasion were important in accenting the sense of European cultural and physical distinctiveness. In the early 1600s the English colonists' framing of "Indians" grew out of a rationalization of warfare with them and of the taking of their land. The first English colony was established on Roanoke Island, off what became the colony of Virginia. English commentaries from this era indicate a variable view of indigenous Americans. The colonizer Arthur Barlowe landed in this area in 1584, claimed it for "her highness," and penned this account of indigenous people: "We found the people most gentle loving and faithful, void of all guile and treason, and such as lived after the manner of the Golden Age." Soon thereafter, however, English colonizers attacked these gentle people because they were, as Robert Gray described them, "wild beasts, and unreasonable creatures" or "brutish savages." Moreover, they were not Christians and "worshipped the devil." As Barlowe recounted, "we burnt, and spoyled their corne, and Towne, all the people beeing fledde."[11]

Thinking in military terms, those who founded the Roanoke colony reported to England that indigenous people were scared of English weaponry and could be conquered. "Indian" and "savage" were common terms applied to indigenous peoples by early colonists, although they also used "infidel," "heathen," and "barbarian," all revealing the religious dimension of early framing of indigenous peoples, one that has lasted to the present.[12] Color and physical characteristics got some attention, but seem less significant in this early English American framing of Native Americans than in their subsequent framing of African Americans—a differentiating tendency that would persist over subsequent centuries.

Later English colonists also wrote of their mostly negative views of indigenous peoples. At Jamestown, Virginia, the celebrated Captain John Smith viewed indigenous groups as uncivilized "savages" and "inconstant in everie thing" and "craftie, timerous ... very ingenuous." Smith made it clear that he did not trust the "craftie" indigenous groups that dominated the area at this time. In 1613 the English minister Alexander Whitaker described them as "barbarous people," "naked slaves of the divell," yet still as "industrious in their labour." In 1625 Samuel Purchas described them as "having little of humanitie but shape, ignorant of Civilitie, of Arts, of Religion; moree brutish than the beasts they hunt ... captivated also to Satans tyrallny in foolish pieties, wicked idlenesse, busie and bloudy wickednesse." In these commentaries we again see early framing of Indians as uncivilized, unchristian, and beast-like. A few decades later, the leading English philosopher Thomas Hobbes would point to the "savage people in many places of America" as examples of those whose lives are, in his famous phrase, "poore, nasty, brutish, and short."[13] Of course, their shortened and impoverished lives were often the *result* of English invasions.

The leaders of the Massachusetts colony to the north operated out of a similar imperialistic frame that led them to speak of North America as "unpeopled" and to destroy indigenous communities to secure land.[14] Much colonial language described the Indians as "wild beasts" who should be "removed from their dens" and killed. As one historian notes, "In times of trouble natives were always wild animals that had to be rooted out of their dens, swamps, jungles."[15] Here we glimpse another important dimension of European framing of the "other," one that animalized them and placed them well down the great-chain hierarchy. Significantly, in 1637 one dissenting colonist, Thomas Morton, wrote disapprovingly of this colonial framing of Indians. He described the "new creed" of fellow European colonists as holding that the "Salvages [savages] are a dangerous people, subtill, secreat and mischeivous." Morton disagreed: "I have found the Massachusetts Indian more full of humanity then the Christians."[16] A major dissenter from the hostile Eurocentric framing of Indians, Morton himself was persecuted for his views and positive relationships with Indians.

In most of these commentaries the powerful European American frame not only focused on the subordinated "others," usually negatively, but also on the oppressors themselves, usually very positively. From the beginning, this dominant frame was unidirectional and emotion-laden: The "others" are portrayed negatively and are mainly to blame for intergroup conflicts, while whites are portrayed as virtuous and rarely to blame for such conflicts.

At an early point in North American colonization, the dominant framing accented the view that European Americans were "virtuous republicans," to use Ronald Takaki's apt phrase. Spanish, English, and other European conquerors rationalized the oppression of indigenous peoples in Eurocentric religious and moralizing terms. European American colonists' framing of the new society portrayed themselves as rational, ascetic, civilized, and sexually controlled, while Native Americans and African Americans were stereotyped as irrational, hedonistic, uncivilized, and oversexed. Researchers have recently demonstrated the religiously repressed nature of many European colonists, with their obsessive fears of the "dark others," the irrational and unvirtuous non-European peoples who were thought to be the opposite of Europeans. The European Americans who saw themselves as virtuous republicans increasingly resented what they had given up, and thus often portrayed Native Americans and African Americans in terms of the things they had given up. The European American thus created a "pornography of his former life . . . in order to insure that he will not slip back into the old ways or act our half-supposed fantasies."[17] Clearly, there is strong counterpoint thinking here: "The Indian became important for the English mind not for what he was in and of himself, but rather for what he showed civilized men they were not and must not become."[18]

Note here the central importance of the European American notion that it is the "others" who are irrational and emotional. In this view rationality equals emotionlessness, and irrationality equals emotionality. Yet, from the beginning to the present, European Americans' fears, angers, and jealousies about other racial groups have signaled their own powerful and often destructive emotions, no matter how much they attempt to repress an overt consideration of them.

Early Framing of African Americans

Before the colonizing of North America, early European travelers to Africa had returned to northern Europe with views accenting some positive features of Africa and Africans, but also citing what they viewed as their supposedly ugly, unchristian, and uncivilized character, the latter two views much like those Europeans had of indigenous Americans. Sexual imagery played a role in early European views as well. Just prior to the colonial era early English mapmakers put images on maps that would become more central in later white framing, such as images of large genitals on black male and female figures placed onto maps. However, as one sees in the sympathetic Othello (African) character in William Shakespeare's 1603 play by that name, by the time of English colonization of North America in the 1600s there was still ambiguity in English views of people of African descent. A fully developed negative inferiorization of Africans did not emerge until a little later, with the North American colonization.[19]

The first twenty Africans imported into the new colonies were purchased off a Dutch-flagged ship with "victuals" (foodstuffs) by the European colonists at Jamestown, Virginia, in 1619. Their labor became so valuable that the numbers of those enslaved grew rapidly. By 1650 there were 300 African Americans in Virginia; by 1700 about 6000; and by the time of the revolution in the 1770s about 270,000, nearly half that largest North American colony's total population. In the first two decades of colonial development the early Africans bought off slave ships were sometimes enslaved for life and at other times treated by the colonists more like indentured servants. However, while some were freed after long terms of service in the earliest decades, by the 1660s most were enslaved for life. At an early point in time, English servants in the colonies are recorded as insisting that they cannot be made into "slaves" by their masters or political authorities, signaling they saw slavery as something only non-Europeans should endure.[20]

Even in these early decades the position of the "Negro" workers was never equal to that of the European American indentured servants. The sense of European superiority and Negro inferiority is in the legal and other colonial records from the beginning. Early European views of the dark color of African Americans appear in comments of Captain John Smith on those first twenty Africans (called "negars") imported at Jamestown in 1619, as well as in court decisions and legal statutes soon after that date in Virginia and Massachusetts. As early as 1624, colonial court cases were making it clear that people of African ancestry were framed as socially inferior and physically distinctive in a negative way. The first reference to a "negro" was in a 1624 proceeding, when the Council and General Court of Virginia mentioned a certain "John Philip, A negro ... Christened in England 12 years since," who testified in a court case against an English colonist. Imposed inferiority was clear in European colonists' framing of a man as "negro," a physical color-coded name (from the Spanish for "black") and identity assigned to him by English colonists and not chosen by African Americans. Indeed, the color-coded identity of none of the other trial participants is mentioned in the legal account. That account indicates that Philip was a Christian, which meant that he had more legitimacy in European eyes. If a negative framing of black Americans as inferior had not already been in place, neither "negro" not "christened" would have been relevant to mention.[21]

Just six years later, in another Virginia case, an English man who was found "lying with a negro" was condemned to be whipped "before an assembly of negroes & others for abusing himself to the dishonor of God and shame of Christianity." The man, Hugh Davis, was viewed by the court as having defiled himself with someone physically inferior and was punished before African Americans and others. A "negro" woman's inferiority is here officially indicated, perhaps for the first time in North American history. In another example, an English colonist who had sexual relations with a "negro" was punished for "dishonoring" God by doing public penance in a church. Such forbidden sexual relations were framed as a religious violation. In their laws and court decisions early European colonists made clear their concern, indeed obsession, with intergroup sexual relationships. Strong emotions are evident in early laws against intergroup sex and marriage, with both considered to be "unnatural." In 1662 Virginia established the first law officially banning interracial sex, and in 1691 a law against interracial marriage was enforced by banishment. Again, we see the ways in which these English colonists saw themselves as virtuous and those they oppressed as venal and unvirtuous.[22]

Laws passed in other colonies indicate a similar framing. In a 1690s preamble to a South Carolina slavery law, white lawmakers comment on those enslaved: They "are of barbarous, wild, savage natures, and ... constitutions, laws and orders, should in this Province be made and enacted, for the good regulating and ordering of them, as may restrain the disorders, rapines and inhumanity, to which they are naturally prone and inclined."[23] Here the terms "barbarous, wild, savage" not only conjure up notions of African Americans as uncivilized, but also views of the latter as dangerous, rebellious, and criminal—a distinctive racial stereotyping relating to emotional white concerns about African Americans rebelling against enslavement, against good "laws and orders." Notice the biological implications of the language of "natures" and "naturally." Again we observe similarities in European American framing of African Americans and Native Americans.

These examples reveal that European colonists, no matter how lowly their social positions, were considered superior to African Americans and were regularly treated as such by laws and political action. As legal expert Leon Higginbotham has shown, colonial court cases reveal how concepts of group inferiority and superiority were early and firmly established: Make clear English superiority and "negro" inferiority in all things social, punish in public those who violate these understandings, and rationalize these understandings using a strong framing that accents physical (especially color) notions and religious ideas.[24]

Africans and African Americans were early viewed in colonial laws and in other ways as personal property of European Americans. European American lawyers, judges, and other high officials did much to create this dehumanized framing of African Americans. A 1669 Virginia statute asserted it was not a felony for a master to kill an enslaved African American who was stubborn, for that was only a matter of property. In 1671 the General Assembly declared that sheep, horses, cattle, and Negroes could be inherited by a white orphan.[25]

In the first century of colonial development we observe an important defining and naming process associated with a strong white racial frame. In 1680 the prominent minister Morgan Godwyn, who lived in Barbados and Virginia, concluded that "these two words, Negro and Slave ... [are] by custom grown Homogeneous and Convertible; even as Negro and Christian, Englishman and Heathen, are by the like corrupt Custom and Partiality made Opposites."[26] This was certainly the view of established colonial law by this time. (Later on, writing in the mid-eighteenth century, Quaker leader John Woolman similarly pointed out that "whites" of the "meanest sort" would never be enslaved and accented the role of color in whites' enslavement of black Americans: "This is owing chiefly to the idea of slavery being connected with the black colour, and liberty with the white: and where false ideas are twisted into our minds, it is with difficulty we get fairly disentangled."[27]) Not only were the words "Negro" or "black" already in the mid-seventeenth century synonymous with "slave," but the white frame-makers had imposed a new identity on the culturally diverse Africans. Older sociocultural identities of Africans were partially or totally destroyed by this imposition of an oppressed situation and identity.

Early European colonists also called those of African descent "negars," "mulattos," and "Moors," in all cases accenting them as physically distinctive and racialized. From 1619 onward the physical features, especially the black "complexion," of African Americans were an increasing obsession in European colonists' minds and in those of their descendants. In 1676 one colonial commentary insisted that a "blackamoore" was not physically beautiful; and in 1680, Godwyn, the English minister, wrote a pamphlet on slavery in which he noted the importance of skin color: "their Complexion, which being most obvious to the sight . . . is apt to make no slight impressions upon rude Minds."[28] In addition, with more lighter skinned, multiracial African Americans appearing in the last decades of the seventeenth century, whites' framing of African Americans adopted the "one drop of blood" rule. All children with obvious (to whites) African ancestry inherited a parent's condition of racial inferiority.[29]

In contrast, the earliest references to European colonists are to "Englishmen," "Irish," "Scotch," "Christians," or just "men" and "persons." The term "white" as a color designation for European traders and colonists was in occasional use before the English developed the American colonies, but its regular use comes in later decades of the seventeenth century. Moreover, in the English language of the European colonists, prior to the development of African American enslavement, the word "white" had uses that were mostly positive, such as "gleaming brightly," as for a candle, while the word "black" had mostly negative meanings like "sooted." The word "black" had long been used by the residents of England metaphorically, to describe evil. It was soon adopted by early English colonists for the purpose of naming dark-skinned Africans.[30]

Over this first century of colonization, legal statutes reveal an increasing use of "white" for English Americans, as in this 1691 Virginia law: "whatsoever English or other white man or women . . . shall intermarry with a Negro, mulatto, or Indian man or woman . . . shall . . . be banished from this dominion forever."[31] Both "white" and "black" were not temporary or unattached words, for they were defined within the ever-growing white racial frame. In its racial usage the word "white" was mainly conceptualized in contrast to the word "black"—initially and most powerfully by those who defined themselves as "white." These language developments were a clear indication of the institutionalization of African American slavery and of its racialized rationalization. Increasingly, the word "white" defined who European Americans were, and who they were not. Whiteness was a "terrible invention," as W. E. B. Du Bois put it, one that further solidified European thinking into an extensive either/or framework and came to symbolize for whites civilization and "ownership of the earth." While some contemporary analysts view the accentuated solidarity of North American whites as being a more recent invention—perhaps only after the Civil War—whites were in fact already a distinctive racial group with shared cultural heritage and in a clear racial hierarchy no later than the late seventeenth century.[32]

Who Made the Broad Racial Frame, and How?

Numerous scholars and popular analysts have viewed the concept of "race" as "a folk classification, a product of popular beliefs about human differences." Certainly, the thinking of ordinary European Americans about Native and African Americans became increasingly racialized over the seventeenth century, but much development and propagation of that racist framing came from the European American *leaders*. While people at all social levels have used racialized categories in sorting out and shaping their everyday experiences, the white leaders such as judges, ministers, merchants, doctors, slaveholders, and government officials have usually been the most important in developing, codifying, and propagating strong social categorizations such as that described by the term "race." Since at least the mid-1600s a powerful racial framing has been explicitly, actively, and profoundly developed by the ruling elite, an elite that has over the centuries created and consistently communicated this important framing by means of schools, churches, the legal system, and the media. As anti-Indian genocide and African American enslavement became ever more important in North American development, the European American elite aggressively crafted a well-developed white racial frame designed to defend overseas colonialism and imperialism.

European and European American *scientists* played an important role in shifting the old great-chain-of-being view from a theologically oriented hierarchy with God at the top to a more secular hierarchy that accented "species" or "races" of human beings. Already, by the mid-1600s, these scientists and their associates were designating and writing about dominant and subordinated groups in colonial areas as different "species," which were viewed as part of a natural order to be investigated by the sciences. They were among the first to use the word "race" in English, a word borrowed from the Spanish word "raza." In its earliest usage the English word "race" was employed in various ways to classify people and animals, but one of its important uses was for breeding groups and stocks, with a clear linkage to inheritable traits.[33]

By the 1670s British, French, and North American scientists and social analysts had laid the groundwork for a strong concept of a hierarchy of biologically distinctive "races," which has persisted over the centuries. Central to this effort in the 1670s was England's Sir William Petty, a leading anatomist and philosopher. Petty viewed and named "blacks" as physically and culturally inferior to "whites." Drawing on European travelers' accounts of the Americas and Africa for data, he began a manuscript on the "scale of creatures" and accented hierarchical gradations among human beings. He speculated there were unchangeable human "species" or "races" that were breeding groups and were characterized by physical and cultural differences.

Petty asserted that the Africans who lived near Africa's Cape of Good Hope were the most "beastlike" of all the "men with whom our travelers are well acquainted."[34] The notion of people of African descent being "beast-like" and lower on the "race" hierarchy than people of European descent was a notion that predated Petty, but he was apparently the first to enumerate the array of physical differences in a detailed way:

> I say that the Europeans do not only differ from the aforementioned Africans in color, which is as much as white differs from black, but also in their hair which differs as much as a straight line differs from a circle; but they differ also in the shape of their noses, lips and cheek bones, as also in the very outline of their faces and the mould of their skulls. They differ also in their natural manners, and in the internal qualities of their minds.[35]

Even at this early point in the elite shaping of the white racial frame, the influential Petty, a charter member of the English Royal Society, emphasized much that has persisted in that frame since his time—major physical differences in color, hair, nose and lip shape, facial and skull differences, as well as the concepts and words "white" and "black" for categorizing the groups involved. Like later white analysts, Perry accented intellectual ("qualities of their minds") and cultural characteristics ("natural manners") that he and other English observers assumed to be closely associated with the distinctive physical characteristics.

A few years earlier in 1665, a summary of the conclusions of French scientists and other analysts about "Negroes" had been published in English, and Perry may have made use of it. Drawing on French experience with

Caribbean slave plantations, this "scientific" account similarly accented certain physical characteristics:

> And to shew that the tincture of the skin is not the only particularity observable in Negroes, they have many other Properties whereby they are distinguish'd from other Nations; as their thick lips, saddlenoses, coarse short hair, the horny tunicle of the eye, and the teeth whiter than the rest of men.

The French statement accents strong stereotypes about the mental capacities of Negroes:

> Not to mention the Qualities of their minds, which are so ignorant, that though they have plenty of Flax, yet they want Cloth, because they want skill how to work it; they abound with Sugar-canes, yet make no trade of them, and esteem Copper more than Gold, which they barter for the like weight of Salt; and are wholly ignorant of Laws and Physick. Which ignorance renders their spirits more base and servile than those of other Nations; and they are so born to slavery.[36]

In addition, in the 1680s the prominent French scientist Francis Bernier was apparently the first to come up with a sorting out of human beings into four differentiated race-like categories: Europeans, Far Easterners, Negroes, and Lapps.

In the last few decades of the 1600s, thus, important members of the British and French scientific elites were accenting an array of physical, mental, and cultural distinctions that differentiated in their minds people of European and African ancestry. In their racial framing, which was designed to rationalize the subordination of indigenous and African peoples, they drew on important reports from travelers and colonists in North America, and the latter colonists were in turn influenced by this elite thinking as it percolated through their colonial ministers and other officials.

Establishing the Racial Frame: The First American Treatises

In this same era the educated white elite of North America was beginning to draft longer treatises that asserted clearly the white racial framing of society that had already appeared briefly in commentaries of judges in early colonial court cases. Let us examine two treatises, one against and one for slavery, by prominent New England judges and entrepreneurs. Their views of African Americans reveal that a strong and well-developed white racial frame was firmly in place in North America by the late seventeenth century.

Very few accounts of the racial views of white colonial leaders and intellectuals have survived from the early eighteenth century, but there are two that are revealing. In his 1700 treatise, *The Selling of Joseph*, the successful business leader and prominent Massachusetts judge, Samuel Sewall, wrote what was apparently the first attack on slavery by a white American. Citing biblical sources and using human rights language in arguing against slavery, Sewall asserted that, "And all things considered, it would conduce more to the Welfare of the Province, to have White Servants for a Term of Years, than to have [Black] Slaves for Life." In spite of these anti-slavery views, however, Sewall viewed African Americans from a strong racial frame. He argued that few whites

> can endure to hear of a Negro's being made free; and indeed they can seldom use their freedom well; yet their continual aspiring after their forbidden Liberty, renders them Unwilling Servants. And there is such a disparity in their Conditions, Colour & Hair, that they can never embody with us, and grow up into orderly Families, to the Peopling of the Land: but still remain in our Body Politick as a kind of extravasat Blood.

He later adds:

> Moreover it is too well known what Temptations Masters are under, to connive at the Fornication of their Slaves; lest they should be obliged to find them wives, or pay their Fines. It seems to be practically pleaded that they might be Lawless; 'tis thought much of, that the law should have Satisfaction for their Thefts, and other Immoralities.[37]

Clearly, the reality of slavery had a great shaping impact on the general worldview of leading white figures early in our colonial history. In these revealing comments from a prominent judge and business leader we observe much about the importance of slavery, even in New England. (About 1715, a fifth of those enslaved in the colonies were in the North.) Slavery is important enough in the northern colonies to motivate Judge Sewall to write a pamphlet.

In his pamphlet we observe key elements of a strong white racial frame. He accents physical differences—especially skin color, hair type, and "Blood." We observe the view, shared by Sewall and by slavery supporters as well, that freed African Americans do not "use their freedom well," do not have "orderly families," and are prone to "thefts and other immoralities." Even this opponent of slavery has trouble understanding how difficult life is for black Americans who are free or might become free, for they obviously do not have the same resources as better-off whites. Like Thomas Jefferson some decades later, Judge Sewall cannot envision the full social integration of black Americans into the "body" of white America. His inability or unwillingness to analyze the oppressive structural conditions in which all African Americans lived can be seen in the deceptive way ("Temptations Masters are under") he raised the issue of sexual relations forced by white men on enslaved black women. From the beginning, this suggests too, systemic racism involved *gendered* racial oppression.

Angered by this anti-slavery pamphlet, the Boston merchant, slave trader, and judge on the same court as Sewall, John Saffin, decided a few months later to reply. Also citing biblical passages to support his inegalitarian view of naturally "different Orders and Degrees of Men in the World," Saffin defended the institution of slavery vigorously and concluded with a vicious poem, "The Negroes' Character," apparently the first anti-black poem in North American history. Saffin attacked the character of black Americans in much the same way that the white frame often does today:

> Cowardly and cruel are those Blacks Innate,
> Prone to Revenge, Imp of inveterate hate.
> He that exasperates them, soon espies
> Mischief and murder in their very eyes.
> Libidinous, Deceitful, False and Rude,
> The Spume Issue of the Ingratitude.
> The Premeses consider'd, all may tell,
> How near good Joseph they are parallel.[38]

In this early and strong racist framing, Saffin sounds much like his abolitionist colleague Sewall. He asserted that "Blacks" were innately "Cowardly and cruel," were "Prone to Revenge," often had "Mischief and murder in their very eyes," held "inveterate hate," and were "Libidinous, Deceitful, False, and Rude," and ungrateful. Saffin is aggressively rationalizing his legal right to be a slave trader, that is, to take property in black bodies for his profit. Just in these brief excerpts from the minds of New England business leaders and judges, we observe key elements of the persisting white racial frame: a heavy accent on physical distinctiveness and strong racial stereotypes and images of black immorality and crime, family disorganization, cruelty, hate, deceit, and sexuality. Most of these early stereotypes, images, and interpretations are still part of the modern white framing.

In the treatises by Sewall and Saffin, as well as in some colonial court cases, we observe that the racial framing of African Americans was religiously sanctioned and circulated broadly to rank-and-file citizens by leading officials in this relatively new country. Very important in this regard were prominent New England ministers like Cotton Mather and Jonathan Edwards, who were among the earliest North American intellectuals to aggressively defend the racist hierarchy. Like other colonists, they viewed African Americans and Indians as inferior. In a 1706 treatise, Cotton Mather argued that whites should try to "Christianize Negroes" to save their souls as well as those of their slavemasters. Christianizing Negroes, whom he describes as "creatures" and "barbarians," will make them willing to work harder for slavemasters and keep them from "magical conversations" with the devil. Mather commented thus:

> What shall I do that this poor creature may have cause to bless God forever, for falling into my hands. The state of your Negroes in this world, must be low, and mean and abject; a state of servitude. No great things in this world, can be done for them. Something then, let there be done, towards their welfare in the world to come.[39]

He added that those enslaved should be treated as "thy neighbours." This influential leader accepted slavery as God-ordained and necessary for African Americans because they were lowly, "brutish," and "stupid" creatures. He viewed a Christianizing education as enabling Negroes to become "men" and not be "beasts."[40] At an early stage, this powerful rationalizing frame was insisted upon by colonial economic, legal, political, and religious elites—men who actively fostered the increasingly omnipresent racial framing by means of communications in white-controlled churches, schools, and newspapers.

In these comments from New England judges and ministers, we note again that the early racial frame had strong visual, visceral, and emotional dimensions. There were numerous other examples of how complex and detailed this early framing was. For example, writing in the early 1700s, Edward Long, a Jamaican slaveholder whose writings were read in the North American colonies, accented the "natural sloth" and "bestial or fetid smell" of enslaved Africans. His writings indicate that stereotypes of odor were another part of the early white frame. Like Thomas Jefferson later in this century, Long also viewed those enslaved as close to apes in intelligence and behavior and propagated stories of their "amorous intercourse" with apes.[41]

Most white leaders throughout the colonies seem to have held a similarly positive framing of whites and a similarly negative framing of African Americans and Native Americans. Consider Quaker Pennsylvania, the colony where many whites reportedly were opposed to slavery. This colony's treatment of free black Americans made clear how central the racial frame was. White officials made certain that officially "free" black Americans faced severe laws prohibiting such activities as intermarriage and "loitering" (unemployment), for which the punishment was enslavement. While black Pennsylvanians were not numerous enough to present an economic threat to whites, they still were stereotyped as lazy, criminal, and a physical threat to white women. Here as elsewhere, African Americans also "constituted a psychological challenge to the status of free whites; the greater number of free blacks and the higher their status, the more their presence undermined the status of the general white population."[42]

Assessments of ordinary whites' views of African and Native Americans in this era have to be made mostly on the basis of official laws and public events in newspapers, for we have very few surviving records that directly indicate their views. One 1684 report has a brief quote purported to be the language used by white plantation overseers for enslaved workers: "Dam'd doggs, Black ugly Devils, idle Sons of Ethiopian Whores."[43] Even in this fragmentary excerpt we have clear references to an ugly color, devil-like character and idleness, and oversexed women—emotion-laden stereotypes suggesting that rank-and-file whites shared with the elite a common racial framing of African Americans.

Summary and Conclusion

Strikingly, the anti-black subframe of the dominant white racial frame was fully in place by 1700, as we have seen in commentaries by white scientists, intellectuals, ministers, and other leaders writing between the 1660s and the early 1700s. These elites are the ones, most centrally, who polished, established, proclaimed, and circulated this white frame to the larger population, which in turn used the ideas in their own ways. These elite commentaries focus on at least these major emotion-laden stereotypes and images of black Americans, who are alleged:

1. to have distinctive color, hair, and lips;
2. to be bestial and apelike;
3. to be unintelligent;
4. to have a disagreeable smell;
5. to be uncivilized, alien, and foreign;
6. to be immoral, criminal, and dangerous;
7. to be lazy;
8. to be oversexed;
9. to be ungrateful and rebellious;
10. to have disorganized families.

In the white mind the first four emotion-laden and stereotyped images are thought to be about black Americans' physical and biological character, whereas numbers five through ten are thought to be about their alleged deviant culture and moral character. Collectively, they rationalize the theft of black labor and the many brutalities of enslavement. Early on, black Americans are viewed by whites as very different and "unvirtuous Americans." In each case, most whites have long seen themselves as the opposite, as better-looking physically, intelligent, and culturally and morally superior, as the "virtuous Americans." Given these dimensions of their racial framing, whites routinely viewed African Americans as "problematical" for the white-dominated society.

One important question that arises in thinking about this early framing is: why is there such a heavy white focus on just one group, that is, on African Americans? Many categorizations that people make in their important interpretive frames utilize prototypes—that is, they feature a primary example for each major category. From the beginning, the white racial frame has made the prototypical "superior" racial group to be white American and the prototypical "inferior" racial group to be black American. In developing the white racial frame, whites early focused it on black Americans, which is the main reason that they remain so central to that frame today, a centrality some analysts call "black exceptionalism."

One reason for this centrality is that African Americans' time of experience with white oppression is the longest for any North American racial group except Native Americans. African Americans constitute the only large immigrant group brought in chains, and they have had the longest history of racial oppression entirely *within* this country's white-controlled economy and political system. Certainly, Native Americans have suffered very great oppression at the hands of whites for at least as long a period, but historically they have not been as central to the dominant white racial framing and to large-scale labor exploitation within white society.

From the first decades, black Americans have been at the core of the racist system because they are the group whose incorporation and subjugation have been given the greatest attention *by whites*. Whites as a group have devoted enormous amounts of energy to oppressing African Americans—initially for their wealth-creating labor and later for a range of other economic, social, and ideological reasons as well. Indeed, in the Civil War many thousands of southern whites gave their lives, at least in part, to maintain this central oppression of African Americans. In contrast, whites on the whole have put less time and physical and mental energy into exploiting and oppressing other immigrant groups of color, if only because the latter have been in this country in large numbers for much shorter periods of time.[44]

Before the first century of North American colonization was completed, the dominant white racial frame already had targeted Native Americans and African Americans and already had five dimensions that numerous scholars today cite as the important characteristics of the contemporary white-racist ideology in the United States: (1) classification of human groups as discrete biological entities; (2) such groups ranked hierarchically in an inegalitarian way; (3) their outer physical qualities linked to their inner or cultural qualities; (4) such qualities considered inheritable; and (5) each exclusive "race" unalterably differentiated from others by God or nature.[45] I agree with this listing, but close examination of the court cases, treatises, sermons, and books of the white intellectuals, officials, and other leaders in this chapter demonstrates that the white racial frame is about much more than ideological classifications, stereotypes, and concepts. These passages from the early European American colonists clearly illustrate other aspects of the early white framing of the "others" whom they subordinated. They reveal clearly an array of racist images, visceral emotions, distinctive smells, emotion-laden interpretations, and propensities to act—in regard to both virtuous European Americans and the African Americans and Indians who are lacking in virtue.

We can now turn to the further development and use of these elements in the white racial frame over the next two centuries. From the mid-1700s to the late 1800s the white racial frame became ever more developed and spread aggressively from the Atlantic coast across North America as whites expanded westward.

CHAPTER 4

Extending the White Frame

The Eighteenth Century to the Twentieth Century

During the eighteenth century whites in the North American colonies varied in their framing and discriminatory treatment of African and Native Americans. In some cases the groups suffered similar discrimination within the colonies. For instance, in one 1705 colonial statute blacks, Indians, and criminals were all barred from holding office, and deceased Indians and blacks could not be buried with whites. In other cases, colonial whites were more concerned with black than Indian ancestry. Thus, some colonial laws asserted that those with just one black great-grandparent were legally a "Negro," while only those with one Indian parent were legally an "Indian."[1]

The anti-Indian part of this era's white racial framing was somewhat different from that for African Americans. During this period whites sometimes did assert positive views of Native Americans and, as we will see in the case of leaders like Thomas Jefferson, they periodically depicted them as human, albeit usually paternalistically as lesser humans than whites. The white framing of indigenous peoples was still often negative, even viciously so, yet sometimes mixed with positive commentary and not as universally negative as for African Americans. One reason is that Native Americans were usually part of separate nations rooted in their own territories and regularly fought back collectively against white attempts to take their lands. Some Native American groups made alliances with white Americans against the British, and Native Americans were much less often in enslaved positions within white communities. Native Americans usually had access to the means of collective resistance to enslavement unavailable to Africans torn from their homelands. From the earliest contacts, European American leaders and intellectuals sometimes offered, albeit often backhanded, compliments about Indian courage, intelligence, and cooperation against the British.

Eventually, many whites even came to frame Indians, especially once they were killed off or forced beyond white-controlled territory, as heroic symbols of the Americas and its natural strengths, while "negroes" were not seen as really American or as having major positive characteristics that should be recognized, but rather were framed negatively as subordinated labor and contrasting symbols of darkness opposite to dominant whiteness. Indeed, Indian images were added by whites to U.S. money, such as the U.S. Indian-head penny and nickel, because Indians were viewed as heroic vanishing symbols of a white-conquered "American wilderness."

Historian Winthrop Jordan has suggested that Native Americans and African Americans were both viewed early on as "primitive" and as "two fixed points from which English settlers could triangulate their own position in America: the separate meanings of Indian and Negro helped define the meaning of living in America."[2] Indians and black Americans are said to be fixed points against which whites worked out their own position and identity in North America. However, prior to such contacts the European invaders already had a strong positive identity as Christians and "civilized" Europeans. Thus, it was European Americans' choice to create and name the social positions of "Indian" and "black" in their system of racial framing and oppression. These were *not* already fixed positions in their societal universe. From the beginning whites fully controlled the dominant racial framing for both groups and imposed new social identities on them.

Killing Indians: White Unity and Framing in the Eighteenth Century

In the eighteenth century American colonies, the national-origin and religious diversity among European-origin groups created significant interethnic tensions. Over time, however, these European-origin groups came to be seen as fully white. Seventeenth century and eighteenth century European American wars against Native Americans, and later the British, were important in solidifying diverse nationality groups into one "white nation." Whites' racial consciousness was strongly reinforced during the Indian wars and the late 1700s revolutionary war, and whiteness early became central to the definition of "American." Whites frequently grouped diverse Native American societies together as "savage" and "treacherous" and used the collective word "Indians" for them, a racialized framing that again rationalized the use of violence against them. Indians who fought back were asserted to be less than human and depraved murderers, a part of the anti-Indian subframe of the white racial frame. Like their predecessors, eighteenth century colonists periodically framed Indians as animals—"beasts of prey," as Colonel John Reid put it in 1764 or as "animals vulgarly called Indians" and a "race" who had no right to land, as Hugh Brackenridge put it in the 1780s.[3]

In this revolutionary era, the white framing of Indians asserted that there were essential links between their supposedly inferior character and biology and their allegedly inferior cultures. Retrospective accounts by white soldiers who fought in the Indian wars emphasized their biological otherness. A shared "white" identity was often proclaimed by these soldiers, as well as by white writers in newspapers. Interestingly, white officers in military units were less likely than rank-and-file soldiers to assert openly their whiteness, but did discuss the color and physical characteristics of the Indians—sometimes terming them "blacks" and thereby making a connection in their framing to black Americans. Ordinary soldiers accented their whiteness as a sign of racial superiority, whereas officers already had a strong sense of class and racial superiority. Ordinary soldiers linked their political rights to their asserted white identity. The propertied colonial elite had to entertain the idea of universal white male suffrage because of their alliance with ordinary white soldiers in fighting the Indians and the British army.[4]

The assertion of strong white identity and acceptance of privilege by ordinary whites provide early examples of the "public and psychological wage of whiteness" later described by W. E. B. Du Bois. From this revolutionary era to the present, most working class and middle class whites have accepted a higher position in the racial hierarchy and racial privileges (symbolic and status capital) from the white capitalist elite in return for giving up much class struggle against that elite, a class struggle that would likely have brought them significant economic and other benefits. Although the white working and middle classes do not have the societal power and resources of the elite, they have received many privileges and socioeconomic resources that stem from their generally advantaged position in the racial hierarchy.

The Declaration of Independence: Officially Framing Indians and Black Americans

Soon after the French and Indian wars ended in the 1760s, numerous colonial political and business leaders decided to revolt against Britain and issued a famous Declaration of Independence. Much has been written about this document, but its highly racialized sections have received less attention than they deserve, especially the one directed at Native Americans. Two passages in the working draft indicate the racial framing of Thomas Jefferson, the Declaration's primary writer, and also of the influential men who signed it. Jefferson sought to include the following passage about the African slave trade in the document, but it was vetoed by fellow slaveholders:

He [the British king] has waged cruel war against human nature itself, violating its most sacred rights of life and liberty in the persons of a distant people who never offended him, captivating and carrying them into slavery in another hemisphere, or to incur miserable death in their transportation thither.... Determined to keep open a market where men should be bought and sold, he has prostituted his negative for suppressing every legislative attempt to prohibit or to restrain this execrable commerce. And that this assemblage of horrors might want no fact of distinguished die, he is now exciting those very people to rise in arms among us, and to purchase that liberty of which he has deprived them, by murdering the people on whom he also obtruded them.[5]

In this long passage in the draft of the Declaration, Jefferson hypocritically blamed King George for the slave trade, one in which he and his slaveholding peers had played a major role. In this white framing of enslaved black Americans, Jefferson expressed fears that the British were inciting them to rebel. Slave uprisings were a recurring concern for slaveholders, which is one reason they framed enslaved black men as dangerous. Even as these white men cried out for freedom, they could not bring themselves to add this passage recognizing that "crimes" were "committed against the liberties" of another people and thus to condemn the slave trade, the latter being too central to their prosperity and racialized social world.

Numerous analysts have paid attention to this deleted passage, but very few have analyzed the importance of another racialized passage that remained in the Declaration of Independence:

He [the British king] has excited domestic insurrections amongst us, and has endeavoured to bring on the inhabitants of our frontiers, the merciless Indian Savages, whose known rule of warfare, is an undistinguished destruction of all ages, sexes and conditions.

The Declaration's statement on Indians proclaims emotion-laden racial stereotypes held by Jefferson and his colleagues in all the colonies: (1) Indians are not really "adults" but are easily manipulable by the British king; and (2) indigenous peoples are viewed collectively and negatively as "merciless Indian Savages" who make war immorally on women and children.[6] (Implicit too here is a strong framing of whites as virtuous.) These two racially framed commentaries for a document supposedly about liberty and equality suggested that the new country was to be a white republic where African and Native Americans would not be equal to whites.

Over the next decades Jefferson's views of Native Americans became more complex. In 1785 he published his major book, *Notes on the State of*

Virginia, the first ever by a secular American intellectual and one whose racist commentaries were cited by white political leaders and media commentators over the next century—indeed, by white supremacists on websites to the present day. In that book Jefferson's comments about Native Americans are paternalistic and romanticized. They are said to be noble but lesser human beings: "We shall probably find that they are formed in mind as well as in body" much like whites.[7] He does not view indigenous Americans as a separate race or threat to white racial purity, as he does for African Americans in the same section of this book. Like George Washington and other founders, Jefferson even envisions a future blending of white-assimilated Indians and whites into one society, a reality he could not envision for enslaved African Americans if they were ever freed.[8]

In 1813 Jefferson sent a letter to Baron Alexander von Humboldt describing his view of the U.S. treatment of Native Americans. He begins in a paternalistic tone, again suggesting the possibility of the incorporation of Indians into white society:

> You know, my friend, the benevolent plan we were pursuing here for the happiness of the aboriginal inhabitants in our vicinities. We spared nothing to keep them at peace with one another. To teach them agriculture and the rudiments of the most necessary arts, and to encourage industry by establishing among them separate property. In this way they would have been enabled to subsist and multiply on a moderate scale of landed possession. They would have mixed their blood with ours, and been amalgamated and identified with us within no distant period of time.

But then he shifts back to describing Indians as "unfortunate" men collaborating unwisely with the British enemy in the War of 1812:

> On the commencement of our present war, we pressed on them the observance of peace and neutrality, but the interested and unprincipled policy of England has defeated all our labors for the salvation of these unfortunate people. They have seduced the greater part of the tribes within our neighborhood, to take up the hatchet against us, and the cruel massacres they have committed on the women and children of our frontiers taken by surprise, will oblige us now to pursue them to extermination, or drive them to new seats beyond our reach. ... The confirmed brutalization, if not the extermination of this race in our America, is therefore to form an additional chapter in the English history of the same colored man in Asia.[9]

In the Declaration of Independence, Jefferson's statement on the "savage Indian" implied a rationalization of their extermination, and here he continues with that argument. In spite of his periodically paternalistic views, Jefferson asserts the necessity of government policies aimed at exterminating or fully subordinating the Native American "race." By this time in history Jefferson thought he could see that Indians were vanishing—that is, were being killed off or forced westward as whites expanded across the continent. This enabled him and later whites to speak sometimes of the "noble" Indian, which became part of complex white imagery of Native Americans that has lasted to the present.

White paternalism toward Native Americans is evident in court decisions handed down during Jefferson's era. Shortly after 1800 a prominent judge, St. George Tucker of the Virginia Court of Appeals, issued a decision arguing that the Virginia Bill of Rights did not apply to "a black or mulatto man or woman with a flat nose and woolly head" who had challenged "false imprisonment" in slavery. Tucker did rule that the Virginia Bill of Rights applied to a "coppor coloured person with long jetty black, straight hair," by which he meant an Indian, and to "one with a fair complexion, brown hair, not woolly or inclining thereto, with a prominent Roman nose," by which he meant a white person.[10] Tucker's important ruling reveals that the relatively few surviving Native Americans had some rights, at least officially in Virginia, while African Americans had none. It also shows just how complex and extensive the white frame was at the time, with its accents on an array of particular physical characteristics.

More White Framing of Native Americans

From Jefferson's day to the end of the nineteenth century, whites moved westward from eastern states and engaged in one displacing or genocidal attack on Indian societies after another, until many Indians were killed off and most of the rest were forced onto white-controlled "reservations." This bloody oppression was, yet again, rationalized with anti-Indian images of the old white frame. Take the example of Colonel Lewis Cass, who led troops against several Indian nations and served as Secretary of War under the slaveholding President Andrew Jackson. (Jackson was famous as a bloodthirsty Indian-killer and creator of the "Trail of Tears" march that forced surviving eastern Indian groups at gunpoint into western areas.) Colonel Cass wrote an article about Indians in 1827 in which he asserted that all people should value riches, honor, and power, but that there

> was little of all this in the constitution of our savages. Like the bear, and deer, and buffalo of his own forests, an Indian lives as his father lived. ... He never attempts to imitate the arts of his civilized

neighbors. His life passes away in a succession of listless indolence, and vigorous exertion to provide for his animal wants, or to gratify his baleful passions.[11]

Again we note a member of the white elite articulating with obsessive emotion the old stereotypes of animal-like, lazy, oversexed, and uncivilized Indians. For Cass and most other whites of the nineteenth century, to be civilized one had to be saturated in Western cultural values.

Later in that century, in a paper on "the significance of the frontier in American history," historian Frederick Jackson Turner accented a similar theme and helped subsequent generations of whites to rationalize what they have interpreted as the advance of "civilization" (Western culture) against "savagery" (Indian cultures) and "primitive Indian life." In Turner's racist framing, there was once a western frontier that was a place of "hostile Indians and stubborn wilderness." Indigenous peoples appear in his analysis as natural objects, like mountains, that whites had good reason to replace with their supposedly superior society.[12]

As historian Richard Drinnon has explained, about three hundred years of Indian wars perpetrated by whites generated a racial framing that mostly hid the obvious truth about Native American humanity and hardened European Americans to their brutally oppressive actions. This enabled them to engage in "dispossession and extermination or uprooting in an atmosphere fouled by self-congratulation and by sighing regrets over the Native American's utter unworthiness of their disinterested benevolence."[13] The omnipresent white racial frame served to legitimate the othering process, the theft of lands, and the killing, which got worse as the frame became ever more entrenched. To the present day, such framing of indigenous Americans has continued to cloud whites' understandings of the reality of the often genocidal conquests whites long engaged in—and of their many contemporary consequences.

The Enlightenment Era: Framing African Americans

The early white racial framing of Indians and African Americans had emerged just before the eighteenth-century Enlightenment era and the rise of modern science, but the scientists and other thinkers of this Enlightenment era expanded this racial framing. They joined their natural science interests to the study of human issues, often aggressively linking physical characteristics to human moral and social characteristics. They applied their supposedly scientific methods to placing peoples of color down the human hierarchy. In the 1730s, for instance, the influential Swedish botanist Carl Linnaeus distinguished categories of human beings—white, black, red, and yellow. While he did not use the word "race," he did think in racial terms as he directly associated skin color with particular cultural traits, with whites being regarded as superior. Like earlier European and American thinkers, he argued that Europeans were "inventive, full of ingenuity, orderly, and governed by laws," but that "Negroes" were "lazy, devious, and unable to govern themselves."[14]

This era of the European Enlightenment is typically depicted by historians and others as the beginning of modernity—with its dramatic increase in science and reason, rejection of old dogmas, and liberating ideas of freedom. Enlightenment thinkers, such as Britain's Adam Smith and North America's Thomas Jefferson and Ben Franklin, together with many followers, proclaimed in speeches and writings that expanded human freedom was centrally important and individual achievement was the measure of a person's worth—the white liberty-and-justice frame. Even today, encyclopedia articles on this Enlightenment era often do not mention its extraordinarily seamy side—its expanding colonialism, imperialism, and slavery, and its elites' rationalizing these oppressions in interpretive frames.[15] In fact, the accenting of individual freedom created a need for explanations of individual impoverishment and subordination such as slavery. In this era the white racial frame was further emphasized and enhanced, for it continued to explain for whites (and others) why many people, especially Indians and African Americans, were so impoverished or apparently unworthy.

During this era, as earlier, many European Americans, especially slaveholders, defended the enslavement of African Americans as a major way to develop white prosperity in the ever-growing American colonies. Arguing that whites could not handle labor in the harsh open fields, white apologists for slavery still framed the growing numbers of enslaved African Americans as mere pro-perty. African Americans were like the "axes, hoes, or any other utensil of agriculture," to quote one Georgia slavery advocate. Numerous pro-slavery advocates, such as English American naturalist Bernard Romans, spoke in white-framed terms of inborn flaws, viewing "treachery, theft, stubbornness and idleness" as "natural to them and not originated in their state of slavery."[16] The stereotyping and imaging of black women as oversexed and dispensable was often dramatically presented. In the 1730s, for example, the white editors of a Charleston, South Carolina, newspaper published a notice directed to white men that arriving soon were "African ladies ... of a strong, robust Constitution ... able to serve them by Night as well as Day. When they are Sick, they are not costly, when dead, their funeral Charges are but [little]."[17] In addition, the white view of black men was still, as earlier, that they were oversexed and dangerous because they supposedly lusted after white women.

The first white abolitionists in some colonies were Quakers, and they recorded the views of their kinfolk and friends. Anthony Benezet, a Pennsylvania Quaker, wrote that slavery supporters held "in their Minds, that the Blacks are hardly of the same Species with the white men, but are Creatures of a Kind somewhat inferior."[18] John Woolman, a Quaker abolitionist, spoke of African Americans as "our Fellow creatures," yet also as "far from being our Kinfolk" and "of a vile stock."[19] In this era, as earlier, African Americans were viewed by a great many whites as a separate species, and were distanced as "vile" even by white abolitionists.

The Founding "Fathers" Frame African Americans

In the late colonial era and early United States, the reality of slavery continued to have a great shaping impact on the racial framing of most whites, including those with great power. In white leaders' framing the physical features of enslaved African Americans received much attention. In the 1750s Benjamin Franklin, the famous liberal intellectual of the founding era, framed his conception of white virtuousness with an obsessive concern for the country's demographic composition:

> The number of purely white people in the world is proportionably very small. . . . Why increase the sons of Africa, by planting them in America, where we have so fair an opportunity, by excluding all blacks and tawneys, of increasing the lovely white and red?

He further argued that the number of mixed-ancestry Americans would likely grow with an increased slave trade, and white "amalgamation with the other color" would produce "a degradation to which no lover of his country, no lover of excellence in the human character can innocently consent."[20]

Franklin not only framed African Americans in terms of negative stereotypes, such as of their character, but also revealed a strong aesthetic bias and obsessive fear of their skin color degrading highly prized whiteness. Stereotyping, imagery, and racialized emotions again appear together. Although mainstream history books often do not record it, Franklin was at this time a slaveholder. He and his family enslaved African Americans for decades before he became an active abolitionist later in life.

Other major founders such as Thomas Jefferson, James Madison, and George Washington were slaveholders and framed African Americans as racially inferior. Jefferson, the framer whose views have influenced many since his time, was himself influenced by earlier scientific work of men like William Petty, including their views of black Americans. In Jefferson's *Notes on the State of Virginia*, he articulated a well-developed white frame with strong anti-black images, stereotypes, and emotional arguments: Black Americans smell funny, are natural slaves, are less intelligent, are physically ugly, are lazy, are oversexed, are ape-linked and animalistic, are musically unsophisticated, cannot think well, and cannot if freed ever be socially integrated into white American society. If freed, they must be shipped out of the United States. Founders George Washington and James Madison did not write as much about African Americans, but they shared Jefferson's highly racist framing of those they enslaved.[21] In the peak era for U.S. slavery, the late eighteenth century and first six decades of the nineteenth century, the circulation of racist ideas continued to emerge substantially from leading slaveholders and their associates. A well-developed racial frame was constantly supported by the legitimating discourse of the elite whites who controlled major institutions, including the economy, law, politics, education, and religion.

Ironically, white Americans' conceptions of their own freedom and of justice developed within a societal system grounded in the extreme racialized oppression of Native and African Americans. Over the decades before and during the revolutionary war with Great Britain, white Americans who were mostly of British ancestry crafted a liberty-and-justice frame that they articulated aggressively as they pursued their break with a mother country considered to be oppressing them and suppressing their liberties. Yet much in this liberty-and-justice frame contradicted their strong racist framing, which rationalized the oppression of African and Native Americans. Observations of black enslavement played a role in white minds as the source for a metaphor they applied to their own "enslaved" political situation vis-à-vis the British king. In the revolutionary era, white colonists frequently insisted that they must not be treated as "negroes" or "Guinea slaves" by the British. Near the beginning of the revolutionary war, General George Washington asserted that the time had come "when we must assert our rights, or submit to every imposition, that can be heaped upon us, till custom and use shall make us tame and abject slaves, as the blacks we rule over with such arbitrary sway."[22] Numerous other whites spoke in similar fashion.[23]

A major part of the ideological effort directed by American revolution-aries against the British included the explicit construction of the aforementioned liberty-and-justice frame. This important framing, which has persisted for centuries, was articulated aggressively after the mid-1700s as the white colonists sought to break away from the British empire. This perspective was famously asserted by Patrick Henry at a March 1775 meeting of Virginians considering revolutionary action. Henry gave his speech to urge white Virginians to fight the British. This is a portion of his speech that was preserved:

For my own part I consider it as nothing less than a question of freedom or slavery; and in proportion to the magnitude of the subject ought to be the freedom of the debate. . . . And judging by the past, I wish to know what there has been in the conduct of the British ministry for the last ten years, to justify those hopes with which gentlemen have been pleased to solace themselves and the House? . . . Are fleets and armies necessary to a work of love and reconciliation? . . . Has Great Britain any enemy, in this quarter of the world, to call for all this accumulation of navies and armies? . . . They are sent over to bind and rivet upon us those chains which the British ministry have been so long forging. . . . If we wish to be free—if we mean to preserve inviolate those inestimable privileges for which we have been so long contending—if we mean not basely to abandon the noble struggle in which we have been so long engaged, and which we have pledged ourselves never to abandon until the glorious object of our contest shall be obtained, we must fight! . . . There is no retreat but in submission and slavery! Our chains are forged! Their clanking may be heard on the plains of Boston! . . . Is life so dear, or peace so sweet, as to be purchased at the price of chains and slavery? . . . I know not what course others may take; but as for me, give me liberty, or give me death![24]

Assuming this version of his speech is roughly accurate (it was first printed only in 1817), we see much here that supports the idea that Henry was a leading "radical" in the American Revolution, a man willing to give his life for the ideals of freedom. He asserted such views in speeches and letters and was later a strong supporter of adding the Bill of Rights to the Constitution. Yet, he here counterposes "freedom" to "slavery" and repeatedly uses the metaphor of "chains and slavery" to describe conditions faced by white colonists. At this point in his life, Henry had been a slaveholder for years, and he left some sixty-five African Americans enslaved at his death. Clearly, the white founders' frequent references to their "enslavement" reveal how central African American slavery was to colonial society and to whites' defensive framing of the racially oppressive society they maintained.

The founders' views were fundamentally hierarchical and increasingly made use of the new term "race" in its modern sense. They were influenced by the ideas of European thinkers, who were in their turn influenced by the racial framing of white American thinkers and the reality of African American slavery and Indian wars in North America. In Europe the eighteenth century Enlightenment was anything but enlightened on racial matters. Leading Western thinkers such as Immanuel Kant and David Hume advocated and enhanced the white racial frame. Hume viewed "negroes" as inferior "breeds of men." The West's most celebrated philosopher, Immanuel Kant, taught social science courses explicitly articulating very racist ideas. He asserted that "humanity exists in its greatest perfection in the white race" and that there is a hierarchy of "races of mankind" with superior whites at the top.[25] Like Jefferson and other U.S. intellectuals, Kant used the concept of "races" in the sense of biologically distinct, hierarchical categories. Similarly, the prominent German medical professor Johann Blumenbach developed an influential and hierarchical "race" classification, with those he named "Caucasians" (Europeans) at the top, and Mongolians (Asians), Ethiopians (Africans), Americans (Native Americans), and Malays (Polynesians) down the ladder.[26] In this long Enlightenment era, new North American and European scientific and philosophical traditions were aggressively grounded in influential ideas about whites' biological, cultural, and social supremacy.

Drawing on these scientists and philosophers, popular writers then provided much instruction and misinformation for ordinary people in North America and Europe; they adapted elite-framed ideas for the public. The popular media that aggressively circulated this well-articulated white racial frame in the late eighteenth century and early nineteenth century were mostly newspapers and other printed materials, with a growing number of cartoons communicating negative imagery targeting Native and African Americans.

The Mid- to Late Nineteenth Century: More Racist Thinkers

In the mid-nineteenth century slavery continued to substantially shape the political-economic worldviews of leading figures. North and South, white officials and intellectuals proclaimed versions of the dominant white frame in defending each region's political and economic interests. White southerners emotionally and aggressively insisted on their system of slavery as creating a better regional civilization. In an 1837 speech in the Senate, influential Senator John C. Calhoun, a former vice president, articulated with emotion the preposterous view that southern slavery was a "positive good" for African Americans:

> Never before has the black race of Central Africa, from the dawn of history to the present day, attained a condition so civilized and so improved, not only physically, but morally and intellectually. In the meantime, the white or European race, has not degenerated. It has kept pace with its brethren in other sections of the Union where slavery does not exist. . . . I appeal to all sides whether the [white] South is not equal in virtue, intelligence, patriotism, courage, disinterestedness, and all the high qualities which adorn our nature.

But I take higher ground. I hold that in the present state of civilization, where two races of different origin, and distinguished by color, and other physical differences, as well as intellectual, are brought together, the relation now existing in the slaveholding States between the two, is, instead of an evil, a good—a positive good.[27]

Calhoun operates out of a strong version of the white racist frame with its language of the "black race" and "white race" and a rationalization of slavery as improving supposedly uncivilized Africans.

During this era official reports reveal that white officials also periodically worked to declare a disproportionate number of free black Americans to be "insane." Those black Americans were listed as insane at a rate eleven times greater than those who were enslaved, and much more often than whites. Drawing on such records, defenders of slavery like Calhoun argued that black Americans were better off in slavery than in freedom, which supposedly inclined them to insanity.[28]

In this era an anti-black framing was not confined to the South, but was widely shared across the United States and in Europe. Writing extensively about his 1830s travels in the United States, the French official and influential analyst of U.S. democracy, Alexis de Tocqueville, was critical of slavery and of slaveholders like Calhoun who insisted U.S. states had a right to nullify federal government acts with which they disagreed. Nonetheless, de Tocqueville also viewed African Americans from a white racial frame:

Among these widely differing families of men, the first that attracts attention, the superior in intelligence, in power, and in enjoyment, is the white, or European, the man preeminently so called; below him appear the Negro and the Indian. . . . The Negro has no family; woman is merely the temporary companion of his pleasures. . . . The Negro, plunged into the abyss of evils, scarcely feels his own calamitous situation. . . . He admires his tyrants more than he hates them, and finds his joy and his pride in the servile imitation of those who oppress him. . . . If he becomes free, independence is often felt by him to be a heavier burden than slavery.[29]

De Tocqueville was an influential liberal intellectual in the United States and Europe of his day. Moreover, since his insightful book recounting his travels, *Democracy in America*, was published, he has become somewhat of an icon in U.S. intellectual circles and is often cited as one of the first social scientists and one with a clear understanding of U.S. democracy. Although critical of some U.S. political and economic institutions, including the tyrannical aspects of U.S. slavery, even he was unable to transcend the dominant racist framing of African Americans.

This very racist aspect of his U.S. analysis has been ignored by most social analysts who have used his work, to the present day. In de Tocqueville's view, whites were necessarily dominant in the racial hierarchy and superior to Indians and "Negroes." He asserted numerous racist stereotypes, such as that black men have no real families and are oversexed. Holding to an extremely insensitive perspective like that of other leading whites, de Tocqueville also asserted that black Americans did not feel the calamity and pain of their situations and could not manage freedom from slavery. In his book he later added, again parroting old racist framing, that the enslaved black man's "physiognomy is to our eyes hideous, his understanding weak, his tastes low; and we are almost inclined to look upon him as a being intermediate between man and the brutes." Although de Tocqueville was probing and critical in regard to U.S. democracy and the system of slavery, he accepted much white-racist framing of African Americans quite unreflectively.

The Continuing White Obsession: African Americans

From the beginning of the nineteenth century to its end, a great many whites in all social classes had become rather obsessed with black Americans. In the 1880s the abolitionist and political leader Frederick Douglass, who had been enslaved, made an eloquent speech on this obsession at a celebration of the 1863 Emancipation Proclamation:

> Go where you will, you will meet with him [the black American]. He is alike present in the study of the learned and thoughtful, and in the play house of the gay and thoughtless. We see him pictured at our street corners, and hear him in the songs of our market places. The low and the vulgar curse him, the snob and the flunky affect to despise him, the mean and the cowardly assault him, because they know . . . that they can abuse him with impunity. . . . To the statesman and philosopher he is an object of intense curiosity. . . . Of the books, pamphlets, and speeches concerning him, there is literally, no end. He is the one inexhaustible topic of conversation at our firesides and in our public halls.[30]

Douglass aptly captured the many ways in which black Americans had become the center of whites' racist thinking, imaging, and emotions. Notice the diversity of social arenas where the white frame was imbedded and perpetuated. Douglass observed negative images and conceptions of black Americans in treatises of well-educated whites and in plays in theaters attended by ordinary whites. He saw black Americans attacked in large numbers of books, pamphlets, and speeches—all ways in which the elite articulated its racist framing among themselves and to the masses of whites. Douglass speculated that black Americans were the inexhaustible topics in private backstage settings where only whites were present. He also found them in broadside pictures on street corners and heard mocking in racist songs. This white obsession was more than mental, literary, and discursive, for African Americans were also being made the targets of violent curses and emotional assaults by whites.

Evidence for this racist obsession can be found in all decades of the nineteenth century. The print media, the primary mass media of this era, were full of anti-black cartoons and other visual and verbal depictions that constantly reinforced anti-black and pro-slavery views, North and South. For example, the prominent artist Edward Clay published a popular series of anti-abolition prints with aggressive caricatures of white-black couples and multiracial children to show whites' disgust with the idea of liberating enslaved African Americans and with the abolitionists' ideal of equal-status interactions between whites and blacks. Like whites before and since, these nineteenth century whites imaged and framed dangerous black men as lusting after white women. Indeed, this white obsession with interracial sex and marriage led to a new English word, "miscegenation," fabricated by white New York journalists opposed to such relationships. An important and emotion-laden element of the white racial frame has long viewed sex across racial lines as unnatural, probably because many whites have viewed black Americans as less than human and/or interracial sex as a threat to white racial purity. Ironically, this negative framing is profoundly hypocritical, for it has never stopped many white men from forcing sexual relationships on black women—from the first decades of colonial development through centuries of slavery and Jim Crow segregation.[31]

The segregated South after the Civil War was especially marked by a continuing white obsession with racial purity. Numerous laws stipulated that people with any "ascertainable Negro blood" were to be regarded as and legally segregated as "Negroes."[32] Not surprisingly, this concern over "blood purity" was a major force lying behind the commonplace laws banning interracial marriages. Even into the 1950s, a majority of U.S. states—including all southern and most southwestern states—had laws prohibiting interracial marriages, most specifically marriages between white and black or Asian Americans. From the end of the Civil War in the 1860s to the decades of the 1950s and 1960s, the white frame's view of black men as sexual threats to white women was quite intense and often used to rationalize white violence against black men. Moreover, the gendered racism that most whites also directed at black women routinely viewed them as having "jungle bunny" sexual desires and procreative abilities. Some contemporary scholars have even speculated that the preoccupation of many white men with alleged black male hypersexuality reflects some deep white psychological problems, perhaps growing, at least in part, out of collective guilt over the extensive white male role in the rape of black women over centuries.[33]

During the slavery and legal segregation eras, newspapers and other print media were important in circulating the dominant racial frame to most whites, including new European immigrants who came in ever larger numbers from the 1830s to the early 1900s. In newspapers and magazines highly racist cartoons and drawings, coupled with written portrayals framing African Americans negatively, taught whites of all nationalities, ages, and classes the white racial framing of African Americans. Cartoons accented "ugly" (to whites) physical characteristics: distinctive hair, skin, lips, and odor. Such physical traits were accented in palpably tangible, visual, and emotional ways and commonly linked to other negative cultural images of black Americans.

Perhaps more important than the print media in spreading old and new aspects of the white frame were other forms of popular entertainment, especially minstrel shows and, later, vaudeville shows. A great range of racist imagery, stereotyping, and emotionality was communicated in popular entertainment settings from the early nineteenth century onward. White performers in blackface were popular with working and middle class white men. Such shows spread the racial frame across the country, especially among the illiterate. The minstrel performances celebrated whiteness by indicating that the audience members, mostly white workers, were not like the "darkies" negatively portrayed on stage. Black men were mocked vigorously as "Zip Coon" dandies, and black women were stereotyped as sexualized and promiscuous. "Aunt Jemima" imagery originally surfaced in an 1870s minstrel show, later becoming widely circulated on commercial products. Minstrelsy was a critical way that key visual images, stereotypes, emotions, and interpretive understandings of the white racist framing were spread to illiterate whites, new immigrants, and younger whites.[34]

The minstrel shows perpetuated and reinforced a vicious and tangible version of the anti-black framing and operated across social class lines. They were popular with middle class and elite whites, including U.S. presidents such as John Tyler and Abraham Lincoln. Lincoln was fond of minstrel shows and the "darky" joking of white performers. He was not the racial saint of historical mythology. While he did oppose slavery, he routinely operated out of and helped to spread the white racial frame, viewing free and enslaved black Americans as racially inferior, supporting Jim Crow laws, and articulating a view of the future United States as an assertively white country. Other influential whites were similarly fond of the highly racist minstrel shows. Not long before his death, Mark Twain expressed great concern for the decline in the "real nigger show," the white minstrel performances. He was typical of leading whites in this favorable view of minstrel shows.[35] The constant media and minstrel portrayals helped to cement negative images of African Americans in the white racial frame as the counterpoint to positive white views of whites and whiteness, for all social classes.

Systemic Racism in the North: Paternalism and Violence

The South is too often the main focus of sustained commentaries on systemic racism in U.S. history. Yet, before and after the Civil War, the nineteenth century North was a difficult and dangerous place for African Americans. Whites' anti-black actions there too were often out of an intense white racist framing of white and black Americans. For example, during the 1840s and 1850s, a relatively light-skinned African American, William Allen, secured a very good education and became a professor at New York Central College, at the time the only college that had ever hired a black man and one of few with white and black students. Allen became acquainted with a white woman, and they decided to marry. In early 1853, when local whites found out about the pending marriage, including most of her family, they organized to prevent it. Armed white mobs attempted to tar, feather, and kill him, and he was lucky to escape. In a book he wrote about these experiences, Allen notes that at the "announcement of the probability of the case merely, [white] men and women were panic-stricken, deserted their principles and fled in every direction." One nearby town even passed a resolution that "Amalgamation is not part of the Free Democracy of Granby." Some newspapers editorialized that Allen should be killed, and even some white supporters were persecuted. Again we observe that the white racial frame is far more than a matter of racist stereotypes and ideology, for it includes strong racialized emotions and inclinations to violence to protect whites' proclaimed racial interests. In Allen's view the "so-called free" men and women of color of the North were as oppressed as those in the South.[36]

In this era, as earlier and later in North American history, much of the white frame was compatible with other political and economic frames. Thus, even the minority of whites who were critical of slavery, such as the eighteenth century Quaker abolitionists, articulated anti-black stereotypes. We also observe this orientation among white abolitionists in the nineteenth century. Even Harriet Beecher Stowe, author of the anti-slavery novel *Uncle Tom's Cabin*, argued in the 1850s that the "negro race" was different from the "white race":

They are possessed of a nervous organization peculiarly susceptible and impressible. Their sensations and impressions are very vivid, and their fancy and imagination lively. In this respect the race has an oriental character, and betrays its tropical origin. . . . When alarmed, they are often paralyzed and rendered entirely helpless. . . . Like oriental nations, they incline much to outward expressions, violent gesticulations, and agitating movements of the body.[37]

What were then considered liberal white views tended to be paternalistic versions of the dominant racial frame and often played up the supposedly childlike qualities and necessary dependency of enslaved and free black Americans. Even Stowe, a fierce opponent of slavery, could not see past her racist framing of African Americans as impressionable and handicapped by bodily expression.

During this era the everyday actions of most white abolitionists reflected paternalism toward and discrimination against African Americans. For example, in the anti-slavery movement's offices of the 1840s and 1850s, the leading intellectual, Martin Delany, noticed that African Americans were in a "mere secondary, underling position, in *all* our relations to them."[38]

Extending the White Frame: Other Americans of Color

During the mid-nineteenth century the white-controlled system of racial oppression and its rationalizing frame were substantially extended as white entrepreneurs and political leaders brought in yet more labor and territory of people of color, again mostly for the purpose of generating more white wealth. These new oppressions began on a large scale in the 1840s with a U.S. military invasion and conquest of northern Mexico, which brought new lands and more than 100,000 Mexicans within the new U.S. boundary, and in the 1850s with the importation of Chinese contract laborers by white companies, such as railroad firms. Those European Americans who imported Chinese laborers and annexed large areas of Mexico by force already had a strong white racial frame in their heads. That age-old frame, from the beginning centrally focused on white superiority and black inferiority, has long been adaptive and multidimensional, and its central racist doctrines have regularly been adjusted and extended to new social contexts and groups. White political and economic leaders, as well as scientists and intellectuals, quickly imbedded the Mexicans and the Chinese in this society's white-controlled hierarchy of exploitation and in its expandable rationalizing frame.

In the southwestern United States few white colonizers invading northern Mexico in the 1830s and 1840s viewed the Mexicans as white, but placed them down at the bottom of the racial hierarchy with Native Americans and black Americans. One white land agent wrote that Mexicans were "swarthy looking people resembling our mulattos, some of them nearly black." The famous Texas politician and slaveholder Sam Houston spoke of Mexicans as inferior "half-Indians." Other whites wrote that Mexicans had a "filthy, greasy appearance."[39]

In 1848 Senator John C. Calhoun, the former vice president quoted previously, was actually opposed to the U.S. annexation of Mexico, but in speaking against that he revealed yet more elements of the increasingly common white-framed perspective on Mexicans:

> We have never dreamt of incorporating into our Union any but the Caucasian race—the free white race. To incorporate Mexico, would be the very first instance of the kind of incorporating an Indian race; for more than half of the Mexicans are Indians, and the other is composed chiefly of mixed tribes. I protest against such a union as that! Ours, sir, is the Government of a white race. The greatest misfortunes of Spanish America are to be traced to the fatal error of placing these *colored races* on an equality with the *white race*. That error destroyed the social arrangement which formed the basis of society. . . . And yet it is professed and talked about to erect these Mexicans into a Territorial Government, and place them on an equality with the people of the United States. I protest utterly against such a project. Sir, it is a remarkable fact, that in the whole history of man, as far as my knowledge extends, there is no instance whatever of any civilized colored races being found equal to the establishment of free popular government, although by far the largest portion of the human family is composed of these races. . . . Are we to associate with ourselves as equals, companions, and fellow-citizens, the Indians and mixed race of Mexico? Sir, I should consider such a thing as fatal to our institutions.[40]

The politically influential Calhoun put Mexicans into the "inferior Indian" and "mixed-race" subframes of the dominant white racial frame, accenting that they were not white but down the racial hierarchy. He feared any attempt at political equality and viewed Mexicans as unintelligent and incapable of participating in a "free popular government," which of course the slavery-oriented United States government was certainly *not* at that time.

The racist framing of Mexicans and other Latin Americans was not limited to the Southwest. Just before the 1840s Mexican American War, a Boston newspaper published a poem, "Their Women Wait for Us," that revealed northern framing of people of Latin American (mainly Mexican) descent:

> The Spanish maid, with eye of fire, At balmy evening turns her lyre
> And, looking to the Eastern sky, Awaits our Yankee chivalry
> Whose purer blood and valiant arms Are fit to clasp her budding charms.
> The man, her mate, is sunk in sloth—To love, his senseless heart is loth:
> The pipe and glass and tinkling lute, A sofa, and a dish of fruit;
> A nap, some dozen times a day; Somber and sad and never gay.[41]

Accenting "Spanish" female hypersexuality and male laziness, this stereo-typed and emotion-laden imagery draws substantially on the pre-existing white framing of black Americans. In his language of "pure blood" and "chivalry" the white poet again accents the white superiority that had already been framed this way for many years.

Whites outside the newly conquered "New Mexico" area of Mexico that was seized in the Mexican American War tended to view all the new Mexican Americans as not white and inferior, but the handful of powerful whites in that area had a different viewpoint because they were a statistical minority. Between the 1840s and the 1880s, these powerful white invaders decided to share power with the established Mexican elite there. Because whites sought statehood—delayed for decades because the territory was not majority white—they developed a perspective that viewed the Mexican elite as inferior but still as European and "Spanish." Although many in the Mexican elite had Indian ancestry, the white elite decided they were "white enough" to play an important political role.[42] This small Mexican American elite played a coordinating political, and thus oppressive, role between the Anglo whites and the poor Indian, Mexican American, and enslaved African American populations there. The Mexican American elite emphasized their relative "whiteness" in order to relate well to the more powerful white-Anglo elite. Again we see the control that powerful European Americans had over the definition of U.S. racial groups. Whites from the eastern United States emphasized traditional white framing and defined the Mexican American elite, temporarily, as white enough to assist in expanding Anglo control over the territory. This history may help to explain the fluctuating accents on whiteness and non-whiteness in some parts of the Mexican American population from that time to the present. Laura Gómez accents the significance: the "twenty-first-century legacy of Mexican Americans' history as off-white" is that they are "sometimes defined as legally white, almost always defined [by whites] as socially non-white."[43]

In addition, from the 1850s to the early 1900s the Chinese workers, and later Japanese and Filipino workers, brought by white entrepreneurs into the West faced extensive exploitation and other oppression, which was repeatedly rationalized by the dominant racial frame. When the economy entered a depression in the 1870s white labor leaders, newspaper editors, and politicians racially framed Chinese American workers, and thus as allegedly taking job opportunities from whites. Chinese workers were physically attacked by white workers and verbally attacked by white politicians and editors supporting the white workers.

Asian Americans were stereotyped as heathen, docile, crafty, and dirty, and called by new white-crafted epithets, such as "Chinks." White leaders and the white public viewed Chinese Americans as an "alien race," as inferior foreigners and not real "Americans." Again we see elements of the older racial frame—heathen, docile, alien in culture, racially inferior—that were developed to negatively frame African and Native Americans also used to racialize Asian Americans. Somewhat new emphases can be seen in the anti-Asian subframe, especially accents on foreignness and deviousness. These negative images reached the highest social class levels. For example, in the famous 1896 *Plessy v. Ferguson* Supreme Court decision that upheld Jim Crow segregation of black Americans, the one dissenting white justice to that decision, John Marshall Harlan, gratuitously penned this racist framing of Chinese Americans: "There is a race so different from our own that we do not permit those belonging to it to become citizens of the United States. Persons belonging to it are, with few exceptions, absolutely excluded from our country. I allude to the Chinese race." More than a decade earlier, the 1882 Chinese Exclusion Act had been passed by the U.S. Congress, a law effectively cutting off most Chinese immigration until its partial repeal in 1943.[44]

Excluded Chinese workers were replaced in western states with imported Japanese workers, who were economically exploited and viewed and attacked from the dominant white racial frame. They too were stereotyped as docile, servile, and devious. Around 1900 the white San Francisco mayor attacked Japanese immigrants as "unassimilable" and threatening white workers' jobs; a Sacramento newspaper editor asserted that the Japanese Americans were "for various reasons unassimilable, and a dangerous element." Other West Coast newspapers generated campaigns against the white-termed "yellow peril"—that is, Japanese and other Asian Americans. Such racist agitation forced the U.S. government to negotiate with the Japanese government to voluntarily prohibit Japanese immigrants. In these cases, the racist framing of Asian immigrants had exclusionary consequences that shaped the demographic contours of U.S. society—that is, this society now has far fewer Asian Americans than would have been the case without this extensive discrimination.[45]

The importation of Chinese, Japanese, and Filipino workers was linked to U.S. military expansion in the Asia-Pacific area. In the 1890s the U.S.

military defeated the Spanish in the Spanish-American War and added the Philippines to its empire, with the country's white leadership aggressively framing this as indicative of the "manifest destiny" of whites to expand everywhere. Invasions were then, as later in U.S. history, justified from the old white frame. In 1899 the British official and prominent U.S. visitor, Rudyard Kipling, celebrated the U.S. annexation of the Philippines and whites' philanthropic "burden" to civilize so-called uncivilized peoples in his famous poem "The White Man's Burden: The United States and the Philippine Islands." The first lines demand action: "Take up the White Man's burden—Send forth the best ye breed . . . To wait, in heavy harness, On fluttered folk and wild—Your new-caught, sullen peoples, Half-devil and half-child."[46] Such negative poetic framing of Asians and others as heathen, demonic, and childlike dependants by an important European official and its publication in a major U.S. magazine indicated the widespread acceptance of this visual imagery in the U.S. and European elites, an imagery closely linked to the U.S. governments' moves in an imperialistic direction.

In this era the contrast between the way in which Asian and Latino Americans were exploited, subordinated, and racialized in the dominant white frame, and the way in which millions of new European immigrants to the United States were treated and constructed, is quite dramatic. For about one generation, European immigrant groups, such as those from Ireland, eastern Europe, and southern Europe, were viewed by native-born, northern European whites as inferior "races" well below the "Anglo-Saxon race" on the U.S. racial hierarchy, but this view changed in a relatively short period of time. As European immigrants and their children gave up much of their homeland cultures and aggressively adopted many aspects of the dominant U.S. culture of whiteness, they were increasingly accepted by native-born whites into the "white race."

Significantly, from the 1830s to the early decades of the 1900s millions of European immigrants and their children adopted the white racist frame's negative perspectives on African Americans and other Americans of color as an important part of their incorporation into U.S. society. Entering during the 1830s and 1840s, for example, poor Irish immigrants were viewed from the prevailing racial frame as an inferior "race," and indeed as "not white," by many of the then dominant English Americans. Most of the Irish soon assimilated to the dominant culture and were taught how to conceive of themselves as fully white by their ministers, priests, business people, politicians, and other leaders. They were pressured and manipulated by white elites, including their leaders, into accepting the already-dominant racial framing denigrating blackness and privileging whiteness. Most came to operate out of this traditional racist frame—such as by attacking or excluding free black workers in competing for jobs in the northern cities. Later, at the turn of the twentieth century, Italian and other southern and eastern European immigrants and their children—after a period in which nativist whites viewed them as inferior "races"—assimilated to the dominant white culture and bought aggressively into the dominant white racial frame, thereby firmly identifying themselves as "white" and getting out from under the negative racial imagery. Many European immigrants and their descendants pressed for a privileged place in the socially constructed "white race," whose privileges eventually included such things as greater personal liberty, better-paying jobs, access to an array of government programs just for whites (such as homestead lands, better public schools, and, later, home mortgage and veterans programs), and the right to vote.[47]

At the same time, as part of being "white," they actively framed African Americans and other Americans of color as racially inferior and discriminated against them. Over time the dominant racial frame has been reproduced and transmitted within numerous immigrant groups and across many generations of Americans.

The Jim Crow Era: Scientific Racism and the Elites' Racial Frame

From the middle of the eighteenth century to the middle of the twentieth century, influential physical and social scientists regularly defended and extended the racial framing and oppression of African Americans, Native Americans, and other Americans of color. For most of this era most white American and European physical and social scientists enthusiastically accepted the view that biologically determined "races" actually existed. For example, during the slavery era, medical researchers and other influential scientists developed a pseudo-scientific terminology to describe black Americans who resisted enslavement as mentally ill or to portray them as naturally inclined by their "blood" to be resistant. Physician Samuel Cartwright wrote about black runaways as having a disease he called "drapetomania" and of black Americans being susceptible to "dysaethesia aethiopis," a disease caused by "black blood" that in the brain created "ignorance, superstition, and barbarism." As with Senator Calhoun's view noted previously, black Americans were viewed as requiring the lessons of the slavery system to improve their supposedly diseased mentality.[48]

Systemic gendered racism was part of the scientific-racism frame as well. Some white researchers in the mid-nineteenth century did medical experiments to prove white-racist stereotypes of black women, including the stereotyped notions of an alleged biological propensity for black women to engage in prostitution. Other white researchers experimented on enslaved black women in order to develop new surgical techniques for eventual use on whites. The "father of gynecology," J. Marion Sims, did much brutal and violent experimentation on enslaved black women without anesthesia. To this day, Sims is regarded by many in the health care system as a hero of modern medicine.[49]

During the legal segregation decades after the Civil War era, there was a significant expansion of the scientific legitimation of the white racial frame, sometimes labeled "scientific racism." Like earlier white philosophers and scientists, most late nineteenth century and early twentieth century scientists held to the view that there were specific "races" with distinctive physical characteristics that were inherited, and that they were arranged in a natural hierarchy of inferior and superior races. They developed a scientific-racist view of people of color across the globe as innately and permanently inferior to whites. The broad ideas of these scientific racists were not supported by careful scientific observations of all human societies, but usually by slanted reports gleaned from European missionaries, travelers, and sea captains who had contacts with selected non-European societies. While presenting themselves as objective, these scientists frequently tried to marshal evidence for the significant differences among human "races" that the imperialist officials in their governments had decided were important to highlight.[50]

The towering scientific figure of the nineteenth century, England's Charles Darwin, applied evolutionary ideas to the development of human races. He viewed the evolutionary process of natural selection as at work in Europeans killing off indigenous peoples, and for him black people were a species category somewhere between whites and gorillas. In his view, like that of other European and American biologists, the "civilized races" would eventually replace the "savage races throughout the world."[51] Similarly, U.S. social scientists like Yale University's William Graham Sumner adopted a "social Darwinist" perspective that viewed humanity as engaged in a life-and-death struggle, one in which the superior white race would win out over the inferior darker races. Black Americans were seen by scientific racists as a "degenerate race" whose alleged immorality was genetic and a matter of biology. U.S. social sciences early developed substantially in connection with white attempts to rationalize the enslavement and segregation of African Americans. The first explicitly named "sociology" books were written by Henry Hughes (*Treatise on Sociology*) and George Fitzhugh (*Sociology for the South*), both published in 1854 and both asserting the white-framed view of black enslavement as a positive social good.[52]

Over many decades of Jim Crow, from about the late 1870s until the 1960s, much social science analysis accented, reinforced, and legitimated older racist views of African Americans and other Americans of color. In the North and South social scientists periodically used "graphs, charts, and other paraphernalia to prove the Negro's biological, psychological, intellectual, and moral inferiority."[53] Emotion-laden anti-black images and stereotypes from the old white frame—such as stereotypes about physical deficiencies, low intelligence, and cultural inferiority—were legitimated by leading social and physical scientists, as well as by politicians and business leaders. Scientists like Nathaniel Shaler, a prominent Harvard dean in the late nineteenth and early twentieth centuries, argued that African Americans were racially inferior, uncivilized, and an "alien folk" in the United States, and would eventually become extinct under ongoing evolutionary processes.[54]

Such views were common among prominent U.S. scientists for decades. During the 1920s Carl Brigham, a Princeton psychologist who later helped to develop the College Board tests, argued from World War I psychometric tests on draftees that the relatively low scores of black draftees showed that they were of "inferior racial stock." Operating out of an aggressive version of the white racial frame, Brigham envisioned sterilization of racially inferior Americans as a good policy for dealing with them.[55] Lothrop Stoddard, a Harvard-educated historian, used a globalized version of the white frame in his widely read book *The Rising Tide of Color*. He insisted with emotion that the "white race" was, and should continue to be, the "indisputable master of the planet."[56]

For decades during legal segregation, a great many white business and political leaders viewed the world from an aggressive and emotion-laden version of the dominant racial frame. President Theodore Roosevelt (1901–1909) was well-known for outspoken agreement with tenets of the new scientific racism. President Woodrow Wilson (1913–1921) advocated the superiority of European civilization over all others and acted to increase the racial segregation of black Americans within the government during his terms. President Warren Harding (1921–1923), a fan of Stoddard's white supremacist book and cozy with members of the Ku Klux Klan, rejected "any suggestion of social equality" between white and black Americans. Prior to becoming president, and much like German Nazi intellectuals, President Calvin Coolidge (1923–1929) articulated in a popular magazine important scientific-racism arguments: "Biological laws tell us that certain divergent people will not mix or blend. The Nordics propagate themselves successfully. With other races, the outcome shows deterioration on both sides."[57] Again, we observe that the dominant racial frame was not something coming from the margins of society, but rather something arising substantially from its political, business, and intellectual center.

Jim Crow, the Supreme Court, and the Southern Elite

During the slavery and Jim Crow eras, the Supreme Court was a clear manifestation of white dominance, for only elite white men served on it.

Examining the justices' decisions on racial matters during most of the legal segregation era, one finds that they regularly reflect the dominant white-racist framing and routinely ignore or dismiss the civil rights counter-frames of Americans of color. Between the 1870s and the 1930s, Supreme Court decisions regularly eroded the civil rights that African Americans had theoretically gained under the 14th and 15th amendments that were added to the U.S. Constitution in the Reconstruction era. In the influential 1896 *Plessy v. Ferguson* case, a nearly unanimous court (one dissenter) upheld a Louisiana law requiring white-black segregation in public accommodations. In this decision the justices asserted that they as white men knew better than black Americans what impact racial segregation had on them:

> We consider the underlying fallacy of the plaintiff's argument to consist in the assumption that the enforced separation of the two races stamps the colored race with a badge of inferiority. If this be so, it is not by reason of anything found in the act, but solely because the colored race chooses to put that construction on it. . . . Legislation is powerless to eradicate racial instincts or to abolish distinctions based upon physical differences.[58]

Not only did these elite white justices frame their decision with racist notions like "racial instincts," but they felt a need to lecture black Americans on what *they* should feel about white-imposed segregation, ignoring the black experience and counter-frame. In his dissent, Justice John Marshall Harlan argued for civil rights for black Americans. The 13th amendment made unconstitutional "the imposition of any burdens or disabilities that constitute badges of slavery or servitude," which is what legal segregation did. Nonetheless, even Harlan expressed a strong version of the dominant racial frame in an added comment: "The white race deems itself to be the dominant race in this country. And so it is, in prestige, in achievements, in education, in wealth, and in power. So, I doubt not, it will continue to be *for all time*. . . ."[59]

Gradually, from the 1930s to the 1960s, desegregation lawsuits brought mostly by black civil rights lawyers resulted in scattered Supreme Court decisions that paid some attention to the black counter-frame accenting civil rights for black Americans. In a key 1938 case, *Missouri ex rel. Gaines v. Canada*, some white Supreme Court justices for the first time in U.S. history openly ruled in favor of the black perspective on racist segregation—in a ruling against law school segregation. Other university desegregation cases preceded the 1954 *Brown v. Board of Education* decision, one hailed by many as pioneering action on the part of brave Supreme Court justices breaking with conservative white racial framing and being far in front of the country's citizenry and leadership.[60] Yet, in *Brown* nine white male justices had very *belatedly* taken seriously the civil rights perspective articulated by the NAACP lawyers and rejected totalitarian-like segregation still operating in seventeen states. The *Brown* decision's years-late delivery reflected persisting resistance from numerous white justices who had routinely articulated a strong white-racist framing of racial segregation. The Court's action was not on the cutting edge on issues of desegregation, for most African Americans were well ahead of the Court in counter-framed understandings of Jim Crow and the need for effective legal action against it. With the help of well-placed, white supremacist judges and U.S. Senators, legal segregation of African Americans and others in numerous institutions persisted into the late 1960s.

For a time after *Brown*, the federal courts paid some attention to the black civil rights counter-frame and pressed forward slowly with desegregation. Several Supreme Court justices were fearful about ordering speedy implementation of their 1954 *Brown* decision. A second *Brown* decision, a 1955 decision designed to implement the first, did not represent the views of most African Americans about undoing racial oppression. In this weak decision the Court's white judges took a position more acceptable to most whites and the dominant racial frame: They sent back the *Brown* desegregation cases to district courts "to take such proceedings and enter such orders and decrees consistent with this opinion as are necessary and proper to admit to public schools on a racially nondiscriminatory basis *with all deliberate speed* the parties to these cases."[61] Neither of the two *Brown* decisions explained to the public the anti-civil-rights reality or immorality of racial segregation, and neither mandated the steps necessary to end actual racial segregation. The justices' foot-dragging and lack of forcefulness reflected a concern with the racist framing of the white majority. And their dilatory decision, as well as more recent Supreme Court decisions backing off of enforcing desegregation in schools, explain the general failure in the United States to meaningfully integrate the majority of public schools.

The hostile racial framing by many whites of the *Brown* decisions made clear the continuing power of the dominant white frame. In one dramatic and emotional response, white congressional leaders from the South issued a "Southern Manifesto." Signed by nineteen Senators and seventy-seven House Members from southern states, the document condemned Brown: "The unwarranted decision of the Supreme Court in the public school cases is now bearing the fruit always produced when men substitute naked power for established law."[62] This manifesto points to northern states, which it argues had pioneered in segregation. Separate but equal, the writers declared, "time and again, became a part of the life of the people of many of the States and confirmed their habits, traditions, and way of life." They argued that this brutal system of extreme inequality in school facilities "is founded on elemental humanity and commonsense, for parents should not be deprived by Government of the right to direct the lives and education of their own children." Here they operated out of a strong white framing they did not seem to recognize, for they meant *white* parents and children. A fifth of the southern population was African American, yet they wrote their defiant manifesto as though it represented the view of all people in the South.

Reacting against *Brown*, these members of Congress drew on racial fictions from the dominant frame, including notions about the virtues of whites and the goodness of a segregated society. They argued for the myth of happy racial relations in a segregated society noted in a previous chapter: Desegregation "is destroying the amicable relations between the white and Negro races that have been created through 90 years of patient effort by the good people of both races. It has planted hatred and suspicion where there has been heretofore friendship and understanding." Theirs is a perspective coming exclusively from the traditional white worldview. These powerful whites held to a strong "states' rights" perspective, one that assumed that white southerners had the right to veto federal action—a perspective that was first developed during the slavery era as a way of protecting the anti-democratic interests of elite white slaveholders.[63]

The single-mindedness of this racist framing can be seen in commentaries of many white journalists after *Brown*. In the 1950s and 1960s, influential *Richmond News-Leader* editor, and later national columnist, James J. Kilpatrick, asserted that the South had "a sense of oneness here, an identity, a sharing, and this quality makes the South unique"; for him and many others like him the South was a "state of mind."[64] He titled his book *The Southern Case for School Segregation*. Again, in such widely expressed sentiments the southern advocates of Jim Crow were thinking only in terms of the views of the white majority. They meant the "white southern case." Black southerners mostly did not, and still do not, share such dreamy views of oneness, sharing, and beneficent white-black segregation that have long been part of white segregationists' fictional framing of southern society.

Numerous white political and business leaders outside the South did not publicly support *Brown*, including President Dwight D. Eisenhower. They too could not see beyond the dominant white-racist framing of these historical events. Historian Robert Caro describes Eisenhower's racist views and collusion in southern resistance to dismantling the racist system: "Not once during those six years [after *Brown*] would Eisenhower publicly support the ruling; not once would he say that *Brown* was morally right, or that segregation was morally wrong." Indeed, Eisenhower openly sympathized with white segregationists' racist views in private settings with friends.[65]

Conclusion

Out of this era of slow and grudging desegregation progress our contemporary era of continuing, and still systemic, racism has emerged. Without the black counter-frame (see Chapter 8) and the civil rights organizations and protests that it spurred and legitimated, the significant changes in overt and legal segregation in the 1950s–1970s era would almost certainly not have taken place. This era of significant legal and other societal racial change was substantially the result of many black Americans being willing to risk lives and livelihoods to bring down Jim Crow and to set the country again on the track to becoming a real democracy. Their efforts, and those of the small minority of whites who actively supported them, changed some of the segregated and other white supremacist ways that U.S. society had operated with since the Civil War. No longer was much overt racial discrimination legally permitted. Schools were officially desegregated. Jobs off limits to workers of color were officially opened up. Voting was now permitted. Some black politicians were elected. White police officers were supposed to treat black people with greater respect, and openly violent white supremacist groups were no longer tolerated. In addition, other Americans of color, often inspired by the black civil rights movement, engaged in protests that helped to bring down numerous overt signs of racial oppression and to move the country in the direction of real multiracial democracy.

Since the late 1960s, moreover, one effect of the legal desegregation progress brought substantially by the civil rights efforts of Americans of color has, ironically enough, been a renewed assertion by whites of white virtuousness. Since the 1960s, increasing numbers of whites have repeatedly insisted that they, and the United States generally, are fair, tolerant, and "no longer racist" and that the continuing social, economic, educational, and political problems faced by Americans of color are mainly of their own making. In the next chapters, we will examine this perspective on U.S. society, which is actually a refurbished version of the old white racial frame.

CHAPTER 5

The Contemporary White Racial Frame

Over the decades since the civil rights movements of the 1950s, white responses to numerous public opinion surveys have suggested that the level of white-racist stereotyping and other racist framing has declined substantially. Survey researchers and psychologists doing lab studies have found that white responses to typical questions about their racial stereotypes and prejudices indicate that in recent years whites as a group have become much less prejudiced toward African Americans and other Americans of color. Such survey results have frequently been interpreted by some researchers and numerous media analysts to mean that for the most part "racism is dead" in the United States.[1]

Is Racism Really Dead?

This interpretation of U.S. society is mistaken, and there is much social science data revealing why. For one thing, typical opinion surveys on whites' racial views are phone polls that ask brief questions and get brief answers, the latter usually forced by the pollster into a limited array of choices. At best, these surveys give a surface-level reading of white racial views. Even more importantly, such opinion surveys are seriously limited by the fact that many whites give the pollster socially desirable answers that accent white virtue or colorblindness and disguise their actual racial framing of society. Psychological research has found that many white respondents alter comments on racial issues to appear unprejudiced. Opinion surveys target, at best, a few elements of the white racial frame and miss much of its broad and deep framing of U.S. racial realities. Psychological researchers who have probed more deeply into the white mindset have found that more indirect and subtle measures indicate that anti-black views and other negative racial subframes are still quite common.[2]

Research data from social science projects using in-depth interviews and other qualitative research methods have come to the same conclusion. Thus, one important study of white students at three major universities found that their responses to brief attitudinal survey items were often different from those they gave during in-depth interviews. For example, while 80 percent of the large sample of white students approved of racial intermarriages on a survey item, substantial in-depth interviews with a smaller but similar student group found that only 30 percent consistently stayed with this racially liberal viewpoint, with the others backing off and indicating difficulties they had in their minds when it came to such intermarriages.[3]

A diverse array of evidence points to the reality that the old white racial frame, albeit with some contemporary alterations and refurbishing, remains powerful and pervasive. Research shows, indeed, that it is still learned and used at young ages, including by young white children. In an ethnographic field study at a multiracial daycare center, one of my graduate students, Debra Van Ausdale, observed numerous incidents that illustrate this point well. Consider this set of events. One day, Van Ausdale observed a white three-year-old, Carla, getting ready to lie down at the school's nap time. The child started moving her cot. When asked why by her teacher, little Carla replied: "Because I can't sleep next to a nigger," pointing to a black child nearby. Carla further explained: "Niggers are stinky. I can't sleep next to one!" Assertively applying a centuries-old racist epithet and old racist stereotyping with significant emotion to a social situation in her own way, Carla demonstrated that as a three-year-old she already held important elements of the white racist frame in her head. Later, at a meeting of staff members and her parents, all the adults present insisted that Carla did not learn the racist epithet from them. Her father finally remarked, "I'll bet she got that from Teresa. Her dad . . . he's a real redneck."[4] If her father's view is correct, Carla learned important elements of the dominant racial frame in her social network. In this case we observe the learning and use of the anti-black subframe of the dominant racial frame by a child within her important organizational and networking structures, structures that provide opportunities for performances of that conventional frame and insure its recurring reinforcement for those involved.

A racial-analysis paradigm with concepts such as systemic racism and the white racial frame is very useful for social analysts seeking to probe deeply and understand better the ways that young whites like Carla and the adults around her feel, think, and act on racial matters. The conventional focus on concepts of "bias," "prejudice," or "stigma," such as in most survey analysis of racial attitudes, is usually too superficial. Recall the important dimensions of the traditional white frame as it is revealed in everyday applications. Today, as whites move through their lives, they frequently combine racial stereotypes and biases (a beliefs aspect), racial metaphors and concepts (a deeper cognitive aspect), racialized images (the visual aspect), racialized emotions (feelings), interpretive racial narratives, and inclinations to discriminate within a broad racist framing. The contemporary frame not only encompasses verbal-cognitive stereotypes and articulated values, the important conceptions of what is desirable or undesirable on racial matters, but also important nonlinguistic elements such as racialized emotions, images, and even smells.

Fostered constantly by political and media socialization efforts and reinforced by a majority of white parents and peers, the contemporary white racial frame is deep and pervasive, with numerous subframes. This dominant white frame shapes thinking and action in everyday situations such as that of Carla and the children and adults around her. Where and when whites find it appropriate, they consciously or unconsciously use this frame in evaluating and relating to Americans of color and in accenting the privileges and virtues of whiteness. One need only read carefully a local newspaper for a day or two or listen carefully to national media broadcasts for a few days to observe how the centuries-old racial frame regularly shapes much of what happens in U.S. public and private arenas.

Learning the White Racial Frame

Children initially learn, and adults continue to learn, major aspects of the dominant frame by means of everyday socialization processes and regular interactions with others. The frame's features are transmitted by an often hidden curriculum taught in families and other social settings. Constant repetition of elements of the frame in everyday interactions like those in the account of Carla is essential to its reproduction across networks, space, and time. Repetition and imitation, including the intonation of verbal expressions and style of nonverbal expressions, build group rapport and facilitate interactions. The dominant frame thereby becomes deeply imbedded in most individuals' minds.[5]

Over the last century many of the sciences have accented the importance of relationships and networks in the physical and social worlds. Contrary to much public and philosophical discussion, the basic unit in society is *not* the individual, but the relationship between two or more individuals in essential and complex relationships and networks. Dyadic interactions, such as mother and child, are almost always nested in ever larger networks of human relationships, eventually building to the level of communities and the larger society. Today, as in the past, whites do not invent most elements of their personal racial framing but adapt them from, and often perform them in, their important networks, which are typically all-white. Researchers have found that whites tend to have much more racially homogeneous networks than people in other racial groups. In literally millions of these kinship and friendship networks, negative stereotypes and images of Americans of color are regularly used, refurbished, and passed along—from one generation to the next and one community to the next. Everyday interactions of friends and relatives in these networks make up the "muscles and tendons that make the bones of structural racism move."[6]

At an early age, white (and other) children learn the white frame in everyday interactions in networks of relatives, friends, and peers. The elements of this dominant frame are acquired by children at home, at school, at play, and from the media. Families play a central role, and racist lessons there tend to be deeply imbedded and well remembered. The little research done on white parents suggests that most offer few explicit lessons about the white frame to children. White children mostly seem to learn the dominant frame and how to act out of it by watching the actions of parents, other adults, and peers. In one research study, we conducted an interview with an older white woman whose mother had once told her that, if children like her were not "good," the "niggers would come in the night and steal us away and use us for their pleasure."[7] Not surprisingly, this respondent reported being intensely afraid of black men since childhood.

Research using photos of white and black faces and good/bad word associations has found that young white children hold anti-black stereotypes and inclinations and that these orientations do not decline in intensity for older groups of children and adults. For example, research using these photo procedures has shown that white preschoolers tended "to categorize racially ambiguous angry faces as black rather than white; they did not do so for happy faces." The important language and understandings of the old white framing of black Americans and other Americans of color are usually learned first in recurring family and friendship settings, and thus become part of a person's "inner speech" that is used to think about and shape racial interactions and other racial actions.[8]

As they get older, children usually learn to hide certain racial views from strangers—not surprisingly, given societal accents on racial pretense in public. In one study using the Implicit Association Test, some Harvard researchers found that six-year-old white children showed an implicit pro-white and anti-black bias in connecting white and black faces to good or bad words, and that the children's self-reported attitudes showed a similar overt racial bias. In the same study older white children and adults also revealed an implicit racial bias in matching white and black faces to good or bad words. However, the self-reported racial attitudes of the older white children revealed less overt racial stereotyping than for the younger children, and the self-reported attitudes of the adults studied showed no overt racial bias.[9] This research study confirms the point made earlier, and documented in a student diary study cited below, that as whites get older most know much better how to hide their racial attitudes in public ("frontstage") settings, such as with researchers, pollsters, or other strangers, and to reserve much overtly racist commentary for the private ("backstage") settings with white friends and relatives.

The Contemporary Frame: Still Accenting White Virtues

Elements of the old white racial frame, often refurbished, continue to be commonplace in whites' everyday thinking and actions. Although nearly four centuries old, this frame has changed rather modestly in much of its pro-white and anti-black core over the centuries. Periodically, of course, important new elements have been added, and some elements have disappeared or become more nuanced. Yet, if the leading racist intellectual among our founders, Thomas Jefferson, were to somehow come back he would recognize much of the contemporary pro-white and anti-black framing, including many of the underlying racialized emotions. He would likely be amazed at the many technological, demographic, and economic changes, but not at much of contemporary whites' framing that emphasizes the superiority of whites and inferiority of African Americans and others of color.

In assessing the pro-white material that is central to contemporary racial framing, one finds much that has persisted over centuries. Many of these elements accent the virtues, privileges, and power of whites and whiteness. The great-chain-of-being idea did not disappear from this white perspective as the country moved from being predominantly agricultural to its advanced urban-industrial period today. That old hierarchical notion has continued over the centuries as a more or less unconscious cultural model essential to the way most people orient themselves in society. Whites as a group remain at the top of the racial hierarchy, and a majority view that as still appropriate. Important white views, values, and framing remain normative, the societal standards to be adopted by children of all backgrounds as they grow up and by new immigrants.

Numerous studies today offer much evidence that the word "American" is often synonymous with "white." In several psychological studies researchers examined how strongly three major racial groups were associated with the category "American." In all the studies their subjects saw African Americans and Asian Americans as less associated with the category

"American" than white Americans. For their white subjects, they found that the association of "American" with whites was positively correlated with the strength of the subjects' own national identification. In important ways, the most intensive U.S. nationalism has become a type of white superiority orientation. White media outlets and politicians also frequently treat the term "American" as meaning "white American." Moreover, for most whites today even the often noted "American Creed" is a white-framed creed with historically white interpretations of its generally rhetorical ideals of freedom, justice, and equality.[10]

Today, whites and whiteness are viewed in positively framed terms by most people who consider themselves white, and often by those who do not. For the most part, whites continue to view themselves individually and as a group to be relatively good and virtuous. This white-framed perspective is mostly unidirectional, with whiteness and whites in the position of mostly being virtuous and the racial "others" as often unvirtuous. As in the past, commonplace white narratives of U.S. historical development still accent whites' superiority and courage over centuries. Implicitly or explicitly, the contemporary white frame accents continuing aspects of this superiority— that is, that whites are typically more American, moral, intelligent, rational, attractive, and/or hard-working than other racial groups, and especially than African Americans and other dark-skinned Americans. Today, in most areas of society, whites as a group are considered virtuous people who act on racial matters mostly in colorblind ways. In political, economic, and other social spheres, most whites manifest a strong sense of personal and group entitlement to what they have. In many settings where racial matters come up, one still hears whites insisting on their general or historical virtuousness: "My family never owned any slaves," "I have worked hard for what I have," "It's not because I'm white," and "We earned it, it is our right."[11]

An Evolving Racial Frame: The "Colorblind" Era

Over centuries of development in North America, the white racial frame has evolved and periodically changed. It is a somewhat flexible worldview that, as it has for centuries, shapes most everything humans do, from thinking and believing to feeling and acting. Significant changes in a positive direction have taken place only during a few major eras, such as during the nineteenth century abolitionist era and during and after the mid-twentieth century civil rights movements. Thus, the 1830s–1860s abolitionist movement helped to bring down the slavery economy. Still, the official abolition of slavery in 1865 did not result in an end to extreme white-on-black oppression, the dominant racial hierarchy, or pervasive racial framing.

Elements of the dominant frame asserting pro-slavery rationalizations were replaced with views of African Americans as still necessarily subordinate to superior whites, but under new structures of official segregation. The partially reworked white racial frame still vigorously legitimated a system of near-slavery called "Jim Crow," with its array of structures of segregation targeting African Americans—as well as over time other Americans of color. Similarly, during and after the 1950s–1970s civil rights movements, which generated the first major civil rights legislation in a century, the dominant racial frame changed, albeit often slowly, in a number of significant ways.

One change in the common version of the white frame was the removal of the idea of legal segregation as essential for white dominance and the gradual adding of a linguistic veneer of "we are colorblind" rhetoric. In many ways colorblind rhetoric, although often apparently sincere, has just papered over what are still blatantly racist views of Americans of color that have continued in most whites' racial framing. Since the 1960s openly segregationist and supremacist views have become much less acceptable. Yet many old racist ideas and other racial frame elements have persisted in forms that are only modestly changed. In addition, government and other public actions designed to bring change in the racist structures, such as the very serious racial inequalities in numerous economic and educational institutions, have been mostly limited to those necessary to maintain social order. When faced with civil rights protests and the need for change, as in cases like the *Brown* decision, white leaders have adopted modest interventions and institutional workarounds—that is, they have made changes in official or legal segregation, but at the same time have usually created weak enforcement mechanisms for new civil rights laws and policies, which mechanisms guarantee the continuation of the dominant racial hierarchy and much of its rationalizing white frame.[12]

Today the contemporary frame's accent on most whites as "no longer racist," "post-racial," and "colorblind" provides new language for what is in fact an old view of whites as a highly virtuous racial group. As we will see below, this white accent on being colorblind has been shown by social science research to be misleading and often a coverup of the substantial levels of blatantly racist framing and action in which many whites still engage. Those who say they "do not see race" in fact usually do see it, and they frequently act negatively on what they see. Substantial research shows that much of the old frame remains influential in white thought and commentary on racial matters, in public frontstage settings and private backstage settings.[13]

There is still much discussion of racial issues in the mainstream media, but frequently such discussion is forced on mainstream reporters and commentators by current events, such as the recurring police beatings and other harassment of black men. In such cases the notion of a colorblind country is temporarily abandoned, although the mostly white reporters and commentators in most areas may express discomfort with discussing such racial matters in any depth. Consider that many mainstream media reports on political campaigns that involve candidates who are not white still insist on accenting the candidates' racial identity whether the candidates wish that or not. Candidates who are not white are frequently mentioned as such, whereas if no racial designation is indicated in a media account, the reader or listener is assumed to know the candidate is white.[14] This is a clear example of *frame assumption*—the assumption that others, especially whites in this case, share one's racially framed understandings.

Candidates who are not white frequently face racial incidents or controversies that force the media to discuss racial matters. For example, in the 2008 presidential campaign of Senator Barack Obama, his racial identity was constantly accented in thousands of media commentaries, including debates over whether he was "black enough" for black Americans or "too black" for nonblack Americans. His racial identity was signaled in media reports on the public's or politicians' discussions of whether "real working class Americans" or "hockey moms" (typically terms for whites) would vote for him. Such racialized commentaries about this pioneering campaign by an African American signaled how fundamental and extensive a non-colorblind framing of African Americans still is. In contrast, there was no media focus on or problematizing of the whiteness of his opponent, Senator John McCain.[15]

During his presidency and second presidential campaign Obama regularly faced much continuing racial framing of a blatant or hostile type, especially from white conservatives. Blatant and hostile racist commentaries and performances could be seen on a recurring basis across the country and were often reported and discussed in the mainstream media. Such recurring events made it evident that assertions of a colorblind and "post-racial" United States were quite premature and generally mythological. Much of this racist framing of Obama has been integrated into an anti-Obama political framing. One observes numerous examples of this linking of racial and political thinking in the contemporary Tea Party movement, a mostly white conservative movement that has had a significant impact within the Republican Party, and on many state elections and legislatures. This movement is made of conservative political organizations that emerged after Obama was first elected. Numerous members have had links to white nationalist groups. One national survey found that those who sympathized with Tea Party groups were much more likely than the general population to believe that too much was being made of the African Americans' problems and to hold that the Obama administration favored blacks.[16]

Research by the Institute for Research & Education on Human Rights found that Tea Party activists were almost all white and placed great emphasis on racial and national identity issues, such as on where Obama was born and his alleged African-ness. Activists showed that they often operated out of a harsh racial framing in their use of racist epithets, distorted racist images of Obama, and numerous Confederate battle flags at political events, the latter common symbols of white resistance to racial change since the 1960s.[17] In addition, out of a strong racial framing, numerous Tea Party members have asserted that "their country" is being taken over by people of color. One recent Tea Party Nation email included an article speaking of the end of the "White Anglo-Saxon Protestant" race because of increases in people of color. Many white Tea Party and other conservatives also seem to greatly fear Mexican immigrants, and many have signaled strong support of anti-immigrant nativistic organizations and laws.[18]

Not surprisingly, a great many white Americans exhibit significant discomfort in talking critically about continuing white racism, including that which is overt and blatant and that which is more covert and expressed backstage in white areas of society. Sometimes this is just a colorblind denial that racial hostility and discrimination persist as serious problems in a supposedly post-racial United States. In other cases this reflects awareness that talking seriously about racism contradicts the omnipresent preference for colorblind "talk." Research by Bonilla-Silva and others has demonstrated the rhetorical devices whites use in everyday conversations, especially with strangers, to try to portray themselves as colorblind and non-racist. Bonilla-Silva has utilized studies involving survey data and in-depth interviews with mostly white students and black and white Detroit metropolitan area residents to examine the "colorblind racism" that dominates much white thinking. His research reveals specific micro-frames whites use to interpret racial issues and the narratives used to present themselves as colorblind.[19] Such strategies are not limited to ordinary whites, for we observe examples of this colorblind approach in frequent assertions by white politicians and media commentators.

The Persisting Racial Frame: Still Preoccupied with African Americans

The contemporary white racial frame, as with earlier versions over the centuries, contains many negative elements targeting African Americans and other Americans of color. Strikingly, from the beginning to the present, whites have placed the anti-black subframe at the heart of this racial framing. Consider this recent account from the diary of a white student at a historically white university with a modest number of black students:

A couple friends were gathered at a house on Saturday evening. They were discussing funny stories over drinks, all the people were white seniors. One person, Adam, told everyone about a game that he and his friends always wanted to play in high school. The game is called "spoons." This is a game where you drive around, find a black male, then you yell the "N" word and throw the spoon at him. If you don't hit him, you have to go get the spoon. This is a game that he heard of, he didn't make it up. . . . The house next door is a black fraternity. There is a house full of people that live next to a black fraternity. They began joking about stealing three Greek Kappa letters from the student neighborhood and putting it on their house so it would be Kappa Kappa Kappa (KKK). This also never happened, but during casual conversation people that are not actively racist joke about extremely racist things.[20]

Such contemporary accounts of racist joking and proposed action—here involving well-educated whites—reveal the character of the aggressive anti-black framing still in a great many white minds. Many whites enjoy such joking. Indeed, a recent study of a huge number of Google searches on the Internet found that a great many (presumably mostly white) Americans in all regions seem to get pleasure from searching out "nigger jokes" and other anti-black humor there, clearly for them a type of racialized entertainment.[21]

Black Americans have long been a central reference point, a negative racial framing against which most whites have consciously institutionalized racism and unconsciously defined themselves. One dramatic historical example, which operated until the late 1950s in the legal system, is the presence of defamation-of-character laws that permitted whites to claim in court that they had been defamed if they were labeled by someone as "black." In contrast, it was *not* possible under the defamation laws for a black person to sue for being labeled "white."[22] Significantly too, being called "Mexican" or "Asian" did not trigger such defamation-of-character laws, again signaling the deep reality of the white frame's central focus on the white-black distinction. To the present day, most whites consider being seriously taken as "black" to be an insult.

Moreover, if pressed to think about or discuss a vague category like "nonwhite people" or "people of color," most whites today will likely think and respond with reference to black Americans unless asked to do otherwise. The continuing white preoccupation with black Americans in recent decades not only underscores the pervasive anti-black stereotypes, ideas, and images of the dominant frame but also reveals deep racial emotions and inclinations. Few white analysts have recognized the significance of this preoccupation. It is mostly African American writers and scholars who have called attention to it. Recall Frederick Douglass's speech in the 1880s about the white obsession with black Americans then: "Of the books, pamphlets, and speeches concerning him, there is literally, no end." More recently, Irene Diggs, a leading African American anthropologist, wrote that

> Nearly everybody in the United States is prepared to discuss blacks, and almost no one is entirely without an opinion on blacks. Most are amazed at the huge amount of printed material on blacks. A complete bibliography would consist of several thousand titles. The intellectual energy spent on blacks in the United States, if concentrated in a single direction, would move the proverbial mountain.

She too pointed up the numerous words, books, and articles contemporary whites in various sectors have regularly written on African Americans. She added that

> blacks are a main divider of opinion in national politics and certainly in local politics. As a secondary problem and as a peculiar influence on all dominant national issues, the presence of blacks has disturbed religious moralists, political philosophers, statesmen, philanthropists, social scientists, politicians, and businessmen. The presence of blacks is interpreted by many Americans as a menace.[23]

Over centuries now, the white racial frame has kept this strong obsessive focus on black Americans as the dominant issue, problem, or reference point in an array of U.S. institutional arenas. Huge amounts of white energy have been expended on preserving systemic racism, including on the written and oral rationalizations of that societal reality.

Nobel-prize-winning novelist Toni Morrison has pointed out that for a long time African Americans as a group have functioned as a key metaphor and fundamental referent for white Americans in public discourse and literature. For centuries, African Americans have been a recurring target of discrimination and a constant negative reference, implicit or explicit, for whites. White concern with black Americans is present

> in the construction of a free and public school system; the balancing of representation in legislative bodies; jurisprudence and legal defini-tions of justice. It is there in theological discourse; the memoranda of banking houses; the concept of manifest destiny and the preemi-nent narrative that accompanies (if it does not precede) the initiation of every immigrant into the community of American citizens. The

presence of black people is inherent, along with gender and family ties, in the earliest lesson every child is taught regarding his or her distinctiveness.[24]

The history and structures of U.S. society involve African Americans as a recurring reference point. Significantly, African American novelists and essayists have often had very insightful things to say about the dimensions and impact of systemic racism. Commenting on the United States in the twentieth century, an earlier African American novelist, Ralph Ellison, added this insight about the white obsession. From Ellison's experience, an African American often feels like "he does not exist in the real world at all. He seems rather to exist in the nightmarish fantasy of the white American mind as a phantom that the white mind seeks unceasingly, by means both crude and subtle, to slay."[25]

Contemporary Evidence of the White Preoccupation

There are a great many historical and contemporary examples of this black phantom dominating particular white minds, for famous and ordinary whites. Take, for example, the legendary Alabama governor George Wallace. As one white reporter has noted, Wallace, long a leading southern and national politician, was obsessed with African Americans and racial matters: "Didn't talk about women. We didn't talk about Alabama football. I mean, it was race—race, race, race—and every time that I was closeted alone with him, that's all we talked about."[26] In the United States, at least in the South, for many white men "race" has often trumped talking about football and women, two favorite male topics.

More generally, the preoccupation with black Americans is evident in recent opinion surveys where a majority of whites greatly exaggerate the size of the black population. In surveys a majority estimate that black Americans make up at least 30 percent of the population, two and a half times their actual percentage. This suggests an emotion-laden conception, dating back to at least Thomas Jefferson, that there are too many African Americans—a demographic situation many whites view as threatening. Such surveys signal too that many whites periodically or habitually view their societal position in relation to the presence and number of black Americans. Conceivably, white concerns today with Latin American immigrants and their descendants may eventually displace African Americans from this demographic centrality in white framing, but this has not yet taken place in many areas of the United States.[27]

Recent social science studies have shown that negative black images and associated negative evaluations have become deeply imbedded in an overwhelming majority of white minds, including those of whites with relatively low levels of overtly expressed prejudice. When given a test of unconscious stereotyping, most whites quickly and implicitly associate black faces (photos) with negative words and traits (for example, evil character or failure). They have more difficulty in linking black faces to pleasant words and positive traits than they do for white faces. Analyses of thousands of tests have shown that nearly 90 percent of whites signal an anti-black, pro-white bias in these face-reaction tests.[28] Moreover, in studies where whites are shown photos of black faces, even for a few milliseconds, key areas of their brains designed to respond to perceived threats light up automatically under brain scans. Also, the more racial stereotyping white subjects revealed on paper-and-pencil psychological tests, the greater their brains' threat responses were when they were shown black photos.[29] Such studies suggest not only that there is significant cognitive stereotyping but also that whites' emotional states, such as fear and anxiety over black images, link to and undergird their white-racist framing and, likely, discriminatory actions in everyday life.

Yet other research on white thought and behavior demonstrates this centrality of African Americans to the contemporary white frame. In recent field studies that I and my colleagues have done, white interviewees and whites who kept diaries have revealed that black Americans are central to their and other whites' identity and everyday thinking. In these studies black Americans are often the non-European group that obsesses or preoccupies a large proportion of whites. In the next chapter I will discuss accounts of racial events recorded by hundreds of white college students who kept journals for us on their everyday lives. In these twenty-first century diaries these students reported that African Americans appear in about three-quarters of the racist commentaries, jokes, and performances that they have observed themselves and other whites doing. All other racialized groups taken together—including Native Americans, Latinos, and Asian Americans—made up about a quarter of the racist performances and other events they recorded. Field interview studies by other social scientists also suggest that the racist socialization of whites regarding Americans of color other than black Americans is usually less thorough and central to most whites' identity, framing, and practices. Interviewing in racially diverse California, for example, Ruth Frankenberg found that white women there accorded a *hyper-visibility* to black Americans and a relative invisibility to other Americans of color in their interviews.[30]

Social science research thus reveals that most whites seem to have a much more developed racial framing of black Americans than of other Americans of color. Contemporary Native American, Latino, and Asian American subframes of the white frame are often strong, but are generally less developed. After nearly four centuries of continuing white discrimination against African Americans in most U.S. regions, African Americans today still remain very central to the dominant white racial frame.

Anti-Black Stereotyping and Imaging: Animalistic Imagery

We can now examine specific aspects of the anti-black subframe. Much contemporary research documents the reality of centuries-old racist stereotypes and images of African Americans still remaining commonplace. A great many white and other nonblack Americans believe or assert that African Americans are violent, criminal, unintelligent, lazy, and oversexed, among numerous other stereotypes and images. In this dominant framing, black Americans are "othered" and often portrayed negatively. In research studies most whites can list the common stereotypes of African Americans, and the level of whites' anti-black stereotyping has been found to be related to their other racist views and to discriminatory actions directed at African Americans.[31]

Among the outrageous stereotypes and images common in the white racial frame today is the old view of black Americans as being linked to apes and monkeys. This was a view asserted by prominent founders like Thomas Jefferson, and it persists today. Ape and monkey imagery has persisted in vicious forms in some areas of white America, as a review of numerous white supremacist websites will reveal. Supremacist groups also still circulate drawings that depict African Americans as similar on various biological dimensions to the apes.[32]

Racist animalizing is not limited to extremist groups. For example, throughout his political years President Obama has seen this animalistic imagery applied, often viciously, to himself or his family. White political officials, political opponents, and many other elite and ordinary whites have often portrayed Obama, his wife, and children as apelike, frequently with a joking cover for these racist attacks. One 2011 example involved a California Republican official who sent acquaintances a photo of President Obama's face placed on a chimpanzee with the hostile caption "Now you know why—No birth certificate!" Several other officials called on her to resign, but like many whites she defended this white framing by insisting she was "not a racist" and that the message "was a joke." She contended she did not know this animalizing was racist. Such ignorance is unlikely because one must know the old stereotyping of black Americans being apelike to understand such a "joke." Yet another Republican official claimed this conventional racist framing of Obama was "light-hearted" and just "fun" that these Republicans often engaged in.[33]

For some years this type of framing directed at the Obama family has been commonplace in white-dominated arenas, including on Internet websites. To take another example, early in 2012 a white federal judge emailed to numerous people a joke about a young Obama talking with his white mother, who in the joke suggests Obama's mixed ancestry might have resulted from wild party sex, jokingly alluding to potential sex with a dog. A "mongrelizing"of black Americans in jokes is an old part of white racist framing. Again, the judge was defensive and said he was not a "racist" and meant this joke only for friends. He soon apologized.[34]

We need to emphasize the point, documented here in numerous other examples throughout this book, that a great many whites derive significant *pleasure* from doing racist commentaries and performances. Yet, when called on this enjoyable racist activity, most know somehow that it is wrong and many thus insist they are "not racist." The frequency of such events, the emotional "fun" whites have, and the often intensely defensive reactions reveal, yet again, the psychological and social depth and importance of systemic racism in a supposedly colorblind era.

In addition, some recent research suggests that the white-framed linkage of black Americans to apelike imagery is often half-conscious or unconscious. Some psychologists have found that the association in many white minds between black Americans and apes remains strong and emotion-laden. In one study, white and other nonblack college students who were exposed to black faces were quicker in recognizing fuzzy drawings of apes than those who were not exposed to black faces. In a second study of white students, researchers found that whites who were subliminally primed with ape images subsequently paid more attention to black faces than to white faces that they were shown. Those not so primed paid more attention to white faces. In a third study white male students presented with black and Asian faces were again more likely to attend to black than to Asian faces when they were primed subliminally with ape images. The association between black faces and apes was thus shown not to be a general white orientation to all nonwhite faces, but mainly to black faces.[35]

In these recent research studies, a remarkably strong association between ape images and black images was found in many white minds. As in previous centuries, black Americans are still often framed, and often seemingly unconsciously or half-consciously, by whites as animal-like and not fully human. Evidently, while most social scientists view "race" as a social fiction and social construction, many whites still view "race" as, to some degree, a biological reality.

Anti-Black Stereotypes and Imaging: Criminality

The ape-like stereotypes and images of African Americans held at some mental level by many whites frequently link to other emotion-laden stereotypes and images, such as those of criminality. For centuries, a central negative image in the white frame has been that of the "criminal black man." Not surprisingly, recent social science studies have shown the blacks-as-apes stereotyping has serious behavioral implications. In one study researchers found that white students' blacks-as-apes mental connections, subliminally primed by ape-related words presented to them, shaped their willingness to accept *more* police violence against a black criminal suspect than against a similar white criminal suspect when these students were then shown videos of such police violence. Moreover, a content analysis of hundreds of Philadelphia newspaper articles discussing black and white death-eligible criminal defendants found that English words eliciting apelike images in people's minds were more likely to have been used by newspaper writers for black than white defendants. Animalistic imagery is part of the dominant white frame that legitimates whites' targeting of black Americans for discrimination, including discriminatory policing. These researchers conclude that the visual and verbal dehumanization of black Americans as ape-like assists the process by which some groups become targets of societal "cruelty, social degradation, and state-sanctioned violence."[36] Notice too in these studies that the racist framing of black Americans need not have been conscious for it to have had negative effects on the way whites think or act.

Much research shows that a great many whites connect black Americans as a group with crime, while they do not easily associate whites as a group with crime. The image of black Americans as criminal remains an important part of the contemporary anti-black subframe. Note the recent comments of William Bennett, former U.S. Secretary of Education, who on a talk show stated that, "if you really wanted to reduce crime, you could—if that were your sole purpose—you could abort every black baby in this country and your crime rate would go down." After focusing only on black babies, Bennett backed off by saying that such actions would be "an impossibly ridiculous and morally reprehensible thing to do, but your crime rate would go down." Even though the conservative Bennett backed off and said this was a hypothetical he did not agree with (and used the "I am not a racist" strategy), we observe how firmly imbedded in some white heads, including those of the white elite, this connection between African Americans and crime remains.[37]

The mainstream media are partially responsible for perpetuating this racist framing. The criminality image is constantly reinforced in the media, especially in local news programs that are major sources of news for most Americans. Most local media operate routinely out of the dominant racial frame and thus accent blue-collar crimes by black Americans and other people of color in news programming, commonly ignoring some white crime, especially white-collar crime. One research project on local news programs found that news stories about violent crime that listed a suspect featured black suspects in a much higher proportion than was warranted by their actual arrest rate. Other research on local television stations has found that black suspects accused of crimes are much more likely to be negatively portrayed in on-air photos than are similar white defendants. In addition, in local television news programming whites are greatly over-represented as crime victims, while black Americans and other Americans of color are regularly over-represented among those said to be the criminals.[38]

Gendered Racism: Images of Black Women and Men

Another important dimension of the dominant racial frame is its gendered-racist character. The frame's negative portrayals of women and men of color, including black women and men, have similarities, but they are not interchangeable. Consider negative portrayals of black women. In a recent study, social scientists had three groups of mostly white students view three different videos—with one group viewing a video with a strongly stereo-typed image of a black woman as a house-keeper/mammy, another group viewing a strong stereotype of a black woman as a sexually aggressive "jezebel," and a third group viewing a nonstereotypical image of a white man retrieving a morning newspaper. Then the groups were asked to observe mock employment interviews, one with a black female applicant and another with a white female applicant, both with similar abilities and answers. After this observation of employment interviews, the subjects were asked to determine if a list of positive, negative, and neutral adjectives indicating character traits fit the person in the employment interview they observed. The mostly white subjects who observed the black interviewee linked her more quickly with negative character adjectives than with posi-tive character adjectives. The opposite was true for those who had observed the white interviewee. In addition, when asked to assess a black or white job applicant, the subjects who had viewed the jezebel video and also observed the black interviewee responded more quickly to jezebel-type (sexual) adjectives than to other adjectives.[39]

Viewing one black woman in an interview was enough of a cue to stimulate these subjects to draw on the negative sexual image of the black woman, one long part of the dominant racial frame. These quick associations of positive and negative adjectives with white women or black women indicate a knowledge of old gendered-racist stereotypes of black women, as well as a deep, often automatic, acceptance of them.

Today, the mainstream media remain central to the perpetuation of this gendered-racist framing. In spring 2007, some radio commentaries by popular talk show host Don Imus included blatantly racist comments about a successful and mostly black women's college basketball team. He laughingly called these talented college students "nappy-headed hos." Famous for barbed comments, Imus brought the harsh and sexualized framing of black women usually reserved for the white backstage out into the public frontstage, and he got fired. Yet, because executives wanted him, he was soon back. The mostly white media executives generally decide what blatantly racist elements from the dominant frame can be openly used by commentators and entertainers on their programs.[40]

Explicit in Imus's emotion-laden imagery is the centuries-old view that black women are not as beautiful as white women. Early in the development of the dominant frame a hierarchy of beauty was produced. In the eighteenth century, for example, Thomas Jefferson made clear in his articulation of the racist frame that white was beautiful and black ugly, a view also asserted by Benjamin Franklin, who revealed an aesthetic bias against the color of the Africans and preference for the "lovely white and red."[41] In contemporary society, black girls and women continue to endure much negative white imaging and commentary on their physical appearance in various settings, including the media, and in recurring advertising that suggests black women's bodies are not as beautiful as white women's bodies. Undeniably, white women have long been the dominant standard for female beauty.[42]

White views of black men reveal aspects of gendered racism, as in the criminality stereotype. For many nonblack Americans, just hearing words like "black man" stimulates a mental image of a large black man with physically threatening characteristics. In research studies subliminal presentations of black male faces, flashed so quickly that the conscious mind does not notice them, trigger negative white responses more so than white male faces. One study gave white subjects a dot matrix with very fast presentations of the faces of young black and white men looking forward. Researchers found that white subjects gave significantly more attention to black male faces than to comparable white faces. However, in a second study using black faces with averted-eye gazes, the researchers found that these black faces did not capture white subjects' attention. Apparently, in this study at least, young black men were especially noticed or considered dangerous only if they were looking directly at a white person. Overall, the researchers concluded that the white view of black men as threatening is "so robust and ingrained in the collective American unconscious that Black men now capture attention."[43]

Significantly, the dominant white standard for what is a "real man" in U.S. society is still white male and patriarchal. The most famous television program with a strong black male figure in U.S. history has probably been the long-running Bill Cosby show. One major study of this comedy series found that most white viewers who were interviewed liked the positive black family portrayal with its strong black male figure, yet many whites did not change their negative views of black Americans and their families generally as a result of viewing that show. Instead, the majority categorized

Cosby's strong father figure and family as "exceptions to their race" and stuck with the dominant racist framing of black Americans as lazy and as capable of succeeding if they would work harder. Significantly, a black television "family" was cited by whites as strong evidence that most black Americans were actually inferior to white Americans.[44]

Such reactions are commonplace. The achievements of individual African Americans such as comedian Bill Cosby or President Barack Obama, and their personal efforts to counter the dominant frame's racist images, often have little impact on the general racial frame because their achievements are viewed by many whites as just "exceptions to their race," exceptions that to whites suggest that their racist framing of a majority of black Americans is still correct. For most people, important information countering their racist framing seldom changes its major elements.

More than Words: Strong Racial Emotions

In most examples of contemporary racial stereotyping, we observe that the verbal elements of the dominant racial frame are frequently linked to significant visual imagery and major emotions. Du Bois suggested that the color bar is created not only by whites' ill will, but also by other powerful motives, by "irrational reactions unpierced by reason."[45] Some emotions are obvious in previous examples we examined, and others become obvious as one reflects on various white actions over the course of U.S. history. Over this history one often observes that a greedy and predatory desire for material wealth has from the beginning been an important motivator of many whites' racial thought and actions, including the killing and enslavement of other peoples. A strong desire for dominance, often associated with an intense white masculinity, seems common in this history as well. Other motivating emotions for such oppression have included a racialized arrogance or an anxiety over possible resistance from those oppressed. Strongly anti-black actions have also entailed a visceral hate dimension, what Joel Kovel has called the "madness" of white racism.[46]

In his sociopsychological analysis of white fear, another important emotion we have noted, Kovel argued that whites typically reject blackness and black bodies because they project their fears, often rooted in childhood, into the dark otherness of an objectified black person. In the childhood socialization process, most whites learn, consciously or unconsciously, to associate black people and blackness with dirt, danger, ignorance, or the unknown.[47] For this reason, a black target of white hostility and discrimination is not seen as "one of us." The racialized others become a general "they" or "you people" to be marginalized or otherwise discriminated against. Over time, racist thought and action also involves a massive breakdown of positive emotions such as empathy, the capacity to experience the feelings of members of an outgroup unlike your own. Holding back or destroying positive emotions, especially real empathy with those across the racial line, seems essential to creating a system of racial oppression.

Today, to take a conspicuous example, strong racist emotions can be seen in white supremacist groups with which hundreds of thousands of whites are at least loosely affiliated. Some fiercely emotional partisans of white supremacy today can be found in white nationalist groups that make effective use of the Internet to peddle extreme versions of the white frame. For example, there is a "Stormfront" website, now the largest explicitly white nationalist site on the Internet, with many thousands of registered users and millions of posts articulating a strong white supremacist framing. In the summer of 2008 this website featured a portrait labeled "Thomas Jefferson, white nationalist," as part of a banner at the top of a webpage. This portrait had a quote from Jefferson: "Nothing is more certainly written in the book of fate than that these people are to be free. Nor is it less certain that the two races, equally free, cannot live in the same government."[48] These white supremacists aggressively accent what they, like Jefferson, view as an absolute necessity—a complete geographical separation of white and black Americans.

Other Americans of Color

Continuing Racist Framing of Native Americans

In some ways the oldest North Americans, Native Americans, are today the most invisible of Americans of color. In public discussions of issues like affirmative action or employment discrimination, Native Americans are usually the Americans of color least focused on and least considered for anti-discrimination policies. They are not currently part of most whites' recurring interactions and experiences. Their relative invisibility to whites may be in part because a significant proportion of the Native American population is out of sight—that is, they live in rural areas or in towns and cities away from the East and West Coasts. They are a relatively small group—because of earlier centuries of white genocide, a bloody history erased in much contemporary memory. Central to maintaining the white frame's image of whites as virtuous involves a collective forgetting about how whites historically reduced this important North American population to national invisibility.

Today, numerous old racist views of Native Americans remain in the contemporary racial framing, including images of Indians as lazy, drug- or alcohol-addicted, criminal, somehow foreign, and not quite American. One Internet-based study of nearly 45,000 people, using *explicit* attitudinal questions, found that the majority said that they viewed Native Americans as being "more American" than white Americans. However, when the Implicit Association Test was used to measure the strength of their positive associations with "American," the white faces in the test were found to be more strongly associated with the concept of "American" than were the Native American faces. Strikingly, this *implicit* bias against Native American faces as somehow more foreign and less American than white faces was found not only for white respondents, but also for people in other racial groups except Native Americans. Researchers found a sharp contrast between respondents feeling they should say that Native Americans were very American in reply to explicit questions asked, yet contradicting themselves with negative evaluations of their American-ness in unconscious responses to real Native American faces.[49]

Other negative stereotypes and images of Native Americans can be found in the mainstream media, school textbooks and popular fiction, and school and professional sports' mascots. For example, in spring 2008 the white host of a North Carolina radio show openly stereotyped Native Americans in a long on-air discussion. Joking with white guests, he mocked Indians as "lazy" several times and claimed his view of Indians was statistically proven. For his likely uninformed listeners, such claims may appear as actual "information" that reinforces the old racist framing of Native Americans. The white host and guests mixed racist joking with serious discussions, including about whether a particular North Carolina tribe had been federally recognized and whether Indians would consider the term "sitting Indian-style" offensive. The host asked a white intern who was marrying a Native American if the latter's grandfather would stand on the road with a "single tear," referring to the stereotyped 1970s "Crying Indian" advertisements. Another white man on the program asked the intern if the couple was "gonna have a teepee-warming party." After listener protests, the show was suspended, but soon returned. As in the Don Imus case, this racist stream of consciousness was permitted to continue, with brief interruption, by executives at one of the country's leading media corporations.[50]

Recent studies of elementary, high school, and college textbooks have discovered many negative stereotypes and images straight out of the old white racial frame. These textbooks often deal briefly with indigenous peoples, but as though they are only part of past history—and that history is described inadequately and inaccurately. Numerous children's books and movies portray Indians with images of Pocahontas-type "princesses," "squaws" (a derogatory term), or male "warriors," all dressed in a stereotyped fashion. In this country one also observes continuing and negative warrior-type framing in the sports mascots used by many high school, college, and professional sports teams in numerous towns and cities, often in spite of

Native American protests. Examples of crude racist imagery out of the frame are the Chief Wahoo caricature used by the Cleveland "Indians" baseball team, the Indian caricature and tomahawk imagery of the Atlanta "Braves" baseball team, and the Indian caricatures used by the Washington "Redskins" (a vicious racist epithet) football team.[51]

Even today, the non-Indian management of these teams, who are mostly but not exclusively white, and many of their supporters see no problem with such extremely racist images and have opposed significant changes. Indeed, some whites have engineered emotional counter-protests against Native Americans who organized and protested this pseudo-Indian imagery. The omnipresent, white-generated parodies of Native American images, sacred chants, face paint, headdresses, and drums for sports fans' entertainment are taken, realistically, by many Native Americans as assaults on them and their cultures, not the least because many of these items have spiritual significance. The sports mascots and related fan gestures are frequently based on old emotion-laden stereotypes of Indians as wild "savages" or bloodthirsty warriors. That is, they are today viewed much like they were in eighteenth century framing, such as that in Jefferson's portrait of "merciless Indian Savages" in the Declaration of Independence. Both Jefferson's racist framing and the contemporary white-controlled framing of Native Americans ignore the historical reality of the truly "savage" European Americans stealing Native American lands by bloody, often genocidal means. Note too that the Indian symbolism chosen by sports teams frames Indians as historical groups and thereby ignores their reality as oppressed and marginalized Americans of color today. The successful white resistance to Native American attempts to get rid of this extraordinarily racist imagery reveals again that whites as a group continue to have the dominant power in determining how the racial frame operates in contemporary society.[52]

The Continuing Racist Framing of Asian Americans

Over the centuries whites, especially in the elite, have been active agents extending the white racial frame, initially developed for rationalizing the oppression of Native and African Americans, to numerous other groups. During the mid-nineteenth century Chinese workers and Mexican farmers and workers were the first Asians and Latin Americans incorporated into U.S. society and its racial hierarchy and framing. They were brought in as part of white expansion in the West, which included recruitment of Chinese laborers for West Coast enterprises like railroads and the imperialistic Mexican American War that brought Mexicans into the United States. Each new group thus encountered and exploited by whites was added to the racial hierarchy and to the white racial frame.

Over the last century whites have continued this process of expanding the racial hierarchy and dominant white frame to include an array of immigrants of color. We do not have space to review this process in detail, but can examine a few important examples. As we previously saw in a diary account where students sang a song mocking the Japanese flash-burned on walls during U.S. bombing attacks, whites view Asians and Asian Americans as available targets for racial stereotyping, imaging, and hostility. The dominant white racial frame includes a strong subframe with distinctive language and images targeting people of Asian descent. Over the last century and more, Chinese, Japanese, and other Asian Americans have been imaged and labeled in many areas as "the pollutant, the coolie, the deviant, the yellow peril, the model minority, and the gook . . . as an alien body and a threat to the American national family."[53] For example, in movies and other media from 1910 to the present, Asian American characters have periodically been pictured as foreigners, outsiders, villains, and criminals. In a process led by powerful whites in the media and in politics, they have been stereotyped as "inscrutable Orientals," poor English speakers, drug dealers, gang members, and dangerous or treacherous.[54] Note too that many such racialized stereotypes and images are variations on preexisting images from the older racist framing of African and Native Americans.

As with other racist framing, anti-Asian framing has significant societal consequences. The negative U.S. framing of the Japanese played some role, albeit one still debated, in the build-up to World War II. From the early 1900s to the 1930s, in the U.S. mass media and in political speeches, moviemakers, writers, and politicians attacked in racialized terms not only the expanding Japanese empire in the Pacific, but also Japanese Americans in California and Hawaii.

The Japanese empire's expansion in the Pacific bumped up hard against the also-expanding U.S. empire in the same area. In the first decades of the twentieth century, white writers set forth many racist images such as that of a devious, threatening, and buck-toothed "Jap." White leaders argued the Japanese were immoral and used the ape imagery for them that had been applied earlier to African Americans. U.S. military and political leaders acted out of an anti-Japanese racist framing that was a subframe of their dominant racial frame. In the middle of World War II, for example, West Coast commander General John DeWitt asserted that "A Jap's a Jap. The Japanese race is an enemy race, and while many second- and third-generation Japanese born on U.S. soil, possessed of U.S. citizenship, have become 'Americanized,' the racial strains are undiluted." DeWitt was echoing the common white racist view. Fearing enemy collaborators in what they had framed as a "large alien population," white leaders moved most Japanese Americans into "internment camps" (actually, concentration camps) in inland areas of the United States. In this extremely discriminatory process, most of these Americans lost land and other property they had worked hard for, and some died or were injured protesting discriminatory treatment. Racist subframes have had serious consequences for Asian Americans.[55]

In recent decades Asian Americans have continued to face much negative framing, with substantial stereotyping and mocking, and consequent discrimination. They are often viewed by whites and others as somehow un-American and culturally inferior or problematical. Their language or speech is frequently mocked, and their physical features are periodically caricatured. For example, the Adidas company recently produced some shoes with a logo with a negative caricature of a buck-toothed, slant-eyed Asian. Similar white-framed images are used in many areas of society. In the late 1990s the editors of the influential *National Review* magazine placed a cartoon-like caricature of then President Bill Clinton and Hillary Clinton as slant-eyed, buck-toothed Chinese figures with Chinese hats, an image critiquing them for Democratic fundraising allegedly involving Asians.[56] More recently, a movie animation company created a Mr. Wong cartoon with a crude caricature of a Chinese "hunchbacked, yellow-skinned, squinty-eyed character who spoke with a thick accent and starred in an interactive music video titled 'Saturday Night Yellow Fever.'"[57] This mocking of Asian people can be seen in the puppet movie *Team America: World Police*, which included a Korean official speaking gibberish in a mock-Asian accent. The movie was "an hour and a half of racial mockery with an 'if you are offended, you obviously can't take a joke' tacked on at the end."[58]

This language mocking and its associated anti-Asian images remain a significant part of the contemporary framing of Asian Americans. Asian American children and adults often are forced to endure hostile mocking such as: "Ching chong Chinaman sitting on a rail, along came a white man and snipped off his tail"; "Ah so. No tickee, No washee. So sorry, so sollee"; and "Chinkee, Chink, Jap, Nip, zero, Dothead . . . Flip, Hindoo."[59] A Toledo radio station's white disc jockey recently phoned Asian restaurants using mock-Asian speech, including "ching, chong, chung" and "me speakee no English." On her talk show prominent comedian Rosie O'Donnell repeatedly used "ching chong" to mock Chinese speech.[60] Language stereotyping and mocking involve racializing sounds and have long been part of the dominant racial frame, and have been directed not only at Asian Americans but also at African, Native, and Latino Americans. Language mocking is usually linked to other important racialized stereotyping and imagery that whites hold in their negative framing of these Americans of color. Researcher Rosina Lippi-Green has noted an essential point about such mocking: "Not all foreign accents, but only accent linked to skin that isn't white . . . evokes such negative reactions."[61]

During the 1960s the "model minority" image of Asian Americans, a significant addition to the contemporary white frame, was added by whites in academia, the media, and the political arena. The main reason appears to have been to counter the anti-racist arguments and actions of black demonstrators in the 1960s civil rights protest era. The model minority imagery, and the term itself, were not created by Asian Americans, but by influential whites. The idea was apparently first articulated by social scientist William Petersen, who in a 1966 *New York Times* article entitled "Success Story, Japanese-American Style" celebrated certain socioeconomic achievements of Japanese Americans. He contrasted their situation with that of black Americans, who were then actively protesting oppressive racial conditions.[62] Some months later, a *U.S. News & World Report* article similarly celebrated Chinese Americans for their hard-work values and argued that if African Americans were like these Asian Americans there would be no need to spend "hundreds of billions to uplift" them.[63] Clearly, whites in elite positions in academia, the media, and government agencies have regularly helped to generate or reinforce this model minority stereotype in the dominant framing of Asian Americans. This imagery is frequently trotted out when elite whites or their acolytes in various groups wish to put down the efforts or character of people of color who are not Asian.

This serves the interests of whites as the top group in the hierarchy. Asian Americans suffer because this imagery conceals the harsh reality of racial hostility and discrimination that they too routinely encounter from whites, which in reality often limits their achievements in society. It also conceals numerous other problems generated for Asian Americans in this white-controlled society, including the significant poverty faced by some Asian American groups. Not surprisingly, thus, one recent summary of research on experiences of Asian American students on campuses shows that the usually white-generated images they face are often quite "negative, such as perceptions that Asians 'don't speak English well,' 'have accents,' and are 'submissive,' 'sneaky,' 'stingy,' 'greedy,' etc."[64] A principal point about the white-generated model minority and other common Asian American imagery is that whites, especially those with significant resources, have the societal power to specify how a group of color is framed in society.

The Continuing Racist Framing of Latinos Today

Latinos currently make up the largest group of Americans of color, with Mexican Americans being the most numerous in this umbrella group. At the beginning of white contacts with Mexicans in the 1830s–1840s, as we have seen, whites viewed the latter out of the old racist frame already constructed for African and Native Americans. This pattern has continued over the last century. During the 1920s a prominent white member of the U.S.

Congress described Mexican immigrants as an undesirable and "mongrel-ized" mixture of the Spanish and "low-grade Indians," but with supposedly troubling African "blood" added in. Again we see a negative view of "racial mixing." Similarly, during this era a white Ivy League professor expressed the fear of many whites that they would eventually be eliminated from the United States because of racial interbreeding and that the "progeny of Mexican peons" would long "continue to afflict us with an embarrassing race problem."[65]

This imagery of being overwhelmed by people "lower" in the racial hierarchy remains strong today in the dominant framing of Latin American immigrants and their descendants. At one 1990s meeting on Mexican immigration in California, a white state Senator expressed opposition to public schooling for children of Mexican immigrants, describing the latter as "on the lower scale of our humanity." Here again, the great-chain-of-being notions about "lower scale" people remains strong in the dominant racial framing. Significantly, the U.S. Latinos who publicly criticized this white Senator's racist comments were attacked in the white-controlled mass media.[66] Using more circumspect language, but making a similar point that the U.S. "civilization" was under significant threat from Latino immigrants, the late Harvard professor Samuel Huntington wrote out of a white racist framing of Mexican Americans, whom he viewed as having a culture inferior to that of white Anglo-Saxon Protestants.[67]

Immigrants from Latin America and their children are today racially framed in various ways. Otto Santa Ana has investigated the language and metaphorical imagery used in reporting on undocumented immigrants in a major West Coast newspaper. His analysis of newspaper articles revealed that the mostly white editors and reporters made frequent use of negative language portraying Latino immigrants as animals, invaders, or disreputable persons. Numerous articles used a framing that animalized immigrants, with similarities to the animalizing of African Americans previously noted. In the newspaper government health and other social programs were described as "a lure to immigrants," and the California electorate was said to have an appetite for "the red meat of deportation." Reporters described immigration agents as catching "their quarry" and spoke of the need to "ferret out illegal immigrants." The reporters' use of strong metaphor-linked words such as "burden," "dirt," "disease," "invasion," and "floods," "explicitly or implicitly, conveyed images of Mexican and other Latin American immigrants as threatening, dangerous, and burdensome.[68]

Whites' negative framing of Mexican Americans and other Latinos can also be seen in how whites have stereotyped and imaged them, much like black Americans, as violent and criminal over many decades. For example, a 1940s report by a white police officer, backed up by his superior in the Los

Angeles Sheriff's Department, alleged that Mexican Americans had a desire for street violence that was "inborn." Reflecting on the 1940s, one prominent white scholar wrote at the time that the Mexican American was justifiably viewed as "'lawless' and 'violent' because he had Indian blood; he was 'shiftless' and 'improvident' because that was his nature."[69] This commentary shows how strong racist stereotypes of Mexican Americans were in the white framing even before recent increases in immigration. Two decades later, a leading historian of the Southwest, Walter Prescott Webb, framed Mexican Americans similarly: "There is a cruel streak in the Mexican nature" and that "may and doubtless should be attributed partly to the Indian blood."[70]

Traditional white racial framing has long accented, often prominently, notions of "blood," violence, and criminality in assessing most Americans of color, including Latino groups. These stereotypes have regularly appeared in movies and television programs. Over recent decades Hollywood films, such as *Falling Down* (1993) and *Gran Torino* (2008), as well as numerous television dramas, have portrayed Latinos as disproportionately violent criminals, drug users, and welfare mothers. This negative framing is found in the views of whites at various class levels. For example, one survey of white college students found them agreeing that Hispanics were more likely than whites to be physically violent, dirty, uneducated, and criminally inclined.[71] Today, many whites continue to racially stereotype and image Latinos in a variety of ways. In this aforementioned survey, white students expressed the belief that, compared with whites, Latinos place less value on prosperity, learning, and "mature love." In addition, the majority of white respondents in another survey believed Latinos "tend to have bigger families than they are able to support," while one-fifth felt Latinos lacked "the drive to succeed."[72]

Recently, social scientists have found strong anti-Latino framing in several regions. In a southwestern study, Hilario Molina has demonstrated from field interviews how the anti-Mexican subframe of the dominant white frame regularly racializes and slanders undocumented Mexican immigrants. Interviewing immigrant day-laborers, he found that they face much strong negative framing from white individuals, as well as from cultural sources such as the mass media. Whites often seemed to fear that Mexican immigrants could not be culturally assimilated, and would bring serious changes in the dominant culture. In addition, these undocumented immigrants reported significant negative stereotyping out of the white racial frame from some Mexican American subcontractors with whom they dealt. In this case, as Molina suggests, the "elite white male remains unseen but active in racializing the social and structural activities."[73]

In a recent interview study of middle class Latinos, political scientist Maria Chávez has shown the range of racial framing and discrimination faced by Latino professionals. One West Coast lawyer described his experiences with whites over a long time and his awareness of being "a minority" thus:

> I'm always aware of it. . . . It's subtle because, for example when I bought my home on [names area] and it overlooks the water. I was outside and I don't know what I was doing and my neighbor says: "Oh, are you the gardener?" . . . And that's what I have experienced for 55 years. . . . As a Latino or Native American or any kind of minority, you're just another wetback or you're just another migrant farm worker or whatever, until you are a professional and suddenly your stature changes. And you have to be aware of it whether it's been brought out to you or whether you've faced it.[74]

Such examples signal how powerful and lasting the white framing of Latinos is, and it is often strong even where there are relatively few Latinos. Indeed, researchers have found this anti-Latino framing to be common in many urban and rural areas of the country.[75]

Whites have included in the Mexican American and other Latino subframes of the dominant racial frame much language mocking, which is again commonly expressed with joking and laughter. Mocking Spanish involves whites, especially in the middle and upper classes, creating derisive terms like "no problemo," "el cheapo," "watcho your backo," and "hasty banana," as well as phrases like "numero uno" and "no way, José." Such mock Spanish by white English speakers generates, overtly or subtly, a negative view of Spanish, those who speak it, and their culture. Mock Spanish, together with associated caricatures of "lazy" or "oversexed" Mexicans, is commonplace in gift shops, boardrooms, and the mainstream media, especially in southwestern areas. Even though openly racist talk is often frowned upon by many whites, nonetheless, this mock Spanish is still used by whites in public and backstage settings. It perpetuates negative stereotypes and images of Mexicans and Mexican Americans, as well as other Latinos, in ways that many may view as harmless. However, as Jane Hill has shown, the significance and impact are quite substantial: "Through this process, [Latinos] are endowed with gross sexual appetites, political corruption, laziness, disorders of language, and mental incapacity."[76] Such repetitive mocking routinely reinforces the anti-Latino frame in the minds of whites and others of all ages and classes.

As we have seen, throughout much contemporary racial framing of Latinos (and Asian Americans) there are recurring negative references to them as immigrants and in some sense "foreign." One commonplace view of Latino immigrants and their children is that they cannot be fully incorporated into U.S. society. The framed notion is that they do not want to adapt, or do not adapt well, to the dominant English language and Anglocentric cultural traditions. However, this often uncritically accepted idea of "assimilation" is problematic, because for more than a century it has developed substantially within a strong racist framing of society. The idea of assimilation is usually accompanied by an explicit or implicit insistence on *one-way* adaptation of immigrants, especially immigrants of color, to the white-dominated culture and racial hierarchy. Even the scholarly literature on immigrant incorporation tends to use the term and idea of assimilation uncritically. Indeed, the conventional white racial frame and U.S. racial hierarchy are often, consciously or unconsciously, assumed by many analysts to be part of the normal nature of this society and something that naturally has to be accommodated by new immigrants of color. Today, for the most part, whites will reciprocally "assimilate" only to aspects of new immigrants' cultures that do not threaten white dominance, such as to some immigrants' music or food preferences.[77]

As a matter of everyday reality, Americans of color, including immigrants from Latin America and Asia, are more or less forced to accept much of the existing white racial frame and racial hierarchy. The mostly white-controlled media and schools aggressively press them to conform constantly over their lifetimes. They learn that they must more or less conform to many white-normed and white-framed societal realities, so that they can survive in this still racially oppressive society. Indeed, they adapt much more cooperatively to many of these societal pressures, such as in learning the English language, than a great many whites are willing to give them credit for.[78]

This pressure to conform has numerous negative consequences. One of the striking things about the white racial frame today is how widespread many of its essential elements are across this society. Even many new immigrants of color, such as recent Latino and Asian immigrants who have been interviewed recently, carry important bits of the white frame in their heads, frequently imbibing them from a now global U.S. mass media before they have arrived in the United States. They, as well as other Americans of color who have been in the country for a long time, often accept significant parts of the dominant white racial framing—sometimes including negative framing that whites have historically directed at their own groups. Americans of color that I and my colleagues have interviewed often buy so strongly into the white framing of yet other Americans of color that they do not trust or relate well to the latter. Such cross-racial framing makes intergroup cooperation in the struggle against white racism more difficult.[79]

Conclusion: Some Scholarly Impacts

The white racial frame is pervasive. One finds it operating in obvious and unexpected places, influencing much in U.S. society and in global society. Even white scholars, researchers, and others with much education frequently think and write, consciously or unreflectively, out of a strong and unexamined version of the white frame.

For instance, Joan Herbers has pointed out how certain words and concepts from older versions of the white frame are still used in certain physical sciences. She notes that biological scientists and writers still use the terms "slave-making ants" and "negro ants" because of the behavior of a specific type of ant that preys on other ants. Like the U.S. founders who used slavery as a metaphor for their own political oppression, today some scientists reference the enslavement of black Americans in their scientific naming and discourse, likely without a thought to the larger racial frame from which it comes. Herbers argues that "using the slavery metaphor today is anachronistic, and I submit that it is time to discard it altogether."[80]

Periodically, various researchers in the biological sciences and social sciences reveal that they think and act uncritically out of some old version of the white racial frame. Consider the white researchers Richard Herrnstein and Charles Murray, who in the 1990s made influential arguments that paper-and-pencil "intelligence" test data demonstrated that black and Latino Americans were intellectually inferior to whites. In their view, which has been picked up by popular analysts to the present, certain black-white genetic differences account to a substantial degree for racial differences in test scores.[81] More recently, in 2007, one of the most distinguished physical scientists, James Watson, co-discoverer of the structure of DNA and Nobel prize winner, argued that IQ test data indicated that black people were less intelligent than whites: "All our social policies are based on the fact that their intelligence is the same as ours—whereas all the testing says not really."[82] Typically, the analysts making such arguments are thinking uncritically out of a learned white racial framing. They speak or write as though there is no way to view data showing differential group scores on conventional "skills" tests (inaccurately termed "intelligence" tests) other than their negative framing of the supposedly lesser intelligence of people of color. They do not critically assess the reality that these tests have mostly been created by and/or normed on whites or the fact that much of the tests' substance reflects the (white) culture of those who devised the tests.

In recent years, numerous medical, biological, and social science researchers working on human genome issues have resurrected the discredited racist idea of "race" being substantially a genetic and biological reality. Bioethicist Dorothy Roberts summarizes:

Race is central to every aspect of the new science and technology that is emerging from genomic research—computer-generated portraits of the molecular structure of human populations, biomedical studies searching for genetic cures, personalized medicine tailored to each individual's genotype, reproductive technologies for improving children's genetic makeup, genetic genealogy for tracing ancestral roots, and forensic DNA testing that helps law enforcement catch criminals. This science and technology is redefining race as a natural division written in our genes.[83]

Recently, too, a few social scientists have tried to revive the idea that "race" is actually a genetic-biological reality of great societal relevance.[84]

The medical, biological, and social scientists trying to resurrect the old idea of "race" as a real genetic and biological reality are operating from a very unreflective white racist framing. They show no critical awareness of the centuries-old history of the word and concept "race." "Race" was *not* a product of critical scientific research, but was a category scheme for human beings intentionally adopted by white biological and medical scientists, other intellectuals, and political leaders in the eighteenth and nineteenth centuries as part of a broad racist framing that was central to *rationalizing the large-scale oppression* of Africans and other people of color during the massive expansion of the Atlantic slavery system over several centuries. Their elite descendants extended this rationalizing racist framing of African Americans and other people of color—for example, as "inferior" to "superior" whites—during the long Jim Crow era that followed on the slavery era and lasted until the 1960s.

One reason for this renewed and uncritical accent on biological approaches to "race" seems to be a continuing desire on the part of numerous elite and other whites, as researchers Nelkin and Lindee put it, to remove "moral responsibility" for societal oppression "by providing a biological 'excuse.' Genes are the agents of destiny: We are the victims of a molecule, captives of our heredity."[85] Kaufman and Hall have noted too that this new accent on "genetic determinism cuts both ways, however, for although it absolves the individual from responsibility, it also absolves the society at large."[86]

CHAPTER 6

The Frame in Everyday Operation

To make sense out of systemic racism, we need to consider both its early material development and rationalizing frame and the numerous ways in which it continues to operate in the everyday lives of this country's residents, and thus in the recurring operations of this ever-more-diverse society. The white racial frame is very often translated into discriminatory actions, a crucial point about systemic racism that is examined in this chapter.

Consider this recent account from a Latino college student about violent racism at a historically white northern university:

Freshman year I lived in [a dorm on campus] with Eduardo . . . and I remember we were at this party in the neighborhood. I left early because I was tired, and then later on that night, Eduardo comes into our dorm room bleeding in his hands and face. I asked what the hell had happened to him. He told me the story of how he got beat up by three white males on his way back to the dorm. The reason why he got beat up was because he was . . . on the phone with his girlfriend of the moment, screaming out in Spanish while he walked back. The white guys that beat him up told him that, "This is America, and we speak English only," and beat him up. . . . It's absurd to beat someone up because he was speaking in another language. I had a similar experience on my freshman year, too, where I was called a "Spic."[1]

Observe here the severe impact that these whites' racial framing of young Latinos had on them. The latter are viewed by these apparently well-educated whites as not really American, and in at least one recent case "spic" framing led to a violent attack. These white-racist voices still resonate and create pain across the country well into the twenty-first century, even as many whites prefer the illusory imagery of a "post-racial" America.

Today, the dominant racial frame continues to shape, structure, and rationalize an array of racially exploitative and discriminatory *actions* by whites, and sometimes others. A central aspect of the white frame is its persistent interpretive and motivating power in generating everyday discrimination and other actions, which is one way we know the shape it takes in human minds. Whites still frequently engage in racial performances and discriminatory behaviors motivated by the racist stereotypes, images, narratives, and emotions of that centuries-old frame. The dominant racial framing does not exist apart from actions. Indeed, it was originally created to rationalize an extraordinary array of very discriminatory actions. Today the dominant racial frame still generates, and is reinforced by, a myriad of discriminatory actions in everyday life.

The Frame in Everyday Operation: The Backstage

Much contemporary research shows the destructive reality and consequences of systemic racism. Psychological researchers have found that virtually all whites are aware of major elements in the dominant racial frame, including old anti-black stereotypes, no matter what their personal inclinations to act on them may be. Automatic mental processing brings up commonplace stereotypes in the minds of most people whenever an appropriate stimulus appears, such as a member of a racial outgroup. This research also indicates that very prejudiced people are more inclined to act on the activated racial stereotypes, while less prejudiced people often engage in mental processing that ignores or rejects all or part of triggered stereotypes.[2]

Research studies have found that those who show a strong implicit racial bias on measures like the Implicit Association Test (of different faces) are more likely to engage in overt racist performances and other racist action, including discrimination against people of color. Studies at Rutgers University found that white and other nonblack subjects who revealed greater implicit bias toward black Americans on psychological tests were more likely than other subjects to report engaging in discrimination such as hurling racist slurs, excluding black people, and threatening physical harm to black people. Moreover, in assessing hypothetical university situations, white students with strong racial biases were more likely to recommend budget cuts for black, Asian, and Jewish student organizations (that is, potential economic discrimination).[3] This and other social science research indicates that the dominant racial frame is so deeply entrenched in society and in individual minds that most whites apparently do not realize how routinely they act out of it.

Given that many of the psychological-test studies we have examined reveal a strong racial bias for a substantial majority of whites, it is not surprising that interview studies also show a substantial level of racist performances and other racist behavior. In our in-depth interviewing and other field research, my colleagues and I have found that much blatantly racist thought, commentary, and performance has become concentrated in the social backstage where only whites are present. Much less is performed in the social frontstage settings where there are strangers or people from diverse racial groups present. This is because of pressures to be socially correct (colorblind) in frontstage areas such as workplaces and public accommodations.

Examining these two faces of white racism, Leslie Houts Picca and I analyzed journals from 626 white students at numerous colleges and universities in several U.S. regions. These students were asked to record their observations of everyday events in their lives that exhibited racial issues, images, and understandings. In relatively brief diaries (on average, six to nine weeks) these white students gave us thousands of accounts of racist commentary and actions by white friends, acquaintances, relatives, and strangers—much of it in backstage areas. In addition, some 308 students of color at these colleges and universities gave us several thousand diary accounts of racist events, mostly events that had happened to them or their acquaintances and relatives of color.

The journal accounts offer insights into how the dominant racial frame operates today in everyday life. Let us examine a few examples that show the range of racial performances and other racialized actions. In one journal excerpt a white female student at a midwestern college comments on a trip with two white friends on Halloween:

> I rode in the car with my best friend Abby and her new boyfriend Todd. It takes a little over an hour to get to ... the Haunted Trail ... so Todd decided to put in a little music. I'm not really sure what types of bands played this but it wasn't real music. They were songs about black people and they were very harsh and very gross. The lyrics said things about hanging, and they were good for nothing, and shooting, and such. Todd thought it was hilarious, he loved it! Abby and I were disgusted, I couldn't believe that he actually liked this, and that people would actually seriously say these things. We finally asked him to turn it off and to play the radio. He turned the radio on but he seemed rather reluctant, it seems that he was enjoying what we had been listening to. We asked him if he was racist and he said, "Hell yeah!" I

don't remember exactly what he said now but he talked about how he thought that black people were only good for the sports they played in, how he hated the fact that they all smoked and pretended to be cool. I was surprised that Abby would date someone like this, because we have a few black friends from her school. I know that he wouldn't have said that around just anyone, cuz he would probably get his ass kicked. Other than these comments and his bad choice of music he seemed like a fun guy to hang out with.[4]

Unmistakably, the anti-black aspects of the white frame are not something only found in decades past, for they are still routinely expressed and acted on by many whites. Here a racist framing is aggressively expressed in an everyday interaction. Notice two categories of actors—a central protagonist and two mild dissenters who tolerated the extreme anti-black performance for some time. This account is in an interactive backstage where only whites are present. The protagonist is aggressively white-centered, and he enjoys supremacist music and feels he can impose negative framing of African Americans on white friends. It takes a while for the women to get the music shifted to something else. Many whites enjoy or tolerate such overtly white-racist music, and clearly the mostly white executives who run the music industry sometimes provide the facilities to circulate musical versions of the dominant racial frame in its blatant and subtle forms.

The diarist describes the protagonist as knowing when and where in his social settings to accent blatantly racist views. Whites often speak and act differently in the all-white backstage and the often more diverse frontstage. There is an interesting rationalizing phenomenon: If whites do not articulate racist ideas in public, if they keep them to themselves or just express them in the backstage, then they or their white friends and relatives frequently do not see them as seriously "racist." Articulating blatant elements of the racist frame in private settings seems to be at least acceptable, probably because in their view no one is "really hurt" by that tactic. What is particularly striking here and in numerous other student diary accounts is how the participants describe friends who do blatantly racist performances as "nice," "fun to hang out with," or "not a racist." An accented view of white virtue, a very old concept in white racial framing, seems to override the actual reality of racist performances in many diary accounts. Also, numerous diary entries reveal that these students do not want to describe friends or relatives as "racist," or as doing racist stuff, even when that is obviously what they are doing. This is an important part of the colorblind version of the contemporary white racial frame—the view that one should play down or not see the actual racist behavior that one engages in, or that one's friends and relatives engage in.

In their diaries most of the students and their friends or relatives do not appear as extreme white supremacists like the young man in the previous account, but they still demonstrate much strong anti-black framing in the everyday accounts. Here is a typical example of a white performance of the anti-black subframe, in this case from a diary entry by Hannah, a white student who reports on a night of drinking at a northern college:

> Three of my friends (a white girl and two white boys) and I went back to my house to drink a little more before we ended the night. My one friend, Dylan started telling jokes. . . . Dylan said: "What's the most confusing day of the year in Harlem?" "Father's Day . . . Whose your Daddy?" Dylan also referred to black people as "Porch Monkeys." Everyone laughed a little, but it was obvious that we all felt a little less comfortable when he was telling jokes like that. My friend Dylan is not a racist person. He has more black friends than I do, that's why I was surprised he so freely said something like that. Dylan would never have said something like that around anyone who was a minority.[5]

Old anti-black stereotypes targeting black families, and using animalizing imagery, permeate this performance. The emotion-laden stereotypes have an impact because of their frame resonance: The youthful listeners also have a deeply imbedded racial framing that resonates with these racist commentaries and enables the latter to have much more impact on their thinking and action than they otherwise would have. Indeed, a similar joke about whites would not have had this impact because there is no negative anti-white frame in white minds for such commentaries to resonate with.

Later, Hannah provides reflective commentary that is rather unusual in these student journals:

> It is this sort of "joking" that helps to keep racism alive today. People know the places they have to be politically correct and most people will be. However, until this sort of "behind-the-scenes" racism comes to an end, people will always harbor those stereotypical views that are so prevalent in our country.

In her commentary Hannah offers a rare recognition of how different white performances commonly are "behind-the-scenes." She recognizes how such performances in backstage settings maintain the dominant framing, and thus systemic racism. Nonetheless, even the perceptive Hannah is unwilling to classify her friend as "a racist person." Note too that the dominant racial framing is performed in an intensely interactive setting. The performances emerging out of the dominant frame are frequently essential in integrating white networks, which makes implementing anti-racist changes difficult. Researching an all-white country-and-western group, researcher Nina Eliasoph discovered that overtly racist performances among them, like those of these students, helped to integrate the group socially and to create a type of social capital. Ending racially framed conversations here would likely have contributed to this group's breakup. Knowing the dominant racial frame well includes knowing "how and where it is appropriate to speak about it."[6]

The college diarists wrote numerous accounts about similar performances by relatives operating out of a blatantly racist framing. Note this journal entry from Tiffany about a racist performance by her father, in a midwestern home setting:

> We were watching the news and my father (white male in 40s) noticed that most of the stories they were telling had to deal with primarily black people. Once he started that the negative black jokes poured out of his mouth. He had some customers in the house (we own our own ... repair shop) and he was still telling the jokes. He never thought twice about it. He never thought about what his customers might say or do. Some of the jokes were along the lines of "Why is Tylenol white? Answer: 'Cause if it was black it wouldn't work!" Everyone in the room was laughing and they all had their own responses to the jokes. One lady (around 30 years of age) said "Yeah ... that is true."[7]

Here too is an important social setting, one in which racist commentaries provide a type of "social glue." As they are in about three-quarters of all student diary accounts of racist performances, African Americans are primary targets of this performance, in this case backstage with white family members and customers. The protagonist implies white virtue and asserts a centuries-old stereotype. Notice the frame assumption. In many examples like this, white protagonists make the (usually reasonable) assumption that most other whites, in this case customers, will agree with, or at least not object to, overtly racist performances.

Judging from the student diaries, frequent repetition of racist stereotypes, jokes, language, and images is characteristic of many all-white gatherings. The referents and symbols in racist "joking" and related racist performances in backstage settings and, as well as in frontstage settings, are generally emotion-laden and linked to a shared white frame. Whites frequently use stereotypes, language, and other negative material regarding black Americans and other groups of color often dating back centuries. The categories of racialized performances in our thousands of everyday accounts show us many white protagonists, cheerleaders, and passive bystanders, but extremely few active white dissenters. Backstage events like these operate to regularly build and routinely reinforce the white racial frame and important social relationships and performances that sustain that frame.

Racist Partying: More White-Dominated Areas

At or near many college campuses blatantly racist partying seems very popular. For example, at the University of Connecticut law school white students had a Martin Luther King, Jr., "Bullets and Bubbly" party where they engaged in aggressive racist framing. White students put on baggy clothes and fake gold teeth and held machine guns. Similar parties mocking African Americans and other Americans of color have been "enjoyed" at numerous colleges and universities in various regions, as researchers King and Leonard have described. At South Carolina's Clemson University, numerous white students mocked the King holiday with a "ghetto-fabulous" party and dressed up "in blackface, drank 40s, wore fake teeth grills, flashed gang signs and . . . padded their posteriors to conform to their stereotypes of the Black female body." Moreover, at California's Santa Clara University white students set up a Latino-themed event at which white "women feigned pregnancy, the young men played at being cholo and everyone reveled in the symbols and spectacle they associate with Latinos."[8]

The recurring reality of contemporary white youth's use of racist framing is observed in many settings, including in their participation in various types of holiday entertainment. Consider a study of Halloween events. Several sociologists recently secured 663 journals about Halloween events from college students in several regions. These journals listed *many* examples of white youth engaging in costuming and related actions racially mocking and stereotyping Americans of color.[9] In their research on Halloween issues, sociologists Mueller and Chou asked students in two small college courses to record what they saw at Halloween parties or while trick-or-treating. Numerous racist costumes were reported. For the students in one class, the stereotyped and racially framed costumes included twenty American Indian costumes, four Middle Eastern (for example, terrorist) costumes, nineteen Mexican/Latino costumes, nineteen blackface costumes, and forty other costumed portrayals of African Americans. Racialized costumes were observed in many places white youth frequent—student parties, restaurants and bars, neighborhoods, and church parties. In these numerous cases, mostly well-educated whites were acting out the deep racist realities of this society, often in ways suggesting rebellion against the social changes being attempted by some to reduce such racist stereotyping.[10] Events like Halloween parties provide yet another context in which whites can feel they are more or less in a backstage arena where they can openly revel in their racist performances—and thereby reproduce society's ongoing racist framing and hierarchy. Not surprisingly, when defending such racist performances, most whites say that they are only "good fun" and therefore "not racist."

These partying accounts, and other student accounts considered previously, make clear that the contemporary white frame still has numerous anti-others subframes, out of which many whites of various ages will act as the opportunity presents itself. Indeed, hundreds of thousands of examples of these racist subframes and their everyday use can be seen in the many racist photos, often of racist partying, and racist commentaries on Internet social media such as Facebook and Twitter webpages over recent years.[11]

The Normality of Everyday Racism

In these reports of contemporary racial events from college students and other whites, the protagonists and their supporters frequently take material from the centuries-old racial framing and use it, often innovatively, for their everyday use and individual and group entertainment. Yet, no matter how creatively it is performed, much of this contemporary racist framing of black Americans and others would be familiar to their parents, grandparents, or more distant ancestors. The array of racialized actions recorded in research studies is extensive. Not only do whites of various ages regularly make racist jokes, but they also call black Americans and other people of color the old racist epithets, dress in racist costumes, play supremacist music, mock black entertainers and leaders, yell racist epithets on the street, show racialized fear when black men are near, cross streets to avoid black people, make racist comments to acquaintances of color, and mock those who take exception to their racist actions. In these many performances we see how the white racial frame involves much more than thinking and believing the racist framing, for it also involves talking and acting as well.

Note the distinction that some in these examples make, explicitly or implicitly, between backstage and frontstage performances. Many whites will apparently not do their overtly racist backstage routines in the frontstage with strangers because they fear that they might be "misinterpreted" or inaccurately viewed as "racist." When whites engage in racist performances, some do seem aware of how they reinforce the racist system, yet still do them. Many others appear to be, at most, half-conscious of the fact that their actions play a central role in maintaining that racist system. Certainly, a majority of whites do not seem to view most racist joking, commentaries, and other routinized actions out of the dominant racial frame as morally wrong. Such actions are often viewed as harmless and "no big deal," indeed often just good entertainment. This no-big-deal viewpoint prevents most from perceiving how such performances cause substantial harm, and it links to a common defensiveness when they are asked about their racist commentaries. When challenged, most seem to feel defensive and/or assert their virtuousness. Many say something like, "No, of course we don't intend our jokes to hurt anyone," "They're just jokes," or "You people are too sensitive." Even when they do racist performances, their racial framing accents that they, as whites, still should be considered to be "good" people. The dominant frame not only provides fodder for racist performances, but also one means of excusing those performances. For most whites, at least some racist commentaries and performances are part of the "normality" of U.S. society.

White Racial Framing in Popular Culture

Contemporary popular culture—including the aforementioned Halloween celebrations as well as Hollywood movies, television shows, and video gaming—provides many examples of contemporary white racist framing. These and other popular media are also important in the intergenerational transmission of the white racial frame, and thus in sustaining systemic racism. Significantly, much popular culture periodically targets people of color in racially framed ways.

From the beginning, whites' racist framing has been common in U.S. movies. One recurring frame element in movies is the positive image of the white racial self, which has remained substantially unchanged over many decades. Researching white self-images in movies since 1900, researchers Vera and Gordon have shown that whites are regularly portrayed as noble, brave, and kind, and as natural-born leaders who mostly outshine all others, sometimes including a few villainous whites. One observes what they call "white saviors" in many films from the early pro-Klan movie *Birth of a Nation* (1915) to recent films, such as *Glory* (1989), *Dances with Wolves* (1990), *The Blind Side* (2009), and *Avatar* (2009). As with earlier movies with racial themes, numerous movies made since the 1980s have a central white character who is a "white savior" of people of color.[12] Certainly, these recent movies operate from a more liberal white framing. They are usually more nuanced in dealing with racial issues and often portray some "evil whites" negatively, clearly in an attempt to get audiences to identify with the "good whites" central to these movies.

The popular movie *Avatar* illustrates this point. This futuristic movie about an indigenous people on the moon Pandora centrally accents a white savior figure, here a U.S. soldier. The moviemakers present the peace-loving indigenous people's "god" as preferring a white soldier as their savior-hero, a choice actually inconceivable from the viewpoint of most indigenous people. In *The Blind Side* the white female hero is strong and assertive, while the black football player she assists is portrayed as needy, emotionally troubled, and lacking in personal agency.[13] In these movies, as in movies like *Dances with Wolves* about a white soldier and Native Americans, the "white savior" somehow rescues or attempts to rescue weaker people of color. Very revealing too is the fact that these recent mainstream movies *never* probe issues of institutional and systemic racism. An underlying assumption of these moviemakers seems to be that the only white racism to be concerned about is that of blatantly racist individuals.

While mainstream media portrayals of racialized outgroups such as African Americans have become significantly more positive over the decades since the virulently racist *Birth of a Nation*, contemporary movies and other popular media still perpetuate much racist framing of men and women of color. For instance, many media outlets—including television news and other programs noted previously—disproportionately emphasize negative images of black men, including as street criminals, as well as negative images of black women, including as "welfare mothers." Portrayals of mostly positive racial images of whites and of a white-controlled society, but varying and disproportionately negative images of certain people of color, are still part of contemporary U.S. culture.

Similarly, the video gaming subculture reveals many examples of white racial framing of people of color and of whites. As of 2009, the National Public Diary Group has calculated, nearly 170 million people in the U.S. played video games. Research indicates that game makers and most dedicated players are very disproportionately white, male, and heterosexual. Reviewing existing research, Daniels and Lalone concluded that over recent decades the gaming world generally has been heavily white-oriented "through the makeup of mostly white male game programmers as well as the procedures or systems included in the games themselves. Video gaming is predominantly created by white people and played most often by white people."[14] Thus, numerous popular video games help to reproduce the dominance of straight white men in the society's hierarchies, as well as elements of popular culture that reinforce those hierarchies.

Numerous openly racist games have been created or reworked for white-supremacist movement websites. Games like Border Patrol, which suggests players "shoot the spics," are played on home and office computers by many whites who are not members of such white supremacist groups—including one Georgia city council member who emailed the Border Patrol web link to city employees. Even more serious, because of its much larger audience and extensive socialization impact, is the recurring racial framing in many ordinary video games. For instance, studying closely the popular *Grand Theft Auto* video games, Daniels and Lalone found that the game makers incorporated many racist stereotypes of Americans of color: "nearly every black character, Hispanic, or non-white character is represented as a gang banger."[15]

The data on gaming assessed by these and other researchers reveal that much discussion by the typically white players during and around their playing of popular games involves racist commentary, including racist language. When criticized for racist language and other racist framing, white gamers and other defenders of the video games commonly fall back into the typical defenses we have seen before—"I am not racist," "I did not mean it," or "I was only joking, can't you take a joke?" This response suggests that racist activities that are entertaining are not problematic—and, indeed, that whites get to decide what is racially problematic in society.[16] Not surprisingly, the heavily white gaming subculture mostly downplays the racist framing manifested in numerous games and, by implication, the larger society. In this manner, white racist framing is perpetuated and reproduced millions of times weekly in the mostly backstage settings of video game playing.

We also observe periodic evidence of overtly racist framing in recent television programs, sometimes presented by white and other nonblack producers as supposed satire. Several popular shows, such as Fox's *The Cleveland Show*, have operated openly with a stereotyped racial framing of black Americans. With its mostly white scripting team, *The Cleveland Show* has a black central character whose antics have been viewed by millions. The show makes use of several negative stereotypes of black Americans. One sees overt racism in its initial sambo-referencing theme song with its lyrics of "everybody knows my happy black guy face," a song that was later changed. One pilot plot had Cleveland's very young stepson in a stereotyped black male role of being interested in hypersexualized adventures, and one program had Cleveland as the "whitest black" in the country who finds "true blackness" as a hypermasculine rapper.[17] These images are crude stereotypes fashioned out of an old racist framing of black Americans. While these nonblack producers and writers have meant this to be satire, such satire is frequently not understood by many white and other nonblack viewers who take the presentations as more or less accurate views of black Americans that they share. Such constant presentation of black Americans in stereotyped terms, whether direct or satirical, on popular television programs provides yet more popular culture reinforcement of the age-old anti-black framing in many viewers' minds.

Mostly white executives control most of our mainstream media, entertainment, public relations, and advertising companies, and they obviously work hard to get large U.S. and global audiences to watch or listen to their media presentations and buy their advertised commodities. In so doing these powerful white decisionmakers significantly shape or reshape numerous trends in so-called popular culture. Today, as these numerous examples illustrate, much of our heavily media-influenced popular culture still draws important racialized elements from the dominant white racial frame.

The Diverse Frontstage: The Frame's Negative Impact

The student diaries and numerous other sources we have examined in this chapter reveal that the dominant white framing of Americans of color remains very strong and quite commonplace. This dominant racial framing regularly operates to motivate and shape discriminatory actions by whites in a diverse array of settings. In this country, as elsewhere, everyday lives typically involve a series of encounters among various individuals, and there are often negative encounters between white Americans and Americans of color. In many of these encounters racist stereotypes, images, and emotions from the dominant racial frame play a significant role in generating discrimination by whites, which actions in turn reproduce white interests and continuing inequality.

We need to examine what happens on the other side of this white discrimination. The targets of discrimination are of course real human beings with lives, feelings, and responses to recurring racial hostility and discrimination. Interviews with older African American adults that I and others have done typically reveal that over their lives most have had, literally, thousands of negative experiences, ranging from subtle to covert to blatant discrimination, with white Americans of both genders and various ages and classes. Today, most African Americans have to live everyday lives that are to a substantial degree geographically or socially segregated, substantially because of critical choices made by whites in the past and present to separate and subordinate them. Surveys indicate that a majority of African Americans would prefer to live in mixed-race areas with a significant white population, but many cannot do so because whites historically have made that difficult through discriminatory control of real estate, banking, and political institutions, as well as through choices by white homeowners and renters. Even many middle class African Americans have few white neighbors. The pathological reality of a substantially segregated country, with still major differences in economic assets and continuing housing discrimination, needs to be brought forcefully into contemporary analyses of U.S. racial matters and of government anti-discrimination policies.[18]

One Pew Center survey examined the racial views of white and black Americans. More than 80 percent of black respondents reported widespread racial discrimination in at least one major societal area. Two thirds reported that African Americans often or always face discrimination in jobs or seeking housing. Half said the same for shopping and restaurants. The Pew research report listed the results of a vague question about black progress: Only a fifth of the black respondents felt things were better today for black Americans than five years ago and just 44 percent felt that life would be better in the future. Yet, the white respondents were twice as likely as black respondents to see black gains in recent years, and a majority thought the future would be better for black Americans. A majority of whites still openly deny the continuing impact of systemic racism.[19] White denial of this extensive and severely negative impact has been part of the white frame for centuries. For example, in Jefferson's famous 1785 treatise, *Notes on the State of Virginia*, this founding father confidently asserts that enslaved black Americans do not feel pain as much as whites: "Their griefs are transient. Those numberless afflictions ... are less felt, and sooner forgotten with them."[20] Such a dramatically insensitive view of oppression's impact seems essential to the white racial frame in its past and contemporary forms, and closely linked to the white-virtuousness perspective white Americans have long asserted.

The Impact of Everyday Racism: Frontstage Settings

Today, the expression of racial hostility and discrimination by whites takes an impressive array of damaging forms, from blatant discrimination to more subtle and covert discrimination. Whites who are very racially preju-diced are likely to fully embrace the old racial frame and justify its use with overtly racist explanations. Those who are more racially liberal may inter-nalize much of the frame, yet are more likely to be aware of the parts of it, feel guilty about some parts, and/or try not to act on aspects they believe to be false. Some may draw on the dominant racial frame's material for openly hostile actions, while others may use similar material but in a paternalistic fashion to "help" those racially targeted. Many, especially liberal, whites may select elements of the dominant frame to strongly disagree with, and some-times act assertively out of a counter liberty-and-justice framing of society. Thus, people can hold two or more frames relevant to a particular social setting in their heads simultaneously. Unfortunately, blatantly discrimina-tory actions motivated by the white frame are by no means disappearing.

One example of blatant discrimination can be seen in this recent diary account from a black college student attending a historically white college on the West Coast:

This is one of those sad and angry nights for me. Tonight marks the third time since the beginning of the school year that I've been called a nigger by a bunch of white students on a ... weekend. ... At first I used to wonder where they actually take the time in their heads to separate me from everyone else by the color of my skin. I used to just blame alcohol consumption for their obvious ignorance and racist attitudes, but I have since stopped trying to make excuses for them. I have to admit that at times like this . . . . Sometimes it seems that if I am around all white people, then I become nothing more than a token Black "exhibit" for their amusement. I guess that even I have to be careful not to judge all based on a few bad examples, which more often than not is the fate of many in the black community today. The saddest thing however, is that these people, these college students are supposed to be the supposed crème de la crème, the future business and political leaders.[21]

In racially diverse frontstage settings this student has had to deal with barbed epithets hurled by presumably well-educated whites—indeed, as he says, our future *leaders*. Black Americans have a long history of oppression, and such epithets cause much harm. Racist epithets in the present often trigger individual and collective memories of past discrimination. This diarist, like many African Americans, has a savvy counter-frame that includes his sociological analysis of the recurring oppression he faces. At first, he blamed whites' racist actions on alcohol, but has stopped exculpating them. In these everyday experiences, he is viewed by discriminatory whites, not as another fully human being, but in terms of racist framing that often dates back centuries.

Well into the twenty-first century such accounts of black Americans in regard to racist commentaries or attacks remain commonplace, and we still observe racist framing frequently in hostile voices and actions of many whites, including on school campuses. For example, in one brief period the University of Virginia—a campus partially built by enslaved black labor—experienced several racist events, including racist slurs yelled at African American students, a card with racist slurs placed on an African American student's door, and a "nigger" message put on another dorm door.[22]

Older Americans of color also report much discriminatory treatment. This is often blatant, but also takes subtle or covert forms. Consider these encounters with white framing by two professors in different college settings. The first is an African American professor at a predominantly white institution, who recounts how a white student

went to [my] department and he talked to some white male professors, and he told these white male professors what I had said in my class. And one of the white male professors had said to him that I was right, that such a thing had happened and had occurred. . . . He comes back and tells me that he was having trouble believing what I said, and that he went over to [my] department to see if he could get that documented and validated. And I said, "And?" And he said, "Well, I asked some professors and they said that such a document existed and that you were telling the truth." . . . Some students don't believe what I have to say and they will have to go and ask somebody white before they believe it.[23]

One of the oldest stereotypes in the dominant frame relates to black intelligence and competence. We see this in eighteenth century writings of founders like Thomas Jefferson, who argued that black Americans were very inferior: "Comparing them by their faculties of memory, reason, and imagination, it appears to me, that in memory they are equal to the whites; in reason much inferior . . . and that in imagination they are dull, tasteless, and anomalous."[24] This old stereotype of black Americans as less intelligent and creative than whites had been in the white racial frame for more than a century before Jefferson, and has remained in the frame ever since. In this account even a Ph.D. from a major university is not sufficient to head off the white student's aggressive questioning of a black professor's abilities. We notice too the negative impact such overt questioning, which is recurring, has on those targeted by it.

As we have seen numerous times, the white racial frame today also includes important subframes targeting other Americans of color. In this example a Latino professor makes this clear in talking about a long period of teaching in predominantly white settings:

Ironically, in my two decades of teaching, it has been the naive White student who, more often than not, needed the safety to ask potentially offensive questions without being made to feel ignorant or malicious. Typical of the initial questions posed by both graduate and undergraduate students are, "Oh, Professor Bonilla, but you don't look Latino." or, "How long have you been in this country? You don't even have an accent!" Today, these kinds of questions present opportunities to enlighten them that not all Latinos look or sound alike. . . . Early in my teaching, my frosty reply to such questions tended to be the not so noble, "How many Latinos do you know?" or, "Well that's nice, I can barely tell you have an accent either." I took their inquiries as unwelcome reminders of my relative isolation. . . . They can be so immersed in the "normality" of their White cultural milieu that they neither see it nor understand it.[25]

Again, we observe a frame assumption. White students assume their way of viewing aspects of society, in this case Latinos, and their racialized actions inspired by that view are normal and unproblematic. Because he does not fit their frame's image of what a Latino should look like—presumably he should be darker—he is questioned. The white framing of Latinos frequently assumes speech and accent "problems," including an inability to speak "good English" or the presence of what whites consider a problematical accent. (*All* speakers of English speak with an accent.) We observe the negative and isolating impact of that white-framed action, as well as significant counter-framing and well-honed resistance to discriminatory actions. While these examples of frontstage interactions across the color line stem from college settings, events like these are well documented for numerous other institutional settings for most Americans of color.[26]

When it comes to recurring hostility from whites, the dominant frame not only reveals itself in blatant ways but also in subtle and covert guises. Much subtle mistreatment is accomplished by means of significant facial, postural, or other nonverbal signals. By such signals even liberal whites frequently communicate much information about their stereotyped framing. In a long conversation we recently had about what might be seen by some people (especially whites) as "subtle" discrimination, one savvy African American professional described to me a few everyday experiences with whites operating out of racialized stereotypes and emotions:

> I see it in daily interactions (i.e., the lady at the counter who refuses to touch your hand and take your money, especially when you just witnessed an alternative behavior with the white patron before you). Then there is the cashier who tosses the money to me as I am waiting to receive change. Also, I was asked at a store just before I was to hand my money over, "Are you paying with cash or food stamps?" I asked the so-called gentleman why he asked me this question when he did not ask the white person before me. . . . Then there is the constantly asking me if I need help in a store when I am alone. When I am with whites, I do not get asked at all or very little.

He continues thus:

> I see it when the lone Asian or white female breaks their neck to walk a mile away from me on the sidewalk as I pass. I see it when one white male and I are the only ones in a public bathroom; his nervousness and awkward body language tells me a lot. I see it at work—daily challenges in terms of one's intelligence level—such as voice tones when discussing your ideas that contradict theirs. I see it when white people see me reading academic books at the gym, and I am

asked why am I reading that particular book. When I answer, I get a puzzled look on their face as if something does not compute in their rationale of what I am supposed to be doing as a black man with muscles who enjoys working out. I see it when I am walking with a white woman (regardless of personal status), the white eyes begin to follow you. It is as if you are wearing the "Scarlet Letter" for the white villagers to see.[27]

Notice here the great array of ideas and emotions that whites communicate, often nonverbally, in this one brief account of just a few of a black man's everyday experiences: (1) the emotion-laden fear of touching a black hand, probably out of some white stereotype of "dirtiness" or "danger"; (2) the stereotyping of a black man as too poor for customary courtesy; (3) the obsessive white stereotyping of a black man as shoplifter by clerks (who should know most shoplifters are white); (4) the emotion-laden fear of being alone with a black man signaled by nervousness in body language or movement away; (5) the stereotyping of black intelligence at a gym and work—with an aggressive response to a challenge to whiteness signaled in tone of voice; and (6) the hypersexualizing of a black man walking with a white woman revealing old white fears of "racial mixing."

Extremely blatant discrimination is not necessary for whites to communicate their racist thinking and emotions or to create much lasting harm. Targets of the dominant white framing know that it is present even when whites are not hurling a series of explicit racist insults. Holding that racial frame in their heads, but trying to suppress some overt actions reflecting it, whites frequently send powerful nonverbal signals as their real feelings, the emotions central to their racial framing, leak out into cross-racial interactions. Just a brief listing here of recurring events recently facing one black professional reveals numerous aspects of the centuries-old white-racist framing of black men—criminality, dangerousness, black dirtiness, hypersexuality, fear of their resistance—in a remarkably comprehensive and ugly contemporary display. Note too that there is nothing particularly new about most of this white-framed hostility and discrimination. Indeed, from its targets this is not "subtle" racism.

Such normal behavior by whites is not just discriminatory and very painful to endure, as we can tell from the tone of his comments, but points up how everyday racism is an isolating and alienating phenomenon. People do not experience racism abstractly, but in concrete everyday relationships. The persisting white framing of Americans of color does not exist suspended in the air, but is involved in millions of such face-to-face interactions. It divides people from one other and severely impedes the development of a truly common human consciousness.

This alienating racist system creates much damage to those targeted by it. Du Bois once described being black in the United States as being a person looking out of a deep mountain cave. A black person views

> the world passing and speaks to it; speaks courteously and persuasively, showing them how these entombed souls are hindered in their natural movement, expression, and development; and how their loosening from prison would be a matter not simply of courtesy, sympathy, and help to them, but aid to all the world. . . . It gradually penetrates the minds of the prisoners that the people passing do not hear; that some thick sheet of invisible but horribly tangible plate glass is between them and the world.[28]

The cave metaphor sharply accents the alienating reality of racial oppression. In this narrative, being black is often like being an entombed soul trying to get the attention of white passers-by, but to no avail. The wall of racial separation is too great.

Today, social science studies demonstrate the severe effects that racial dehumanization has on the health of Americans of color. In several interview studies African American respondents who are questioned about the impact of discrimination list many effects—from hypertension and stress diabetes to stress-related headaches and heart and stomach conditions. And the impact is more than physical, for it has serious psychological effects ranging from anxiety to depression to anger and rage. Anger over discrimination remains commonplace and generates physical health problems, emotional withdrawal, and other individual and family costs. In addition, the pain of discrimination in one's workplace may generate chest pains and headaches, which can create a loss of energy. That can mean less energy for family interactions, parental obligations, and church and other community activities.[29] But recurring, everyday assaults of racial hostility and discrimination have effects not just on individuals but also on their networks and communities.

Everyday Interactions: Symbolic Racial Capital

In these accounts of backstage and frontstage actions, we see much evidence of the significant racial capital held by most whites. Such racial capital includes not only economic, political, educational, and social networking capital, but also *symbolic capital.* This valuable capital is at best half-consciously recognized by most whites. Among other features, it encompasses the shared assumptions, understandings, and inclinations to interact in certain traditional ways that whites have mostly learned in families and other social networks. Symbolic capital, including white skin privilege, is a central part of the dominant racial frame and operates to link both white acquaintances and white strangers.

Backstage and frontstage interactions among whites and others examined previously reveal the use and abuse of symbolic racial capital. When whites interact with other whites, they usually receive significant privileges unavailable to people of color. Whites do not have to say explicitly to other whites that "I am white like you and need to use my racial capital to gain privileges" to get privileges. Symbolic capital enables whites to avoid many interactive problems, such as police profiling and similar official harassment, and it facilitates positive interactions among whites in many settings, such as in party settings, job interviews with white interviewers, or gaining access to white political officials. Messages of "I am white like you" are routinely sent out by the physical and cultural markers of whiteness. Living in a society where the dominant framing constantly maintains the prized white identity, and regularly denigrates the identities of racialized "others," a white person is typically taken as having positive symbolic capital and being worthy of racial privileges. This symbolic capital makes it much easier for whites to interact in most white-dominated arenas, and it often shapes how decisions are made and their outcomes.[30] The everyday use or operation of this symbolic capital is often subtle and hard for many whites even to see. Moreover, people of color who are employees in historically white institutions often report that many whites there have significant difficulty in relating well to them.

Most white men, who dominate most meetings of managers in historically white organizations, usually relate reasonably well, drawing on shared experiences, socialization, and language. This is the reality described by the phrase "good old boy network," which is a valuable type of social capital. Such settings are usually fairly comfortable places for most white men to interact. In contrast, white managers often relate awkwardly with the few managers of color in historically white workplaces. Little previous contact with people of color, especially on an equal status basis, is one cause of awkwardness. Research on major law schools by sociologist Wendy Moore reveals a similar pattern. Her data show that these law schools are mostly white spaces in terms of a majority of their occupants' characteristics and their normative structures, racialized spaces where whites rarely think about that discriminatory reality. White students in these schools related relatively easily to each other and to the mostly white faculty members—because of shared white experiences and frame assumptions. In contrast, students of color frequently found the experience there to be alienating and isolating, and that the white students and faculty were often awkward or discriminatory in relating to them.[31]

Conclusion

Numerous research studies and much other data show that the dominant white frame continues to shape and rationalize many discriminatory actions and other racialized actions of white Americans. In these actions, in frontstage and backstage settings, we observe the persisting impacts of old racial stereotypes, images, narratives, and emotions. Significantly, in this chapter we have also demonstrated the very negative impacts of this racial framing and consequent actions for its targets, as well as U.S. society as a whole. Obviously, the targets of racial framing and discrimination are people with human feelings and human responses to the great pain stemming from much racial hostility and discrimination.

In one section we observed how important areas of popular culture—including movies, television shows, and video gaming—regularly reveal major examples of white racial framing still in everyday operation. In much of current popular culture we encounter evidence of how deep and extensive this white racial framing remains, including for the supposedly more liberal white youth who often participate heavily in much popular culture.

Especially troubling too is how often various racialized actions growing out of that white racial frame still provide many millions of whites of various ages with substantial pleasure and enjoyment. The popular culture reality of racist portrayals and performances done or taken as just "good fun" is similar to that observed in the commonplace white joking in backstage settings described in the college student diaries and in the accounts of racist emails sent out and savored by white public officials. Whites' racist commentaries and performances, including those that are blatantly racist, are commonly viewed as acceptable by many because the white performers and observers view them as only joking and as just enjoying themselves. Certainly, after reviewing these data from numerous sources and on diverse social settings, we are left with troubling questions about why so many millions of whites still enjoy and/or tolerate these often very blatantly racist commentaries and performances.

CHAPTER 7

The Frame in Institutional Operation

Bureaucratization of Oppression

Human beings easily rationalize societal oppression, including racial oppression. Researchers Gilles Fauconnier and Mark Turner have explained how in the human mind the accepted views of oppression of a particular group are easily blended with an ordinary bureaucratic frame—and, thus, to produce a view in oppressors' minds of that oppression being just a routine organizational operation of society. This blending makes it easier for such oppression to be rationalized. For the most part, large-scale systems of oppression are not carried out by wild-eyed extremists with major psychological disorders, but by ordinary people in daily routines. During the slavery and Jim Crow eras, most whites viewed extensive forms of racial oppression as normal and supported that with indifference or collaboration.[1]

This general indifference and collaboration remain true for today's serious patterns of racial discrimination and inequality, which are often seen as more or less normal by the majority of whites. The dominant racial frame still views whites as a group to be generally superior and people of color as groups to be generally of less social, economic, and political consequence. One important aspect of this still-dominant frame is that its racial understandings get imbedded deeply in societal organizations and institutions. A majority of whites still view most U.S. institutions as normally white-controlled and unremarkable in that whites therein are unjustly enriched and disproportionately privileged. Another common frame notion views local bureaucratic organizations such as a public school or government agency as properly white-controlled, white-normed, and/or slanted toward white interests.

For a system of oppression to persist for long periods it is necessary not only to develop a strong rationalizing frame but also to build that frame's ideas, images, and emotions into the everyday operation of important organizational structures. In earlier chapters we have seen how this institutionalization of a racist framing operated in connection with early genocidal actions against Native Americans and longterm enslavement and legal segregation targeting African Americans. Today, the system of racial oppression remains highly organized and institutionalized and continues to operate in tandem with our modern economy, strong national government, extensive private and government bureaucracies, and a complex legal system.

U.S. Legal and Political Institutions

The U.S. legal and political system is often celebrated as the world's finest and fairest. Today, a typical statement about the U.S. Constitution by U.S. leaders—including politicians, judges, and law professors—is very positive and uncritical, such as "the greatest Constitution that was ever written." Many everyday references to the U.S. Constitution by leaders and ordinary citizens assert it to be extraordinarily liberty-oriented and freedom-guaranteeing.[2] Usually forgotten in such praise is, as I have shown in Chapter 2, the fact that our foundational document was shaped throughout by the strong racist framing of the white founders and their desire to protect the assets and power most had gained from an economy grounded in land theft and slavery.

From the founding era in the late 1700s until the 1960s, moreover, most federal court decisions on racial matters interpreted the Constitution from a very strong version of the white racist frame and perpetuated over the generations most elements of the system of extreme racial oppression. Extreme legal segregation did not officially end in the United States until 1969. To the present day, the U.S. Constitution and the Supreme Court decisions interpreting it—almost all made over centuries by elite white men—have greatly shaped the basic contours of the legal and political systems, as well as other societal institutions.

Important changes in the system of oppression, such as the official ending of Jim Crow in the 1960s, have come only when many whites have believed those changes to be in their group interest—that is, when there is what Derrick Bell has called "interest convergence" between the interests of the racially oppressed and the interests of whites, especially some in the elite.[3] Consider the Supreme Court decision, *Brown v. Board of Education of Topeka (1954)*. That decision was forced on the court by black lawyers suing to end Jim Crow segregation in schools. The Court decision and its new framing of a desegregated society were grudgingly supported by several white justices, who were under pressure not only from the civil rights movement, but also from some officials in the U.S. state department who worried about how the Soviet Union was using images of rights demonstrators being attacked in its propaganda circulated across the globe. Here two factions of the white elite were contending politically and legally with each other.

The ruling elite has always been overwhelmingly white and male in composition and has for centuries been divided roughly into two socio-political camps—a very conservative camp unsympathetic to populist and expanding-democracy ideas, and a more moderate camp more receptive of some populist and expanding-democracy ideas. The moderate wing dominated the group of founders that gave us in 1776 a Declaration of Independence, with its ringing rhetoric about freedom and equality, while the more conservative wing dominated the founders who gave us in 1787 a U.S. Constitution accenting property rights, one initially without even a Bill of Rights.[4] These two branches of the elite are disproportionately represented in various regions, with more conservatives in the southern elite and more moderates in northern and western elites. As a result, the factions of the white elite have periodically found themselves in some socio-political conflict, such as in certain state and national political contests.

Consider the shaping of U.S. political parties, a process that is substantially about the white racial frame and the divisions within that white elite. For much of the era between the early 1800s and the more recent 1960s, southern members of the ruling elite dominated the Democratic Party (originally the Democratic-Republican Party). Before the Civil War, powerful white southerners, often slaveholders, secured disproportionate influence in that Party and gained much control over the operation of the Congress and other branches of government until that war. After the Civil War and a brief Reconstruction period, when they lost national political power, southern white Democrats regained control of southern political institutions and imposed a brutal system of legal segregation on African Americans. They regained disproportionate influence in national political institutions, most prominently in the U.S. Senate, where they blocked for decades virtually all significant attempts to end legal segregation and expand civil rights, until the 1960s.

After long decades of protests by African Americans, and a World War II in which white Americans found themselves fighting a highly racist German government, some progress in ending Jim Crow and expanding civil rights began during the 1940s. Breaking with the past, and representing the moderate wing of the elite, President Harry Truman (1945–1953) supported a strong civil rights plank in the 1948 Democratic Party platform. This action marked a gradual shift in the dominant white frame; Jim Crow segregation of black Americans was viewed by growing numbers of powerful whites as no longer necessary to preserve most white privilege. Nonetheless, this Democratic civil rights plank resulted in the creation of a States Right's Party by southern Democrats committed to an arch-segregationist version of the white frame. Their almost unanimous commitment to Jim Crow segregation persisted for two more decades.[5]

Eventually, the 1960s civil rights movement, new rights laws, and international pressures led to significant shifts in the composition and tactics of the major political parties. With the right to vote now legally guaranteed, black voters in southern and border states began actively participating in local, state, and national politics, and principally in the Democratic Party. Over recent decades, the Democratic Party has become increasingly more diverse, with a large percentage of its membership today being Americans of color. Over recent years, this increased diversity of the Democratic Party has directly or indirectly triggered the movement of many whites into the Republican Party. Since the 1950s, moreover, southern and border states have increasingly become divided between a mostly white Republican Party centered in white residential areas, especially white middle class areas such as numerous suburbs, and a Democratic Party that is multiracial and centered in many urban working class and lower middle class areas. The Republican Party has also become more oriented to white voters in southern and Rocky Mountain states. The percentage of Republican seats in the U.S. House from southern areas increased from 5 percent in 1954 to 45 percent in 2009, while over this period the percentage of Democratic seats from those areas decreased from 47 percent to 24 percent.[6]

Over recent decades almost all major leaders in the Republican Party have been white, and they and their assistants brought about the Party's resurgence from the late 1960s to the present by using a politics that frequently has intentional appeals to the white racial frame in minds of white voters. The usually white Republican politicians generally deliver to whites a racial framing that accents white interests, a white-oriented political rhetoric, and white-run governments. This Republican resurgence has often been accomplished by making significant use of overt and subtle racist appeals, advertisements, speeches, or codewords. For example, in the later years of the civil rights movement, the late 1960s, presidential candidate Richard Nixon and his advisors made political use of the white backlash against the civil rights movement and civil rights laws in their successful efforts to gain the U.S. presidency.

Then as now, many white voters have feared expanded black political power and elected officials—and what they see as too minority-oriented government programs provided under Democratic administrations. This backlash has provided the Republican Party with the necessary white votes to put into operation for several decades the goal of remaking the political face of much of the United States into one with strong white-Republican influence. Republican political actions taken directly out of the white f rame have often been overt. Thus, in 1980 Ronald Reagan began his first presidential campaign with a pro-states'-rights speech in Philadelphia, Mississippi, where civil workers had been killed some years before by violent white supremacists insisting on southern states' rights. In his 1980s elections, Reagan won the electoral votes of southern states "with thinly disguised appeals to segregationist sentiment, while Democrats were ever more firmly linked to civil rights and affirmative action."[7] Other Republican appeals to white voters have been somewhat more subtle, such as in recurring attacks on "big government," with an implied reference to the government programs thought to help Americans of color. Recall that, while there are several sources of anti-government rhetoric over several centuries now, a major source historically has been the fear of white slaveholders and segregationists—and their white descendants in recent decades—that certain federal government agencies might interfere with white privilege and societal domination.

In practice, since the 1960s, the Republican Party has been the "white party," with relatively few Americans of color strongly committed to it. For example, in elections between 1992 and 2008 the Republican Party got a remarkably small percentage (just 4–12 percent) of black voters. Moreover, in the last few presidential election years the delegates at Republican presidential conventions have been overwhelmingly white. Since 1964 the percentage of black delegates has remained between 1.0 percent and 6.7 percent, while the Democratic Party percentages have been around 20 percent. At the 2012 Democratic convention, an estimated 40 percent of the delegates were black or Latino, while the figure for the Republican convention was less than 10 percent. More than 90 percent of Republican delegates were white.[8] To a significant degree, the white-conservative-Republican political shifts that have dominated much of the political scene since the late 1960s are, directly or indirectly, a result of the white backlash against the civil rights movement and against major socioeconomic and political advances made by Americans of color, including significant movement into numerous historically white institutions.

In addition, the conventional white frame is so institutionalized that mainstream news outlets routinely operate out of it in political reporting. One example can be seen in the 2008 national election, during which most mainstream media and many conservative political groups focused, for months of the primaries and final election, on a story about then Senator Barack Obama's former African American minister, Dr. Jeremiah Wright, because of his comments in a sermon dealing with white racism (see Chapter 8). This media story lasted so long because the image of a supposedly "radical" black minister resonates with the dangerous black man image in the age-old white racial frame. In contrast, a somewhat similar story about the controversial views of an arch-conservative, anti-Catholic white minister who was a supporter of Senator John McCain did not last long in the same mainstream media. There was no negative image of a dangerous white man in the dominant white frame for this news story to resonate with.[9]

The Frame and Unjust Enrichment: Justifying Institutional Processes

One function of the white frame is to justify the great array of privileges and assets held by white Americans as the group at the top of the racial hierarchy. Unjust enrichment and impoverishment have accompanied racial oppression from the beginning. The large-scale resource and wealth gap is substantially the result of societal processes of the reproduction of unjust enrichment for white Americans and unjust impoverishment for African Americans and many other Americans of color over centuries of systemic racism.

The white racial frame provides some social "shrouding"—that is, it attempts to conceal much of the injustice of the systemically racist reality from those who adopt elements of the white framing. This shrouding involves hiding or sanitizing racist realities and entices those operating out of that frame to generally view societal inequalities as normal. Thus, the social inheritance mechanisms that greatly benefit whites as a group are disguised by "whites are virtuous" images of the dominant frame to make the intergenerational transfer of socioeconomic resources and white privileges appear fair, when in fact that transfer often represents the longterm transmission of unjust enrichment across networks and generations of oppressors. This type of unjust inheritance has often enabled later generations of whites to provide better educational, housing, and other socioeconomic opportunities for their children than the later generations of black Americans and other Americans of color whose ancestors, many over six to ten generations, did not secure fair access to such important resources, largely because of massive white-imposed discrimination and racial segregation.

How, when, and where the critical realities of racial oppression are reproduced vary across major institutions and fluctuate with the particular actors making decisions within them. Yet, the effect of white actors operating in public and private organizations in ways that reproduce or enhance white privilege and power has been to keep the overall system of racial oppression and inequality in operation now for several centuries. Sociologist Robert Merton introduced a term for the significant process of resource accumulation and increase over time, what he called "the Matthew effect."[10] (The term is drawn from a Bible verse: "For unto every one that hath shall be given, and he shall have abundance: but from him that hath not shall be taken away even that which he hath.")

Small initial differences in racial, class, or gender inequality tend to build up to large inequalities over time. For example, research on gender inequality in workplaces has shown how small initial advantages accumulate to larger advantages over time. In important workplace meetings, thus, women employees are often less likely than male employees to have comments taken seriously by senior managers, who are usually men. This leads women to participate less actively in subsequent meetings, which means that they are less likely than male peers to accumulate small but important job-related advantages over years. Successful advancement in most workplaces involves parlaying small initial advantages over other employees into bigger advantages, ultimately leading to significant advances.[11] In one project, researchers did a computer simulation of promotions. A very small initial bias in favor of men had huge longterm effects. After numerous rounds of promotions, the small initial advantage resulted in male employees making up two thirds of those at the highest job level.[12]

This substantial advancement for male employees just from the accumulating effects of small initial patterns of gender discrimination is very similar to what results for a great many white workers from the typically large pro-white bias that advantages white workers in most workplaces and other societal settings over many decades. In addition to suffering current discrimination in numerous work and educational settings, black employees and some other employees of color often come into the workplace settings with disadvantages, small and large, from large-scale discrimination in the past against them and their families. Moreover, in many institutional sectors, the "Matthew effect" has regularly worked against black Americans and many other Americans of color over centuries by making the seemingly modest racial advantages that most ordinary white families have historically secured—such as a few hundred acres of farmland given by the government to white families to homestead from the 1860s to the 1930s (but kept from most black families by discrimination)—into large later advantages for them and their descendants.[13] The dominant racial frame plays an essential role in rationalizing and legitimating the many Matthew effects across the society.

The White Frame and Public Policies: Some Examples

Many aspects of systemic racism, including the dominant white frame and deep racial inequalities, have had an extensive impact on many government policies from the country's first years. As we have seen, slavery or legal segregation were in effect for the first 180 years or so of the new United States, thereby routinely affecting how the white officials in major political and administrative positions viewed and shaped U.S. societal and institutional developments for this long era, including that slavery and legal segregation. Since the end of government policies maintaining legal segregation in the late 1960s, whites have mostly remained in control of most major public policy decisions, especially at the national level. As a result, these important government policies have generally reflected their white-framed views, values, and interests. This has been true for policies in regard to national defense, public health, education, criminal justice, and the environment. While most public policy books, and many other social science books, discuss some of these important policy areas, they rarely discuss how systemic racism routinely shapes government policies and the negative impact of many government policies on Americans of color. Most policy books also do not examine well such critical issues for communities of color as continuing racial segregation in schools, environmental racism, and the massive prison complex incarcerating disproportionate and record numbers of Americans of color. Indeed, these and other major issues faced by communities of color have not received nearly the serious policy analysis and supportive government policies they deserve.

A few public policy books do examine the broad issue of the relationship of power to policymaking. Anne Schneider and Helen Ingram have demonstrated that much government policy operates to favor interests of the privileged and politically powerful and to burden significantly the least privileged and politically powerless. The favoritism operates in the construction of policy concepts implemented by powerful decisionmakers, including in the government policymaking process. Biased policymaking by the powerful reinforces existing inequalities in "wealth, status, and power as those who already have the most tend to gain even more from public policy."[14] For the most part, top-level government decisionmakers, a substantial majority of whom are white, have made government policies directly or indirectly favoring white Americans—and often burdening Americans of color and others who cannot protect themselves or their group interests well. We have the space in this book to consider only a few government and related institutional policies, so here we will examine briefly important issues in regard to certain government (and private) immigration, environmental, health care, and imprisonment policies.

Immigration Policies

Over recent decades, the immigration of people of color from Latin America, Asia, and the Caribbean has dramatically changed the demographic makeup of the United States in a more diverse direction. Whites have become a statistical minority in numerous large central cities such as New York, Chicago, Los Angeles, and Houston. At current birth and immigration rates, half the population will be Americans of color by the 2040s. Especially among white Americans, including the policymaking elites, there is much fear and negative racial framing of these immigrants and related demographic changes. Influential policy experts like Harvard's Samuel Huntington and prominent media commentators like Patrick Buchanan have operated out of a strong white racial framing of immigration issues. Many such analysts have worried openly in the mainstream media and in important policy books and articles about the large numbers of immigrants of color they view as very threatening to "Western culture" and "Western civilization." Some have argued aggressively in public policy journals that the essential "white core" of U.S. society is seriously deteriorating. These mostly white analysts often single out legal and undocumented Latino immigrants, who make up a substantial proportion of contemporary immigrants, as a threat to "homeland security" and U.S. national interests and/or as not blending well into the traditionally white-dominated culture and institutions of U.S. society.[15]

In much political and media framing these immigrants of color are viewed as causing employment problems for other Americans, increasing crime rates, or unfairly using government services. Not surprisingly, thus, government policymakers operating out of a strong white racial framing have regularly targeted them with new government policies. For example, in California mostly white politicians and citizen groups worked to get an anti-immigrant Proposition 187 passed in 1994. This proposition attempted to restrict undocumented immigrants' access to various government services, but was overturned by a court in 1999. Yet, this did not keep other state legislatures from attempting to pass anti-immigrant legislation. At the federal level, one important immigrant law was the 1986 Immigration Reform and Control Act authorizing legalization of undocumented immigrants long resident in the U.S., sanctions for employers who hired undocumented immigrants, and screening public assistance applicants for immigration status. One result was significant racial profiling by employers and officials—and discrimination targeting Latinos as a group, including U.S. citizens. Drawing on the white frame, employers discriminated on the basis of racial appearance to be sure they were not hiring undocumented workers. A 1990 Immigration Act was passed to correct these problems, but employers' racial framing and discrimination against "immigrant-looking" native-born workers continues to be reported by researchers.[16]

Nativistic lobbying has pressured the U.S. Congress to pass even more punitive legislation, including the 2006 Secure Fence Act. With a cost in the tens of billions, this anti-immigrant law increased border enforcement personnel and greatly expanded border surveillance technology, including many miles of an expensive border fence. These public policies have cost more than money, however. Over just two decades punitive actions stemming from the anti-immigrant laws have contributed to the deaths of an estimated 6000 undocumented people who have tried to cross an increasingly dangerous U.S. border. The punitive legislation is often motivated by a racially framed concern that many Latino immigrants come, not to work, but to get on government assistance programs. Yet, such stereotyped ideas are strongly contradicted by much research, including that showing a high labor force participation rate of immigrants. Also missing from much hostile framing of undocumented immigrants is knowledge of how government programs work. Undocumented immigrants are legally prohibited from government programs like federal housing assistance, food stamps, Medicaid, and public welfare.[17]

Because of Latino immigration and associated population increases an array of government housing agencies have targeted legal and undocumented immigrants with discriminatory enforcement of local laws. For instance, government agencies in the Northeast have set up new health and safety laws, or begun to enforce little used laws, such as those limiting the number of people living in a house, just to drive Latino immigrants out of mostly white communities. These public policies are white-framed and aggressively favor local white interests, thereby discriminating against those least able to resist such discrimination.[18]

Immigrants of color face many kinds of discrimination. A Southern Poverty Law Center report explains how both legal and undocumented Latino immigrants, as well as native-born Latinos, are frequently "cheated out of their earnings and denied basic health and safety protections." Drawing on white racial framing, local and federal police officers periodically engage in racial profiling and other racial harassment of immigrants of color, as well as native-born Latino and black Americans. According to the Law Center report, local police agencies have enforced immigration laws in ways suggesting "systematic racial profiling" and thus have "made Latino crime victims and witnesses more reluctant to cooperate with police. Such policies have the effect of creating a subclass of people who exist in a shadow economy, beyond the protection of the law."[19] Whatever its location, racial profiling by police agencies is influenced heavily by stereotypes and narratives from the white racial frame. The broader consequences of such discriminatory policies include "relentless vilification" of these immigrants in the mainstream media and their targeting "for harassment by racist extremist groups, some of which are directly descended from the old guardians of white supremacy."[20]

Environmental Policies and Environmental Racism

Government policies on environmental issues frequently reflect the racial framing and interests of local or national white elites and other powerful white groups. These policies affect the health and welfare of people at the local level, and some policies create major problems for communities of color. For example, one major problem is that of toxic waste disposal near communities of color, an issue across the country, from San Francisco to New York City. Frequently, in rural and urban areas, local officials disproportionately locate garbage and toxic waste dumps near areas with large numbers of people of color. Often operating out of a white framing, these mostly white officials tend to view impoverished and working class communities of color as unconcerned about such waste issues and thus as appropriate sites for undesirable government waste facilities. Not surprisingly, such locations are often the easiest to implement politically. Research studies have shown clearly that toxic wastes from dump facilities often seep into groundwater or otherwise create environmental pollution well beyond dump boundaries, thereby creating health problems and other costs for local residents, who are often disproportionately people of color.

Some civil rights and other protest organizations have begun to change the politics around such policy decisions, as have lawsuits brought by local individuals and families facing environmentally related cancers. Assisted by social science researchers, for example, one black family in Tennessee filed a lawsuit against white officials after discovering the latter had long kept quiet about knowledge they had about well water in the area being seriously contaminated. County records showed a nearby landfill allowed dumping of toxic wastes for years, as well as seepage into nearby water sources. As the researcher Bob Bullard, who worked with this family, has explained, this was not an unusual case but one of many examples of official environmental racism: "Governments target communities of color that don't have money, lawyers or power in office."[21]

Recent studies have regularly confirmed that there is a very disproportionate and racialized distribution of hazardous waste treatment and storage facilities in many rural and urban areas. One study using sophisticated geographical techniques to examine racial inequalities in location of waste facilities found that the "magnitude of racial disparities around hazardous waste facilities is much greater than what previous national studies have reported." The findings indicated "factors uniquely associated with race, such as racial targeting, housing discrimination, or other race-related factors are associated with the location of the nation's hazardous waste facilities."[22] Clearly, discrimination by the mostly white policymakers in specifying waste locations likewise means discrimination in who disproportionately bears the burdens of health and other costs from this environmental decisionmaking.

Health Care Policies and Systemic Racism

Many aspects of systemic racism, including the dominant frame and linked discrimination to it, have had extensive impacts on U.S. health care and health policies. Reports from government and private agencies regularly accent "racial disparities" in health care. The Institute of Medicine issued a major report designed to provide input to policymakers. Data on African Americans and other Americans of color showed very significant inequalities in mortality and morbidity. The report described serious inequalities in the provision of health care for medical problems between Americans of color and white Americans, inequalities that exist even when health insurance and incomes are comparable. Like many studies this report accented problems of patient-doctor communication and the absence of adequate health care facilities for communities of color. Unlike other studies, it also noted briefly research showing that the racial stereotyping of white physicians was a likely problem for patients of color.[23]

This report pointed to needed policy reforms involving expansion of access to better health care for Americans of color and a reduction in discrimination in provision of health care. Similarly, a *New England Journal of Medicine* report reviewed inequalities in health care treatments for whites and blacks and called for an increase in research on racial inequality and bias and a policy emphasis on bringing systemic changes in the current inegalitarian provision of health care.[24]

Still, the significance of the racial framing of patients of color among white (and other) medical personnel is only hinted at in these mainstream reports, although much research shows racial framing among white clinicians and substantial discrimination in medical treatments. In these reports a worked-out plan to deal with this racist framing and discriminatory patterns systemic in the U.S. health care system is never offered. A related issue is the curriculum of historically white medical schools where little attention is given to the history of the scientific-racist thinking—such as that discussed in Chapter 4—involved in the development of U.S. medical care. Moreover, strong commitments to the racist notion of real biological "races" are common today among medical personnel and medical researchers, and the history of such racist notions and their contemporary negative effects are rarely presented for substantial discussion in medical schools or journals.[25]

Government and private health policies have yet to be directed at reducing still widespread racial framing—including racist images and ideologies—in the minds of many white medical students and physicians.

Such institutional changes face an uphill battle, for one important survey of (mostly white) physicians found a substantial majority felt the health care system "rarely or never treats people unfairly because of their race or ethnicity."[26]

Public health research has begun to move in the direction of accenting the impact of class structures on health inequalities. Important new research by health researchers Phelan and Link summarizes one major argument: "When we [as a society] develop the ability to control disease and death, the benefits of this new-found ability are distributed according to resources of knowledge, money, power, prestige, and beneficial social connection. Those who are advantaged with respect to such resources benefit more from new health-enhancing capabilities and consequently experience lower mortality rates."[27] This accent on health care inequalities being shaped by class and power structures marks an important shift in public health research, yet even this innovative analysis does not yet adequately address systemic racism in U.S. health care and health policymaking.

Crime and Imprisonment Policies

Among numerous government policy areas where the significant effects of white racial framing and systemic racism can be clearly observed is the institutional arena called the criminal justice system. The U.S. has the most massive incarceration of its citizens of any country. What some call the "prison-industrial complex" is now a segregated Jim-Crow-like system in which a great many black and Latino Americans get very disproportionately imprisoned for crimes that whites also do but suffer much less imprisonment for. In addition, once out of the prison complex, these Americans of color lose many citizenship rights. Current government policies often insure that they lose the right to vote, serve on juries, or get decent-paying jobs. Not only are those formerly imprisoned affected by these post-prison laws, but significant sectors of their home communities are severely affected by their loss of civil and economic rights.[28]

One major reason for the extreme overrepresentation of black and Latino Americans in the prison system is the racially biased character of certain laws and much law enforcement, especially in regard to illegal drug use and dealing. Extreme racial inequalities in this enforcement were accelerated as a result of the 1980s Ronald Reagan administration's expanded actions on the "war on drugs." Officials moved many federal employees to a new drug war, with one racially framed goal being a targeting of drug issues for communities of color, while mostly ignoring the same issues in white communities. Federal policies increased funding substantially for police programs, and the administration spurred media promotion of their new "war." This drug-war expansion was buttressed by local business interests and political officials working to greatly expand the prison-industrial complex locally.[29]

Significantly, at the time of the initial drug-war expansion few Americans in national surveys were concerned about these issues. Yet the Reagan and later administrations vigorously pressed onward, as legal researcher Michelle Alexander suggests, because this drug war "had little to do with public concern about drugs and much to do with [white] public concern about race." Republican administration officials in particular worked hard to get whites to back this "apparent effort to put blacks back 'in their place.'"[30] By means of new public policies, this expanded incarceration of mostly black and Latino Americans put a large percentage of these Americans of color back into a subordinated racial "place." Dramatically, too, researchers have found that whites' racial attitudes and other racial framing, and not actual shifts in crime rates, have been the most significant factors shaping whether whites have supported these expanded and expensive anti-crime measures.[31]

The White Frame and the World Racial Order

Centuries of European and U.S. colonialism and neo-colonialism have created a *world racial order*. Since the fifteenth century, numerous European countries, and later the United States, have expanded globally in imperialist and colonizing ventures that created colonies and military outposts across the world. In the first century of this colonialism the white racial frame became important in rationalizing extensive theft of asset-generating resources from or within colonized areas. This process continued for centuries. Once this global system was in place the rationalizing white frame shaped people's actions in many sectors, not only of the colonizing countries but also of their colonies, including their economies, religious and educational systems, and political institutions. From the beginning this frame was Eurocentric and Orientalist in its accent on the West as superior to other regions.

The scholar-activist W. E. B. Du Bois was among the first to evaluate this globalizing oppression from a critical perspective. He noted the patterns of extraordinarily bloody and racialized subordination that came to people of color across the globe.[32] One indigenous society after another was destroyed or reshaped by the impact of the European and U.S. colonizing invaders and their military, economic, political, and religious organizations. This colonization was frequently defended in terms of a strong white framing that accented white racial and civilizational (usually Christian) superiority and denigrated colonized residents and cultures as racially inferior and uncivilized.

After centuries of European colonialism, and half a century of decolonization, the colonizing and colonized countries have remained interrelated. Today continuing poverty and related economic problems in former colonies are closely linked to continuing prosperity that has persisted over centuries in Europe and the United States. In major ways the stolen labor, land, and resources of these countries continue to be one substantial reason for contemporary prosperity and wealth in Europe and the United States, while leaving most former colonies with lasting poverty and other socioeconomic problems often not of their own making. Even with the demise of direct colonial control, economic neo-colonialism has continued the process of extensive resource exploitation of former colonies. Neo-colonialism means that white-run European and U.S. corporations are still often in control of a continuing process of much resource extraction in many of these countries.[33]

Since declaring their independence, many former colonies' governments have become controlled by local elites that have substantially collaborated in the neo-colonialism process and have adopted significant elements of a white racial framing. Numerous elites in former colonial areas have a more or less worshipful stance toward supposed white superiority in markets, technology, education, and political institutions. Many have adopted elements of this white-superiority worldview and sought thereby to please powerful white officials in the European and U.S. governments, international economic organizations, and multinational corporations.

During and after the colonial era various private agents, such as white missionaries and entrepreneurs, from the United States and Europe have created many white-oriented institutions—churches, schools, businesses, and media organizations—in formerly colonized countries. As these Western actors and organizations have become influential overseas, they have greatly shaped a strong pro-white and anti-other racial framing of much that goes on in the world and, in many cases, helped to form or reinforce a Western-type racial hierarchy internationally.[34]

Today, numerous European, North American, Central American, South American, and South African countries have a Western-type racial hierarchy placing white people, or lighter-skinned people with significant European ancestry, at the top, and darker-skinned people, usually with substantial African or indigenous ancestry, toward the bottom of that racial hierarchy. There is now a world racial order that links more than 200 nation-states together, with nations of color in that global social order still substantially subordinated in one way or another to the nations that are most powerful economically and militarily—typically those former colonizing nations still mostly controlled by whites.

An array of international corporate, nonprofit, and governmental agencies provide the important organizational linkages that in the present day also perpetuate this world racial order. For example, today the maintenance of major elements of this mostly white-dominated international racial hierarchy is substantially done by global economic institutions, such as international corporations, the World Bank, and International Monetary Fund, and by agencies within international political institutions such as some agencies of the United Nations.

Today, the large capitalistic corporations and major government organizations operating globally out of European and U.S. headquarters are mostly racialized in their internal employment and other economic structures. These major international corporations and the markets they have created are substantially controlled by white (mainly male) corporate executives in the United States and the European Union, with some increasing input now from Asian executives, especially in Japanese, Chinese, and Indian corporations. In the present day, the majority of these powerful corporate decisionmakers, even many who are not white, view the world substantially from some contemporary version of the white racial frame. Moreover, since whites play the central role in shaping most of the major norms and structures of international markets and many international political institutions, these are often oriented to white European and U.S. political-economic interests. In their internal and external operations, Westernized global organizations and institutions not only reflect the old racial hierarchy and much of the white framing of dominant Western nation-states, but also periodically take actions that shape nation-state and community racial orders within and beyond their borders—such as by stimulating or reducing the movements of immigrants of color across the globe.[35]

With recurring economic upheavals, such as the near-depression economic crises of 2007–2009 across the globe, many in the world's non-Western elites have been rethinking their conventional acceptance of Western frames of market economics, Western-dominated international relationships, and white-Western superiority. The dominant role of the white racial frame and related class and gender frames in the global political-economic order is now under great pressure to change in significant ways.[36]

The Frame and U.S. Foreign Policy

U.S.-generated systemic racism has had an extensive and lasting impact on U.S. foreign policy and resulting international relations. Many decades of slavery and legal segregation greatly shaped the ways in which U.S. politicians looked out at the world, especially that huge part of it that is not white. In 1789, soon after the U.S. Constitution was approved, the U.S.

Department of State was established and from its beginning reflected the interests of those controlling the country's slavery-centered economy, including major slaveholders who were early U.S. presidents. Similarly, when the U.S. Foreign Service was established in 1924, the country's government was supportive of legal segregation in southern, border, and some northern states. For nearly two centuries the U.S. government's most important foreign policy agencies were established and its policy approaches were developed in the context of extreme racial oppression, an openly advocated racist hierarchy, and an openly proclaimed white-racist frame accenting slavery or Jim Crow segregation and white supremacy. The result was the creation and maintenance of an overtly racist global order.

This global racial order has persisted to the present. As historian Irene Diggs has noted, "United States foreign policy has been colored by the racial composition of countries with whom it has relations, tending to minimize the importance of the largely nonwhite part of the world."[37] As recently as the 1980s Reagan administration, the U.S. government flagrantly ignored the aspirations of peoples struggling to break free of extreme racialized oppression overseas. For instance, this administration was a strong supporter of extreme racial segregation ("apartheid") in the Republic of South Africa.

Today, more than 80 percent of the world's people are not white, yet the majority of the world's peoples and their political-economic interests have only recently been taken seriously—and not yet seriously enough—by the mostly white ruling elites of the United States and many European countries. Most white corporate and governmental elites view the global scene from some version of the white frame, which generally means a condescending view of countries made up principally of people of color and a strongly positive view of Western superiority and global dominance. Moreover, from the late nineteenth century to recent decades, the framing of a "superior" Western civilization and democracy has legitimated dozens of U.S. military invasions of countries in Asia, such as the Philippines, and in Latin America, such as Cuba.[38]

Operating in the minds of many U.S. corporate executives, government officials, and foreign policy experts, the dominant racial frame, coupled with Western class and gender framing, continues to shape significant aspects of U.S. foreign policy. Conceptualizing those countries and peoples that are not white as inferior in culture, civilization, or religion is often a way of using much in the old racial framing without speaking explicitly of "race." Top white officials still often operate with an attitude of civilizational superiority, making it easier to rationalize the U.S. or other Western invasion, domination, or subversion of countries such as South Vietnam, Nicaragua, Iraq, and Afghanistan. Discussions of yet more interventions in non-Western countries periodically appear in the political news. While blatantly racist views of people of color were openly expressed by U.S. foreign policymakers and advisors until the 1960s, today these racist views are usually hidden behind a façade of paternalistic "concern" over the lack of commitment of "underdeveloped" countries to "civilized values" or Western-style "democracy."

Today, U.S. foreign policymakers often operate from a nationalistic perspective with an imbedded white racial framing of other countries. "American" (still typically meaning white American) virtue and superiority are routinely assumed. Indeed, the U.S. government is the only government across the globe to give an annual report card about other countries' human rights behavior. Yet, leading members of the U.S. government tend to get angry when the U.S. human rights record is even modestly questioned by international organizations or non-Western officials.

For instance, U.S. government officials withdrew in protest from a 2001 World Conference Against Racism authorized by the United Nations and held in the Republic of South Africa. U.S. reparations for U.S. slavery and colonialism, as well as issues of Zionism and Islamophobia, were on the agenda. The official reason for this early U.S. departure was because the conference was considering a resolution criticizing Zionism as an example of racism. Yet, there was also a great reluctance by U.S. officials to engage in serious discussions in this international forum of reparations for Western involvement in the Atlantic slavery system and to discuss continuing racial discrimination in the United States. A white framing of the globe among many U.S. officials may also explain the relatively weak commitment to numerous United Nations efforts in recent decades. This U.S. commitment has appeared especially weak when the United Nations general assembly or a major United Nations agency, influenced by the world's population majority of people of color, has made decisions that U.S. leaders consider contrary to U.S. national interests.[39]

Indeed, a majority of rank-and-file Americans, especially of white Americans, mostly seem to share their political leaders' assertive global framing with its strong nationalism and ethnocentrism, which not only accents U.S. cultural and political superiority but also typically sees no need to learn much about other countries and peoples. This nationalistic framing views the United States as the world's "best country." One national poll found that nearly two thirds of 2400 Americans agreed with the statement that "overall the U.S. is better than other nations." Just 3 percent chose "worse," and only 27 percent chose the option of the United States being "a country like any other, and is no better or worse."[40]

This type of ethnocentric perspective inclines a majority of Americans, including powerful white Americans, to mostly ignore many important world events and to stay poorly informed about most of the outside world. We see this in their views of global history and the present global scene. For example, contemporary U.S. and Western European historians often celebrate what they view as the central role of their countries' armed forces in bringing down the German Nazis and their armed forces during World War II. However, fully 75 percent of all Germany's land and air forces were concentrated in the Eastern Front fighting the ethnically diverse armed forces of the Soviet Union. This Eastern Front was the central defining front, the area where eventual German defeat became guaranteed. Today, the ignorance of U.S. citizens about this critical global history—as well as about contemporary world geography, politics, and religion—continues to reveal an ethnocentric, U.S.-centered perspective that is influential in foreign policy circles. Indeed, even as the U.S. government was still occupying Iraq with its military forces in 2008, a survey of the U.S. public in that year revealed that *only one in seven* could even find the large country of Iraq on a map of the Middle East. As one India-born U.S. journalist has noted, U.S. residents typically "speak few languages, know little about foreign cultures, and remain unconvinced that they need to correct this."[41]

Spreading the Frame Globally: The U.S. Mainstream Media

For centuries U.S. individuals, agencies, companies, and other organizations have been active in spreading versions of the white racial frame internationally. U.S. and other Western colonizers, missionaries, and soldiers have done much to spread the pro-white and anti-other aspects of that frame, but today that influential frame is effectively circulated across the globe by a great array of organizations—including, perhaps most effectively, U.S. and other Western media corporations.

Today about a few dozen large media corporations control most of the world's mainstream media operations, including, newspapers, magazines, books, television stations and production, cable networks, record production, and motion picture production and theaters. Much of the material circulated throughout this white-dominated global media system is U.S.-based, and significant portions reflect white-oriented cultural productions and the white racial framing. Most of the world's countries are now important markets for U.S. media productions that periodically make substantial use of racially stereotyped conceptions, understandings, and images. Across the globe hundreds of millions of households regularly get significant information and entertainment from old and new U.S. movies, television programs, videos, and armed forces radio and television stations. Billions of the world's people likely encounter on a regular basis some important elements of the white racial frame—including negative images of African Americans, other Americans of color, or people of color in other countries.[42]

A substantial proportion of the world's population probably holds at least some racial views shaped by the white racial framing that originated in the United States or European countries. One study interviewed fifteen rural Chinese residents of the island of Taiwan (near China) and found that most held stereotyped views of black Americans as self-destructive, dirty, lazy, unintelligent, criminal, violent, or ugly—all features of the white racial frame. The respondents indicated that their racist framing mostly had been drawn from U.S. television shows, movies, and music videos imported into Taiwan. A similar impact has been reported for Latino immigrants to the United States from Central America.[43]

The mostly white corporate executives who control most of the globally powerful media corporations accent a consumerist individualism, and usually downplay important civic values and marginalize local efforts aimed at significant reforms. International journalism tends to be "pitched to the business class and suited to its needs and prejudices; with a few notable exceptions, the journalism reserved for the masses tends to be the sort of drivel provided by the media giants on their U.S. television stations."[44] Escapist entertainment is emphasized, and little that is substantially critical of racial, class, or gender oppression in any country is ever presented.

Conclusion

It is hard to overestimate the centuries-old impacts of the white racial frame on U.S. institutions, including public and private policymaking organizations. Even as this frame has evolved to include new or refurbished older emphases, such as recent accents on a "colorblind" and "post-racial" America, deep structures of white racism remain in place in workplaces, housing markets, banking, policing, political institutions, and other major institutions. While some celebrate certain advances, such as the election of the first black president, many research reports find continuing and systemic racism throughout society, most especially in major organizations and institutions.

In this chapter we see the great impact of systemic racism and its white frame in many policymaking areas, including on national issues of immigration, the environment, health care, and criminal justice. We observe much impact on foreign policymaking. One key reason is that the powerful decisionmakers who are most important in making many policy decisions are mostly whites or others who operate substantially out of a contemporary white frame. They typically pay much attention to the views or interests of white Americans in making decisions that affect not just whites but also people of color, and society generally. The major institutions and organizations of this society are also structured to substantially reinforce this white-interested policymaking.

For multiple reasons, thus, most whites view the mostly white-controlled policy decisionmaking for the country as acceptable and normal, especially as whites as a group are still unjustly enriched and disproportionately privileged in a variety of ways. While not all whites benefit in the same ways from important policy decisions, most do over their lives get significant benefits and privileges as a result. Clearly, for the U.S. system of racial oppression to last for centuries the white racial frame's ideas, images, and emotions had to become deeply imbedded in the everyday operations of the important organizational and institutional structures of society.

CHAPTER **8**

Counter-Framing

Americans of Color

To this point, we have examined the dominant white racial frame and the way that it has developed and impacted this society and others across the globe. In this chapter we consider other important frames that have also developed over the last few centuries, frames that provide alternative or countering perspectives to the dominant framing. Recall that most people are multiframers and carry several perspectival frames applicable to particular situations in their heads at the same time. In examining the contested history of the white racial frame, we discover at least four important categories of frames in everyday operation: (1) the dominant white racial frame itself; (2) a white-crafted liberty-and-justice frame; (3) the anti-oppression counter-frames of Americans of color; and (4) the home-culture frames that Americans of color have usually drawn on in developing their counter-frames.

The Liberty-and-Justice Frame

The second category, the white liberty-and-justice frame, is significant in U.S. history because most white Americans, as well as most other Americans and some Europeans, have articulated some version of this, at least since the seventeenth century. This critical framing appears in the founding documents of the United States, the same documents that made sure that the slavery system would thrive. Notice the centrality of this framing in the "life, liberty and the pursuit of happiness" language in the U.S. Declaration of Independence, as well as in the "establish justice" and "secure the blessings of liberty" language of the preamble to the U.S. Constitution. Liberty, freedom, equality, and justice were well-known concepts for the white founders of the United States.

Where did these founders get their ideas of liberty and justice for this framing? They sought their freedom from the British king, and the circumstances of their conflict with Britain contributed to their goals and views of personal liberty and justice. They also drew on various European and North American sources. Today, the typical scholarly discussion accents European sources, including political philosophers such as John Locke and Jean-Jacques Rousseau. In a 1690 treatise on government, the philosopher read by some U.S. founders, John Locke, asserted his view of social "justice" as universal and part of natural law: "Justice gives every Man a Title to the product of his honest Industry, and the fair Acquisitions of his Ancestors descended to him." For Locke, justice includes the idea that people have a natural right to the product of their labor, including a right to pass that along. Locke also emphasized the importance of what he termed "life and liberty." U.S. founder and intellectual Thomas Jefferson was influenced by Locke and other European Enlightenment thinkers, as we see in the "life" and "liberty" language he put into the Declaration of Independence.[1] It is significant, however, that in important areas of his life Locke, like Jefferson, did not live by these ideals of justice and liberty. Indeed, he was a major investor in the Royal Africa Company, a leading slave trading company, and served on English councils that supervised North American slavery.

Strikingly, the European and U.S. leaders' professed understandings of liberty, freedom, and justice were regularly contradicted by the bloody enrichment of white Americans at the expense of indigenous Americans and enslaved Africans. Their hypocrisy is a major feature of European and North American history. Recall Patrick Henry's famous lines, "for my own part I consider it as nothing less than a question of freedom or slavery," "there is no retreat but in submission and slavery," and "give me liberty, or give me death." I noted earlier the sad irony of this most famous of the founders' speeches: that it was given by a well-off southern slaveholder who left many people enslaved at his death. Clearly, many white Americans' understandings of what freedom and liberty meant were acutely sharpened as they observed millions of enslaved human beings whose lives had little or no freedom. They could see in the tears and words of those enslaved and in their frequent resistance to slavery, as well as in comments of free black leaders and abolitionists, just what freedom and liberty really meant for human beings.

From the American revolutionary era to the present, most whites have held to a cherished liberty-and-justice frame, albeit one that is usually rhetorical and hypothetical when it comes to challenges by Americans of color to racial oppression. When it comes to everyday social interactions, the white racial frame routinely eclipses the liberty-and-justice frame, which tends to be most openly celebrated in personal rhetorical comments or during rhetorical speeches at ceremonies and on holidays. This was true for most whites during the long decades of slavery from 1787 to 1865 and during the long decades of legal segregation from the 1870s to the 1960s. All too often, this is true today as well. At any point over the four centuries of contact and oppression, the European colonizers of North America and their descendants could as a group have broken completely with the white racial frame, conformed to their best ideals of liberty and justice, and fully implemented those ideals for the lives of Native Americans, African Americans, and other Americans of color, but they never have.

Yet, over the centuries some whites have taken this liberty-and-justice frame very seriously and worked to end oppression in the form of slavery, Jim Crow, or contemporary discrimination. For example, the early Puritan dissenter, Roger Williams, was influenced by contacts with Native American leaders in New England and wrote respectfully about Native American culture. He lived with Native Americans for a time, rejected much racist framing of them, sought for white colonists to be fair in land dealings, and used his knowledge of Native Americans to argue for fair treatment.[2]

By the mid-1700s some white Quakers were articulating strong abolitionist views and developing a more authentic liberty-and-justice frame in regard to African Americans. The Quaker leader, John Woolman, wrote accurately about the negative impact of black enslavement on white minds: "Being concerned with a people so situated that they have no voice to plead their own cause, there's danger of using ourselves to an undisturbed partiality, till, by long custom, the mind becomes reconciled with it, and the judgement itself infected." Woolman was an early "social constructionist," for he saw what systemic racism did to all people in society, especially those oppressed:

> Placing on men the ignominious title, slave, dressing them in uncomely garments, keeping them to servile labour, in which they are often dirty, tends gradually to fix a notion in the [white] mind, that they are a sort of people below us in nature.[3]

Woolman recognized the moral contradictions. Whites were taught Christian morality and a liberty-and-justice framing, yet were also taught how to implement and rationalize racial oppression.[4]

Woolman was one of the first to analyze sociologically the connection of skin color to slavery: "This is owing chiefly to the idea of slavery being connected with the black colour, and liberty with the white: And where false

Ideas are twisted into our minds, it is with difficulty we get fairly disentangled."[5] He accented the way in which this oppression becomes normalized as white minds imbed "false" and "fixed notions" about those who are black and "becomes reconciled" to their oppression. In white framing liberty was color-coded: whiteness encompassed liberty, while blackness did not. Since Woolman's day, some whites have periodically joined with black Americans and other Americans of color to accent an authentic liberty-and-justice frame and act assertively on it. Historically, this can be seen in the anti-racist actions of the white abolitionists in the mid-nineteenth century and white civil rights activists in the mid-twentieth century.

Black Resistance: Anti-racist Counter-Frames and Home-Culture Frames

Two other categories of perspectival frames are useful in making sense out of systemic racism and the everyday resistance to it by Americans of color: anti-oppression counter-frames of Americans of color; and home-culture frames that Americans of color have regularly used and periodically drawn on to develop effective anti-oppression counter-frames. Over the long centuries African Americans and others targeted by oppression have developed important counter-frames designed to fight back, or to just survive. This resistance framing began in the first century of European colonization in the Americas. Leaders of racially oppressed groups have long honed a strong counter-frame, as have most ordinary people, the "grassroots intellectuals" in oppressed groups. Although counter-frames were initially developed for survival, over centuries many elements have been added that strengthen and enhance strategies of resistance. Counter-frames have provided important tool kits enabling individuals and groups to effectively counter recurring white hostility and discrimination.

In the North American colonies and, later, in the United States, pressures on African Americans to conform to the dominant Eurocentric culture forced them to become bicultural—that is, to know well the dominant white-determined culture as well as their own home-culture. From the first decades of the slavery system, African Americans have created and sustained a critical home-culture that incorporates important cultural features from their African backgrounds, as well as reworked aspects of European culture, all of which are refined and shaped in the fiery crucible of everyday experiences with North American racism. In spite of the great oppression they faced and constant pressures to abandon African cultures, the diverse groups among those enslaved—Yorubas, Akans, Igbos, and many others—became an African American group with a home-culture that imbedded traditional family values and moral and spiritual elements from numerous African cultures. With important African infusions, these enslaved Americans created their own religion, art, and music, as well as their own perspectives on social oppression, human freedom, and social justice in their new country.

Let me underscore here the importance of this home-culture frame for the everyday lives of African Americans and other Americans of color. Significant elements of this home-culture frame preceded encounters with whites, and thus Americans of color can operate out of it for significant periods of time without concern for or direct reference to white Americans or the surrounding racist society. While the home-culture frame does provide important sources for resistance to oppression and for counter-framing, it is much more than that. As a universal type of human framing, the home-culture frame involves important understandings and values that facilitate everyday life, interaction, and support in family and personal settings. This was true during slavery and legal segregation, and it is today. We need to keep in mind the distinction between the everyday-humanity elements of the home-culture frame and how some elements from it have regularly been utilized for more overt resistance to persisting racial oppression.

Clearly, since the seventeenth century, African Americans have often been restricted by whites in how much they could make overt use of many positive elements of their Africa-influenced home-culture and its often distinctive human framing because of retaliatory repression from whites. Since the days of slavery African Americans have frequently faced aggressive pressures from whites for reculturalization. Africans and their descendants in North America were forced to accept much European American culture, including English, but they still passed along valuable African-origin understandings and other internal cultural elements through oral and written traditions over generations. Because significant elements of this traditional home-culture predated white oppression, enslaved Africans and their descendants have regularly drawn on these positive cultural elements to assist in the ordinary navigations of everyday life, as well as in crafting a counter-frame and its anti-oppression strategies.[6]

Consider the religious orientations of African Americans as an example of this process. For a great many African Americans, past and present, the traditional home-culture and its framing of society have been infused throughout by a positive religious and spiritual imagination that, among other aspects, has often affirmed the common humanity of all people and the sacred importance of justice and equality. This religious home-culture has periodically influenced the development of the black counter-frame of resistance and protest.

Historically, the discourse of most oppressed groups has included counter-framed critiques of oppression not discussed publicly. Enslaved

African Americans frequently drew both on African religious traditions and on Christianity—the latter initially forced on them by slavemasters— to resist white cultural and social dominance. In religious services where whites were present, those enslaved frequently pretended to accept Christian teachings about such things as obedience to authority. When whites were absent, they often blended African religious understandings and their version of Christianity in order to accent ideas of freedom from enslavement. Conceptions of God that many held—for example, the emphasis on God's having led the Israelites out of slavery—were not what slaveholders had envisioned. In the counter-framing of those enslaved, the "Promised Land" could mean the northern states or Canada and thus freedom from enslavement, and a song's "heaven" might be seen as a reality where oppressors would be punished. This was true for African Americans like enslaved Baptist preacher, Nat Turner, a religious man who had recurring visions from God. Visions of deliverance inspired him in 1831 to lead a rebellion by seventy enslaved people in Virginia. Many whites were killed before soldiers put down these black freedom fighters, who clearly had a strong framing of "liberty and justice" in their minds. They had originally planned to begin attacks, as Turner put it, on their white "enemies" on July 4 (Independence Day). The white reaction was fierce. Turner's body was beaten and quartered; and fifty-five other black Americans were executed for actually or allegedly participating.[7]

Enslaved Americans who participated in numerous efforts to revolt took seriously the principle of "liberty and justice." Hidden in the Christian symbolism of some of their music was a strong yearning to be free. Humanistic religious insights and resources from the African American home-culture have been important to the development of strong counter-frames of resistance, from slavery to the present. From the beginning, too, African American Christianity has provided organizational settings within which to critique oppression. Religious gatherings during slavery, including in churches of free African Americans, were important places where they could critically assess society and develop a counter-frame with its resistance ideas. To the present day, African American religious organizations and their leaders have played a very significant role in major protests against oppression, as we have seen in the civil rights protests of more recent decades that have played a central role in bringing down legal segregation.[8]

Early Assertions of the Black Counter-Frame

From the days of slavery to the present, African Americans have a long history of resistance to oppression. No later than the mid-1600s, whites in colonial America were worried about insurrections. White leaders such as

Virginia's influential William Byrd, a major slaveholder, spoke out about the dangers of insurrection that might come from the greedy actions of white slavetraders and slaveholders who were increasing the number of enslaved Africans. In 1710 Virginia's governor, Alexander Spotswood, cautioned the Virginia Assembly that their weak militia should be concealed from "our slaves" lest their "desire of freedom may stir those people" to rebel.[9] White fears of black Americans rising against slavery were already obvious, and such fears accelerated as those enslaved increased dramatically over the next century. Whites had reason to fear; over the long slavery era African Americans engaged in an estimated 250 slave revolts and conspiracies to revolt. Most conspiracies to revolt did not proceed as far as that of Nat Turner's revolutionaries, but were discovered and put down by whites. Nonetheless, they indicated a significant level of collective black resistance and frightened many whites, thereby early on contributing to the "dangerous black man" imagery in the dominant white frame.

During the nineteenth century African Americans frequently protested, first against slavery and later against legal segregation. Before the Civil War there were hundreds of protest meetings and demonstrations by black and white abolitionists targeting slavery. In 1829 a young abolitionist working in Boston, David Walker, published what seems to be the first extended statement of an anti-oppression counter-frame in U.S. history. In his bold pamphlet *Appeal to the Coloured Citizens of the World*, Walker crafted a manifesto for full equality. He wrote to fellow African Americans with revolutionary arguments couched in an anti-oppression framing and aggressively circulated it in the North and South, so much so that southern slaveholders put a $10,000 bounty on his head. Because in 1830 Walker died under suspicious circumstances, some analysts have suspected that he was murdered by whites. If so, this indicates the strong investment whites had in suppressing any type of assertive counter-frame.[10]

Walker's anti-oppression manifesto lays out important elements—critical ideas and resistance strategies—that one still finds in the black counter-frame today. He analyzes the slavery system, and segregation of free African Americans, with blunt language accenting the injustice of these structures. Most whites are "cruel oppressors and murderers" whose oppression will eventually be overthrown. They are "an unjust, jealous, unmerciful, avaricious and blood-thirsty set of beings." Walker's critical counter-frame incorporates a countersystem analysis, one that examines the institutionalized and systemic character of white oppression and calls for its replacement. Walker is perhaps the first U.S. writer to accent the concept of unjust enrichment: Whites seek for African Americans to be slaves to them "and their children forever to dig their mines and work their farms; and thus go on enriching them, from one generation to another with our blood and our tears!" In addition, Walker takes on the stereotyping of the anti-black frame. He notes that whites emotionally stereotype black Americans as "ungrateful," but replies to this framing with historical analysis: "What should we be grateful to them for—for murdering our fathers and mothers? Or do they wish us to return thanks to them for chaining and handcuffing us, branding us ... or for keeping us in slavery ... to support them and their families." He critiques Thomas Jefferson's extensive negative framing of African Americans in *Notes on the State of Virginia*— for example, by explaining that Jefferson's argument that enslaved blacks have limited abilities and are thus naturally inferior to whites makes as much sense as saying that a deer in an iron cage can "run as fast as the one at liberty."[11]

Walker further underscores the contradictions between the extensive oppression of African Americans and whites' rhetorical liberty-and-justice frame. He quotes the phrase "all men are created equal" from the Declaration of Independence, then challenges white readers:

> Compare your own language above, extracted from your Declaration of Independence, with your cruelties and murders inflicted by your cruel and unmerciful fathers and yourselves on our fathers and on us—men who have never given your fathers or you the least provocation! ... I ask you candidly, was your sufferings under Great Britain one hundredth part as cruel and tyrannical as you have rendered ours under you?[12]

Walker does not stop with a critique of the white racist framing, but also accents a positive view of African Americans: "Are we men!!—I ask you, O. my brethren! Are we men?" He builds on what must be one of the oldest elements of black resistance framing. So far as I can tell, the very earliest counter-framing of those enslaved is only indirectly recorded. One rare example is in a 1684 book by Caribbean slaveholder Thomas Tryon. Tryon described an enslaved black man as insisting, "we are not Beasts ... but rational souls."[13] Like his predecessor, Walker accents the humanity and strengths of black Americans. In the *Appeal* he also chides African Americans for not taking more assertive action against oppression and calls on them to actively refute racist claims of whites. Throughout the *Appeal*, Walker accents a vigorous social justice framing of society.

In Walker's brave and revolutionary analysis we see that black Americans early on had a strongly developed counter-frame to the dominant white frame: (1) a strong critique of white oppression; (2) an aggressive countering of negatively stereotyped framing of African Americans; (3) a positive assertion of the full humanity of African Americans; (4) a clear assertion of the American-ness of African Americans; and (5) a strong accent on liberty, justice, and equality for all Americans.

In 1843 an admirer of Walker and prominent abolitionist, Henry Garnet, gave a speech titled "An Address to the Slaves of the United States of America," at a National Negro Convention. Speaking primarily to African Americans, Garnet's counter-framing is aggressive in arguing that those enslaved must assertively rebel against oppression. He offers a structural analysis using the term "oppression" and asserting that white "oppressor's power is fading." Like Walker he argues that African Americans like "all men cherish the love of liberty. . . . In every man's mind the good seeds of liberty are planted." He calls on those enslaved to take revolutionary action: "There is not much hope of redemption without the shedding of blood. If you must bleed, let it all come at once—rather die freemen, than live to be slaves."[14] In spite of some critical reaction, Garnet's address was subsequently published and widely disseminated.

In the 1850s another black abolitionist, Martin Delany, wrote in detail about his anti-racist counter-frame. In a book directed at all Americans, he points out contradictions between the white liberty-and-justice frame and whites' practices: The

> United States, untrue to her trust and unfaithful to her professed principles of republican equality, has also pursued a policy of political degradation to a large portion of her native born countrymen, and that class is the Colored People. . . . There is no species of degradation to which we are not subject.

In addition to assessing the oppression faced by African Americans, Delany makes clear that his resistance framing extends the ideals of the old white liberty-and-justice frame: "We believe in the universal equality of man, and believe in that declaration of God's word, in which it is positively said, that 'God has made of one blood all the nations that dwell on the face of the earth.'" In his analysis he also takes on negative stereotyping in the dominant racial frame. He argues that the "absurd idea of a natural inferiority of the African" was only recently dreamed up by "slave-holders and their abettors in justification" of black enslavement.[15]

Delany attacks anti-black stereotypes and images with a detailed listing of achievements of free and enslaved African Americans. He lists entrepreneurs and professionals who have been successful among free African Americans. He describes how enslaved African workers brought important skills in farming and animal husbandry to North America. Without these agricultural and related skills, the cotton, tobacco, and other important agricultural production would not have been possible. In his view black workers are the "bone and sinews of the country." Indeed, the very "existence of the white man, South, depends entirely on the labor of the black man—the idleness of the one is sustained by the industry of the other." He turns the tables on slaveholding whites, asserting that they are the ones who lazily profit off the labor of others. In addition, we see the idea of the unjust enrichment of whites as part of the black counter-frame. Delany further accents the point that African Americans are old Americans and do not seek to emigrate to Africa, a common idea among whites in his day, but seek liberty within the U.S. society they helped to build. "Our common country is the [1850s] United States . . . and from here will we not be driven by any policy that may be schemed against us. We are Americans, having a birthright citizenship."[16] The counter-frame, at this early point in time, was not just about beliefs, for it also asserted much imagery of freedom and much fervor for liberation from slavery.

Resisting Slavery and Legal Segregation

Nat Turner acted on his counter-framing and took aggressive action against slavery. Delany too acted aggressively out of his counter-framing. In May 1858, he and the white abolitionist John Brown gathered together a group of black and white abolitionists for a revolutionary anti-slavery meeting outside the United States, in the safer area of Chatham, Canada. Nearly four dozen black and white Americans formulated a new constitution to govern what they hoped would be a band of armed revolutionaries drawn from the enslaved population; these would fight as guerillas for an end to slavery. Delany was also among abolitionists who in the 1860s pressed President Abraham Lincoln to recruit African Americans for the Union army. As a result of this recruitment, during the last years of the Civil War several hundred thousand African Americans, the majority formerly enslaved, served as Union soldiers and support troops—and thus did much more at the time to free enslaved Americans than did Lincoln's famous 1863 Emancipation Proclamation.[17]

Most of these soldiers and support troops undoubtedly held some version of the counter-frame in their minds. For example, the formerly enslaved John Washington, who ran away and became part of the Union Army's support troops, described his new situation:

> Before morning I had began to feel like I had truly escaped from the hands of the slaves master and with the help of God, I never would be a slave no more. I felt for the first time in my life that I could now claim every cent that I should work for as my own. I began now to feel that life had a new joy awaiting me. I might now go and come when I please. This was the first night of freedom.[18]

Another formerly enslaved member of Union support troops put it this way: "The next morning I was up early and took a look at the rebels country with a thankful heart to think I had made my escape with safety after such a long struggle; and had obtained that freedom which I desired so long. I now dreaded the gun, and handcuffs and pistols no more."[19] For formerly enslaved men and women, liberty and justice were much more than rhetorical abstractions. Their sacrifices on battlefields and behind the lines helped not only to free those enslaved, but also to put the United States on track to become a freer country.

Although they had the chance to fully implement key features of their own liberty-and-justice frame after the Civil War, most in the powerful white elites in the South and North refused to do so. They encouraged or allowed whites in southern and border states to establish extensive Jim Crow segregation that was backed by anti-black violence, while encouraging or permitting significant de facto segregation of black Americans in northern states. Over time, this legal and de facto segregation generated individual and collective protests from black Americans, including more honing of a strong resistance frame.

The ever-perceptive, formerly enslaved black leader Frederick Douglass developed an extensive counter-frame, first during enslavement in Maryland, then as an anti-slavery abolitionist, and later during legal segregation after the Civil War. In 1852, after he had become an abolitionist leader, Douglass made an eloquent speech in Rochester, New York: "What, to the American slave, is your Fourth of July? I answer: A day that reveals to him, more than all other days of the year, the gross injustices and cruelty to which he is the constant victim. To him your celebration is a sham."[20] Once again, we observe important counter-framing that accents the hypocrisy of the white liberty-and-justice rhetoric, coupled with a strong emphasis on the great injustice done to African Americans.

For decades after the Civil War, Douglass gave speeches that counter-framed Jim Crow segregation as a new type of enslavement for African Americans, as in this 1880s speech: "It meets them at the workshop and factory, when they apply for work. It meets them at the church, at the hotel, at the ballot-box, and worst of all, it meets them in the jury-box." Most African Americans had moved from being the "slave of an individual" to now being the "slave of society."[21] A few years later, also during the early decades of legal segregation, two important black social scientists, Ida B. Wells-Barnett and Anna Julia Cooper, began to develop the idea of gendered racism, a view accenting how gendered the dominant racial hierarchy was. They were among the first to analyze data on the oppressive segregation faced by black men and women, as well as the discrimination faced by women in general, and they made explicit use of counter-frame ideas like "oppression," "subordination," and "repression" in their analyses. Working as a researcher and an activist dealing with violent expressions of white oppression at the turn of the twentieth century, Wells-Barnett developed key analytical ideas about how white oppression is grounded not only in the material reality of economic exploitation, but also in brutal gendering (with related violence such as lynchings) of black men as dangerous to white women and of black women as oversexed. In the decades before and after 1900, black female social scientists were among the first to emphasize the overlapping of institutional racism and institutional sexism.[22]

Working about the same time, and drawing on a centuries-old black resistance frame, W. E. B. Du Bois developed fully a counter-framed view that the United States was pervaded by institutional racism. In *The Souls of Black Folk*, he described the difficult black consciousness created by having to deal regularly with oppression:

> It is a peculiar sensation, this double consciousness, this sense of always looking at one's self through the eyes of others. . . . One ever feels his twoness—an American, a Negro; two souls, two thoughts . . . in one dark body, whose dogged strength alone keeps it from being torn asunder.[23]

This sense of twoness, and the dual roles flowing out of it, have from the beginning been imposed on African Americans by systemic racism. It was early the case, and often still is, that a black American could not openly express his or her true self without risking white retaliation.

Du Bois implemented his counter-frame in actions, such as by helping to found the National Association for the Advancement of Colored People (NAACP) just after 1900 and by being a leader in that organization for decades. He extended his counter-framing to the global sphere as the leading advocate of pan-African nationalism. His globalized counter-frame emphasized the common conditions of, and need for uniting, colonized people of African descent across the world. In 1919, over objections from the U.S. State Department, Du Bois put together the first Pan-African Congress. Attended by delegates from fifteen countries, the Congress pressed for the abolition of all slavery, an end to colonial exploitation, and democratic treatment of people of African descent. This Congress was considered a radical challenge to white dominance and racial framing by white officials in the U.S. State Department and White House.[24]

By the 1930s and 1940s, the pioneering black sociologist Oliver Cox was also developing a counter-framed analysis of U.S. racism as fundamentally structural. In his counter-framing, the sustained exploitation of black Americans for centuries had created in the United States a hierarchical structure of racial classes with whites firmly at the top. The white seizure of African labor in overseas colonialism and North America created a deep structure of institutionalized oppression. He rejected the mainstream social science accent on individual prejudice and bigotry. For him, U.S. racism was not some "abstract, natural, immemorial feeling of mutual antipathy between groups, but rather a practical exploitative relationship with its socio-attitudinal facilitation" of "race prejudice."[25]

The Civil Rights Movement: Out of the Counter-Frame

Over several decades black organization and protests against Jim Crow segregation gradually became substantial and successful. During the last century African Americans, and other Americans of color, have created civil rights organizations that have asserted and implemented an anti-racist counter-framing. One example is the NAACP, which early in the twentieth century inaugurated lawsuits against Jim Crow, which eventually led to the 1954 *Brown v. School Board of Topeka* Supreme Court decision. As suggested previously, both black leaders and black Americans generally were far in advance of the white leadership on racial desegregation issues. Centuries of anti-black oppression have made a majority of black Americans into "everyday intellectuals" who are generally forced by harsh circumstances to develop an institutional-racism framing of society and who have long sought to destroy that racism. As early as the 1930s and 1940s black organizing and voting in the North were substantially responsible for the northern white elite's (and Supreme Court's) increasing concern with taking action against legal segregation. By the end of World War II, the NAACP had 1000 local organizations and a half-million members. Many black (and Latino) veterans returning in the late 1940s from World War II, a war supposedly fought "for democracy," were aggressive in articulating the need for desegregation and joined confrontational civil rights organizations.[26]

From the 1910s to the 1950s, an indication of the increasing expression in action of an anti-racist counter-frame could be seen in the millions of black Americans who abandoned southern states for northern cities, where many could vote for presidential candidates like Franklin Roosevelt and Harry Truman. As presidents, both men were pressured by civil rights organizations to take action against legal segregation. During World War II, under pressure from African American leaders planning a march in Washington, D.C., to protest discrimination, President Franklin Roosevelt issued an executive order reducing discrimination in employment and setting up a Fair Employment Practices Committee. After the war, President Harry Truman took more aggressive action, desegregating the U.S. Armed Forces and establishing a Committee on Civil Rights.[27]

By the 1950s, the black civil rights movement's protests and development of a strong anti-racist counter-frame had created a serious legitimation crisis for the country's white elite. The desire of this elite to protect its national and international legitimacy, including the respect of other world leaders and world opinion, in the face of increasing black protests against Jim Crow was important to the success of continuing civil rights protests. Without aggressive pressuring by African Americans, the white elite would likely not have moved toward desegregation. Important too was the "Cold War" setting in which the U.S. ideology of democracy was proclaimed against undemocratic enemies (especially the Soviet Union) everywhere by the U.S. government. In addition, the wars of the civil rights era—World War II, the Korean War, and the Vietnam War—required substantial mobilization of black workers and soldiers for success, which made it easier for the voices of black leaders and protesters to be heard at the highest levels of white decisionmaking, if only temporarily. In the 1950s the civil rights movement increased dramatically, first with boycotts such as that of segregated buses in Alabama, then in a variety of civil rights protests across the country. The Congress of Racial Equality (CORE) asserted an aggressive black counter-frame and accelerated protest campaigns against housing and employment discrimination in the North. School boycotts, picketing at construction sites, and rent strikes spread. The growing group of organizations oriented toward greater black political and economic power included the youthful Student Nonviolent Coordinating Committee (SNCC). Actions by civil rights groups brought passage of major civil rights acts prohibiting discrimination in employment, voting, and housing. Periodically since the 1940s, many African Americans have come together, at least for a time, and acted in unity to make the United States a freer country.[28]

Essential to many civil rights protests was a dramatic increase in the espousal by black leaders and scholars of a strong anti-racist counter-frame. During the 1960s movements numerous black activists and scholars proclaimed an institutional-racism framing in the tradition of Du Bois and Cox. Activist Stokely Carmichael (later, Kwame Ture) and historian Charles Hamilton demonstrated in their 1967 book, *Black Power*, the importance of institutional racism, of patterns of racism built into society's major institutions today. They contrasted their counter-framed view of institutional racism with the older "race relations" approach focusing on individual white prejudice and individual discrimination. As they showed, institutionalized racism encompassed much more than the beliefs and actions of bigots. In addition, they and others called for a dramatic increase in "black power," especially black political power, and asserted a positive framing of black people and culture under banners such as "black is beautiful."[29] Such developments provoked a strong backlash among many whites.

Note too the continuing importance of African American Christianity and churches in the civil rights movement. Dr. Martin Luther King, Jr., and many other civil rights leaders of the contemporary era have been ministers. As in earlier times, religious leaders and organizations play a significant role in spreading the anti-racist counter-frame and generating protests against oppression. From the slavery era to the present, ministers' sermons, various black celebrations (such as of black history), and church groups' activities have provided much support for the counter-frame that helps people cope with and resist the dominant racist framing of society.

African Americans who have publicly asserted the anti-racist counter-frame have used the language of equality and "liberty and justice for all." In the supposedly post-racial contemporary era, the high level of racial hostility and discrimination still perpetrated by whites routinely contradicts key elements of the white liberty-and-justice frame, which may be one reason that its idealistic language has frequently been used by Americans of color and dissenting whites who seek to reduce discrimination. For example, Dr. Martin Luther King, Jr., often emphasized ideals of liberty and justice, drawing on a centuries-old counter-frame and accenting more meaningfully the important elements of the old liberty-and-justice frame early articulated by the white founders. He made much use of concepts of freedom and liberty, and linked them constantly to the related goal of social justice.[30] King made it clear in a comment about the Montgomery bus boycott by black residents there that the counter-frame also includes a conception of oppression that must be overcome by assertive action:

There comes a time when people get tired of being trampled by oppression. There comes a time when people get tired of being plunged into the abyss of exploitation and nagging injustice. The story of Montgomery is the story of fifty thousand such Negroes who were willing to . . . walk the streets of Montgomery until the walls of segregation were finally battered by the forces of justice.[31]

Significantly, the 1950s and 1960s civil rights movements brought a meaningful emphasis on, and some implementation of, the ideals of liberty and justice back into the U.S. public sphere.

Both Democratic presidents in the 1960s, John F. Kennedy and Lyndon Baines Johnson, seemed to have learned something about the importance of actually expanding liberty and justice from the civil rights movements. An example is Johnson's commencement address at Howard University in 1965, titled "To Fulfill These Rights." There he first accented the "devastating heritage of long years of slavery; and a century of oppression, hatred, and injustice" as explanations for black poverty and inequality. Then he continued:

> *But freedom is not enough.* You do not wipe away the scars of centuries by saying: Now you are free to go where you want, and do as you desire, and choose the leaders you please. You do not take a person who, for years, has been hobbled by chains and liberate him, bring him up to the starting line of a race and then say, "you are free to compete with all the others," and still justly believe that you have been completely fair. . . . We seek not just legal equity but human ability, not just equality as a right and a theory but equality as a fact and equality as a result.[32]

Such phrasing was drawn from the bold language of the black civil rights movement and indicated that this president—and white advisors who wrote the speech—were willing to accent a more authentic liberty-and-justice framing of centuries of racial oppression. However, President Johnson, and subsequent white presidents, soon backed off on this commitment to real justice and equality, for it was clear that major structural changes in racial inequalities were not supported by most whites. Still, for a brief time a few white leaders like Johnson had taken some anti-discrimination action inspired by the black liberty-and-justice framing.

Significantly, today public and private discussions of racially liberal and emancipatory views accenting equality and justice are often identified in many white minds as something distinctively "black"—probably because African Americans have long been the most visible group carrier of a sustained liberty-and-justice tradition, one involving the most extensive civil rights efforts and organization, in U.S. history.

Black Anti-racist Counter-Framing Today

In recent years black scholars and activists have continued to build on the extensive, often positive counter-framing of the civil rights movement era, and some have emphasized a comprehensive Afrocentric perspective including a strong critique of white cultural imperialism. Molefi Kete Asante, among others, has spurred this development, arguing for the distinctive concept of "Afro-centricity" as a counter to Eurocentric culture. Asante and other African American scholars and activists have extensively analyzed this Eurocentric culture, particularly elements that have been absorbed by African Americans. The African American anthropologist Marimba Ani has accented the important parts of a contemporary Afrocentric counter-frame. On the one hand, this strong counter-frame critically problematizes white cultural imperialism that attempts "to proselytize, encourage, and project European ideology." On the other, it underscores the need for African Americans to direct their "energies toward the recreation of cultural alternatives informed by ancestral visions of a future that celebrates Africanness."[33]

This contemporary resistance framing is very evident in the views and actions of rank-and-file African Americans. Before we turn to recent interviews with these Americans, let us summarize briefly some important dimensions of the counter-frame that we have seen in the past and will see in these contemporary interviews: a strong critique of white oppression and its operations; an understanding and countering of negative framing of African Americans; a positive assertion of the full humanity of African Americans, and often of all people; a strong accent on real freedom, justice, and equality; and a recognition of gendered racism faced by black women (and men).

The counter-frame also typically includes honed perspectives on how to deal with white discriminators, including passive and active strategies. For example, in a recent study of black employees in the airline industry, a black female pilot illustrated her direct resistance to hostile racial framing in this interview account:

I have had a lot of rude comments from (white) passengers. But this one time out of Westchester, NY, I had one passenger show up one night, and she saw that I was flying the plane and she didn't want to get on. So, I told the gate agents, "Close the door; I'm getting out of here and she can take the greyhound." They were getting ready to close the door, and she saw that I was serious so she got on.[34]

From much previous experience, this pilot quickly understood the negative white framing of her in this case and decided to risk her job with an active and appropriate response, one asserting both her humanity and her authority. Such resistance teaches lessons of humanity for all Americans, but most especially for many whites who have yet to learn that lesson. In another research study a veteran black police officer described in broader terms his and others' recurring struggle with white racism:

You're looking at a [racist] system that's been built up over the years with a philosophy that's been built up over the years and its taught not only in the educational system, on television, in the media. It's all around you, and you either subscribe to it because it's the easy thing to do, or actually it's the natural thing to do. Or you have to struggle with society and once that struggle, once that fever pitch struggle begins and catches on, I think you'll see some progress, but until that you deal with what you deal with.[35]

Another important element typically in an individual's counter-frame is a developed sensitivity to whites' negative framing of African Americans and to commonplace stereotypes and discriminatory acts, as this black police officer made quite clear:

> After so many years of overt racism and then watching the change over years from those overt acts to covert acts, ... a lot of African Americans have developed an ability to pick up on certain things. I mean, you can pretty much meet someone [and] within two or three minutes and know if they're sincere. And it's wrong, you can say, "Well that's prejudice, and you're prejudging someone," but the truth is the truth. After you've been treated a particular way so long and heard so many things, pretty soon, they come around full circle and you know what certain phrases mean. You know what certain mannerisms mean, because you've seen it thousands of times before and you've seen what it's attached to.[36]

Operating out of a counter-frame that regularly assesses critically the surrounding racist environment, many black Americans regularly question, call out, and challenge racist stereotypes and discriminatory actions when they encounter them.

Another element that is central to both older counter-framing and the contemporary counter-frame is an assertion of positive aspects of black humanity and achievements, such as an accent on the beauty of black women and a commitment to expanding black political and economic power. One black college student put it this way:

> My parents tried to tell me one thing, they tried to instill in me that I was a beautiful person, that my blackness was a beautiful thing, that the fact that I braided my hair was fine, that I didn't have a perm was fine. But when you're like, nine, ten, eleven, you tend not to listen to your parents, and you tend to listen to everything else, which is white people, in my case white people, and all society which is white.[37]

In black family and friendship circles there is often a significant affirmation of black beauty, and thus of full humanity. It is indeed difficult to assert this counter-framing against such a strong positive framing of white beauty and superiority in the larger society. Nonetheless, older generations of black Americans often pass along to youth strongly positive interpretations of black history, traditions, beauty, and humanity.

In much contemporary black counter-framing, gendered racism receive much attention. While some elements of oppression affect all members of targeted groups such as African Americans in similar ways, yet other major elements of oppression vary according to one's position within a targeted group. Thus, numerous scholars and activists have shown how slavery, legal segregation, and contemporary discrimination shape the lives of black women and men in gendered-racist ways.

One scholarly and action-oriented analyst of the intersections of racism, classism, and sexism, Angela Davis, has underscored the point that enslaved women faced gendered racial oppression: They were exploited for their productive labor as workers and their reproductive labor as "breeders" of enslaved children. Another pioneering social scientist, Philomena Essed, interviewed black women in Holland and the U.S. and coined the term "gendered racism." She described how in contemporary societies black women's experiences with discrimination were gendered, how racism and sexism regularly overlapped. From years of experience black women have developed distinctive systems of knowledge that are critical for fighting gendered racism. Sociologist Patricia Hill Collins has shown that a strong black feminist counter-frame highlights and analyzes negative stereotypes of black women—white-generated stereotypes of the docile mammy, domineering matriarch, promiscuous prostitute, and irresponsible welfare mother. These gendered-racist framings of black women, some of which are also applied to other women of color, persist because they are fostered by white-dominated media and undergird recurring discrimination. In research on black women, researchers like Davis, Essed, Collins, Elizabeth Higginbotham, Yanick St. Jean, and Adia Harvey Wingfield have regularly emphasized the importance of liberating women of color from racial, gender, and gendered-racist stereotypes and discrimination.[38]

Today the black counter-frame contains ideals, language, emotions, and images of freedom, equality, and justice, which are often envisioned for all people. There is frequently hope of future societal fairness, of getting "what is rightfully ours"—the modern version of the old "40-acres-and-mule" promise to those freed from slavery after the 1860s Civil War. Today this positive orientation includes an insistence, as with David Walker and Martin Delany, on whites accepting responsibility for racism and on full equality and justice for African Americans. It accents as well the American-ness of African Americans. Consider this excerpt from a 2008 National Press Club speech by Dr. Jeremiah Wright, emeritus minister at Chicago's Trinity United Church and former pastor of President Obama:

> The black church's role in the fight for equality and justice from the 1700s up until 2008 has always had as its core the non-negotiable doctrine of reconciliation, children of God repenting for past sins against each other. ... Reconciliation means we embrace our

individual rich histories, all of them. We retain who we are, as persons of different cultures, while acknowledging that those of other cultures are not superior or inferior to us; they are just different from us. We root out any teaching of superiority, inferiority, hatred or prejudice.[39]

Interestingly, Dr. Wright's earlier sermons asserting justice ideas and condemning the U.S. government's long history of racist actions globally—including one that Wright ended with brief "God Damn America" language in regard to racist government actions—were widely quoted out of context in the mainstream media during the 2008 presidential campaign. Here is a larger excerpt from Wright's counter-framed 2003 sermon, which shows the placement of these famous three words the media took out of context:

> The United States of America government, when it came to treating her citizens of Indian descent fairly, she failed. She put them on reservations. When it came to treating her citizens of Japanese descent fairly, she failed. She put them in internment prison camps. When it came to treating citizens of African descent fairly.... The government put them on slave quarters, put them on auction blocks, put them in cotton fields, put them in inferior schools, put them in substandard housing, put them in scientific experiments, put them in the lowest paying jobs, put them outside the equal protection of the law ... and then wants us to sing God bless America? ... Not God bless America; God damn America! That's in the Bible, for killing innocent people. God damn America for treating her citizen as less than human. God damn America as long as she keeps trying to act like she is God and she is supreme![40]

If Dr. Wright's prophet-like statements are placed in their larger context at the end of a long sermon on societal injustice, one understands he is arguing that, in contrast to the power of God, even the powerful U.S. government is fallible and transitory. It has failed to treat all its citizens equally. His reasoning makes sense and is out of a counter-frame directed against systemic racism.

The mass media's repeated quoting of the "God damn America" phrasing, totally out of its analytical context, caused such a national political frenzy and negative reaction in much of the white population that then presidential candidate Obama was forced to criticize Wright and, after other critical remarks by Wright out of the counter-frame, to break with his former pastor and leave the Chicago church. Moreover, Obama and his mostly white political team seemed to be greatly concerned about negative white reactions to the forthright interpretations of liberty and justice in the black counter-frame.[41]

The use of elements from the black counter-frame runs across a broad continuum. At one end of the frame's use there is a relatively assertive and well-developed anti-racist view that is constantly emphasized in speeches by black officials and in sermons by ministers like Dr. Wright, as well as by many other members of civil rights organizations and organized protest movements. In these important groups and networks there is much strongly critical analysis of the racist dimensions of U.S. society, and the anti-racist counter-framing is mostly conscious, overt, and assertive.

Considering the broad continuum, many black Americans seem to fall in between this very aggressive expression of the black anti-racist counter-frame, and the other end of the counter-frame continuum where there are African Americans who make little or no use of its critical and anti-racist ideas, especially in public. The latter, which include some media commentators, often seem to have conformed aggressively to white norms and customs; and some periodically assert publicly aspects of the white frame's negative views of African Americans. In the past and more recently, one observes this white-framed perspective in strong public commentaries on "disorganized" or "pathological" black families by some black celebrities, scholars, and commentators. Among these more conservative African Americans, modest elements from the counter-framing may be used, such as language about justice, but their use of the counter-frame tends to be much weaker, at least in public, than it is for African Americans like Dr. Wright. In addition, there are many African Americans who fall in between these two ends of the continuum and assert what might be termed a middle-strength version of the counter-frame in their everyday lives, applying it variably as the situations demand. Both the white racial frame and the black counter-frame are variable in their everyday expression depending on individual propensities, family socialization, and requirements of particular social settings.[42]

Throughout the eras of slavery, legal segregation, and contemporary discrimination we see black leaders and rank-and-file black Americans asserting and acting on major elements of the counter-frame, elements that were already present in Walker's anti-racist *Appeal* in the early nineteenth century. Resistance by black Americans over the centuries has made the United States a better country in many ways, and this resistance to white framing continues into the twenty-first century.

Passing Along the Counter-Frame

Where and how do African Americans learn the anti-racist counter-frame? It is not taught in the mainstream media or most public schools and colleges, except those that are historically black. Most educational institutions are in fact distributors and inculcators of the white racial frame. Elements of the black home-culture frame and anti-racist counter-frame are most centrally taught within black families, normally with the support of numerous community organizations. The family has long been the main setting where most African Americans get significant regular doses of the counter-frame. A majority of parents teach their children significant aspects of the counter-frame, including lessons about how to deal with white discrimination.[43]

Over centuries, African Americans have done, as many say, "what they had to do just to survive." In this way they have developed a counter-frame with a strong dose of black pragmatism, a practical perspective toward everyday situations. In everyday encounters with whites African Americans are often cautious and may have to defer to whites and white framing, while with black friends and relatives they can usually be freer and openly discuss negative experiences with whites and ways to counter discrimination. In contrast, whites need not be aware of counter-frames held by people of color, and are often unaware of their own white-racist framing.[44]

The black counter-frame is of course variable in extent and subtlety, and versions of it include subframes that reflect the class and gender realities of black parents and their children. For example, many black working class parents give their children nontraditional first names to provide them with something special—and not conventional European American names. Such naming is a type of resistance to whiteness, an everyday counter-framing. At all class levels, there is often a gendered dimension to the counter-frame and its transmission. Parents and other socializers of black children commonly shape teachings about discrimination to fit a child's gender. Because the white racial frame is itself gendered, with black boys and men generally seen as more frightening and dangerous than black girls and women, teaching the counter-frame is also often gendered. Given the aggressive white targeting of black boys and men for discrimination in areas such as policing, black parents often provide stronger and earlier lessons about being cautious when around white police officers and police brutality for sons than for daughters. Such lessons about being wary of white officers and officials have long been important parts of black counter-framing. Teachings from the counter-frame also tend to be gendered in the case of black girls. Girls are frequently taught a somewhat different array of strategies, some gendered, for dealing with white racism. Thus, many black parents teach their daughters that the white frame's image of beauty is often racially stereotyped, and that being dark-skinned and of African descent is indeed to be beautiful. Such teaching is necessary because over their lives daughters are likely to encounter many positive white beauty images and many negative images of and commentaries on black women.[45]

A few researchers have found that, among black children and young people, having in their minds some critical understandings of how white hostility and discrimination operate can, under many circumstances, increase positive outcomes for these youth, such as better grades and positive self-esteem. Yet other studies show that such awareness of discrimination sometimes links to negative effects, including higher personal stress and classroom conduct issues. Some analysts have viewed these research findings as contradictory, but they actually are not, for the white-racist worlds faced by black children, and adults, create stress and other negative health responses, at the same time that they may create a stronger will to fight—depending on the individual and level of group support.[46]

Much passing along of the home-culture frame and the anti-racist counter-frame takes place in friendship and kinship groups of adults, as well as in various community organizations. Quite important venues are beauty shops, barber shops, and taverns. In one recent study Adia Harvey Wingfield interviewed black entrepreneurs who ran beauty salons. These women often reported going into the hair industry in order to make black women feel beautiful and supported, and they have created black-controlled spaces where women candidly discuss life issues, including counter-framing directed at the gendered racism they face. Wingfield describes these safe spaces:

> By establishing the salon as a soothing, peaceful environment where black women could discuss anything, salon owners were able to create a place where black women and their concerns, issues, and perspectives were fundamental rather than marginalized. . . . The creation of the salon as a safe space allows black women owners to challenge systemic gendered racism by presenting their businesses as a haven from its debilitating effects. Systemic gendered racism in the larger society renders black women invisible, unimportant, and irrelevant. Owners challenge this by consciously establishing salons where black women are central, important, and necessary.[47]

Wingfield also describes the important helping ethic that the salon owners operate from and pass along, to both the black women who work for them and their clients:

> Owners' efforts to value their work, to create safe spaces for black women, and to help other women achieve the financial and social benefits of entrepreneurship are a counter-frame to the systemic

gendered racist ideology that black women and the work that they do are unappreciated and worthless. The helping ideology in particular is a counter-frame to the systemic gendered racist ideology that black women should see one another as enemies or competitors rather than as comrades who collectively face oppressive conditions.[48]

Highly developed understandings of how gendered racial oppression works, and about the strategies that counter that oppression, are passed along in such settings across lines of class, age, and generation.

Black beauty salons are places where black beauty is routinely defined, honored, and enhanced—in resistance to the conventional white framing of black women. While these salons are places where hair is often straightened to conform to a white-framed image of good hair, since the 1960s "black is beautiful" movements many salons have expanded their hairstyling services to include an array of more natural hair styles with African and Caribbean origins, such as braided cornrows, other braiding, afros, and dreadlocks. Adopting natural styles is seen by many black women and men as rejecting white-oriented images of beauty and style. In important ways, thus, these beauty salons are centers of black female resistance to the white-racist framing of black women and its associated discriminatory practices.[49]

An ethnographic study by Reuben May of black men interacting over time in a tavern found that such settings support the development of strong self-identities and counter-frames that involve understandings of discrimination:

> By sharing their experiences with one another, African Americans bolster their confidence in their ability to deal with negative interracial conditions, instead of being adversely affected by them. . . . Patrons' knowledge that others have experienced what they are going through is key for the survival of self-identity, an identity intertwined with the understanding that racial conflict is something that happens everyday in a world that emphasizes race.[50]

In churches, beauty salons, and taverns of their communities, black Americans develop or enhance important home-frames and counter-frames that assist them in making sense of racialized worlds they often find as they venture out of their communities into white-controlled institutions. African Americans of various backgrounds engage in what Elijah Anderson terms "folk ethnography," the development of important knowledge about the realities of their everyday lives, including difficult interactions with whites and other nonblacks in schools, workplaces, government offices, and other settings. The knowledge developed in assessing their experiences, and sharing of this knowledge with others in community places like salons and taverns, help to build counter-frames for dealing with racial hostility, discrimination, and related issues in their everyday interactions.[51]

Variations in the Counter-Frame

There are significant variations in use of key elements of the black counter-frame, just as there are for use of the white racial frame. Each black American or other person of color individually makes use of elements from the pre-vailing counter-frame of their group in dealing with a particular situation, place, and time. Those who are part of a long-oppressed racial group are periodically likely to have to alter their orientations, statements, or actions to please or conform to the framing of those in the dominant racial group. We do not have the space to deal with this matter at length, but let me illus-trate this with an example from President Barack Obama's election cam-paigns. For almost the entire 2007–2008 campaign, Obama mostly kept away from direct discussions of U.S. racism issues. He engaged in a signifi-cant discussion of affirmative action once, only when forced by a journalist; and he gave only one major speech, in March 2008, dealing with U.S. racism—and then mostly with regard to the past and because he was forced to do so by the media-aired comments of his pastor, Dr. Wright.

In spite of Obama's dodging of major racial issues during that first campaign, and his frequent political speeches (such as one critiquing "irresponsible" black fathers) that intentionally played into the white frame's understandings, candidate Obama demonstrated numerous times that he regularly viewed the world from a version of the black counter-frame. For example, in his 2006 book, *The Audacity of Hope*, then Senator Obama listed numerous examples of the discrimination he had faced at the hands of white security guards, restaurant customers, and police officers. He noted having to swallow his anger at discriminatory incidents, as well as fears that his daughters might absorb racist story lines from white-controlled media. He explicitly rejected then, as he likely still does, notions that Americans "already live in a colorblind society."[52]

Clearly, Obama was then, and later on, well aware of the racial hostility and discrimination African Americans have faced in the Jim Crow past and discriminatory present. In his books he used some hard-edged understand-ings from the counter-frame and offered a clear understanding of white-imposed discrimination. He signaled to other black Americans that he realized black Americans' discriminatory situations and inequalities.[53] Nonetheless, Obama has carefully picked the social situations in which he has revealed much about his understandings of societal racism. As a result of this caution, he got the necessary share, 43 percent, of the white vote in his pathbreaking 2008 election. That vote, plus most of the black vote and a significant majority of the votes of other voters of color, enabled him to become U.S. president in 2008. Most Americans of color understand well the racialized tightrope that Obama has had to walk, for they too often walk such a tightrope.[54]

We can now examine some of the resistance efforts and anti-racist counter-frames of other Americans of color. I do not have the space here to go into detail on these efforts, but I will trace out enough material to indicate that African Americans are not the only group to have developed significant resistance efforts and important counter-frames. Let us consider briefly the counter-frames of Native Americans, Asian Americans, and Latinos.

Native Americans and Counter-Framing

Unmistakably, Native Americans have the longest tradition of countering white oppression, including the Eurocentric racial framing. The early European invaders, and their descendants today, have usually viewed Native Americans, who lived in numerous different indigenous societies, as not having had real "civilization" until it was brought by Europeans. However, at initial contact most indigenous societies had home-cultures that were at least as developed and sophisticated as those of European societies. Indeed, many indigenous societies were much more humanistic and egalitarian along class and gender lines than the societies of the European colonists.

Organized Native American protest against white subordination has been substantial over the centuries. The ever widening expansion of the European and European American invaders between the 1500s and the 1890s produced major resistance movements. These were often armed and frequently took the form of wars with European colonists. In North America armed resistance was interpreted from within the home-cultures of the hundreds of indigenous societies that suffered from often violent white invasions. Building on home-culture frames, various Native American groups developed aggressive counter-frames that conceptualized the white invaders as dangerous and as untrustworthy in making treaties. The end of armed resistance after the 1890s did not end significant Native American protests. By the late nineteenth century, new protest organizations had sprung up, each with some counter-framing as part of their thrust. The Society of American Indians, formed in 1911 by a diverse group of Native American professionals, sought to develop national Indian leadership, counter stereotypes and inform the white public about Native Americans, and expand educational and employment opportunities for Native Americans. In the 1940s the National Congress of American Indians, a large advocacy group, was formed; it has long used an anti-racist counter-frame and pressed for tribal self-determination, an end to anti-Indian stereotyping, and expanded education for Native Americans. These and other Native American groups have long fought vigorously for social justice and regularly organized protests against white racist framing and discrimination.[55]

During the 1960s a strong "red power" counter-frame was central to increased Indian activism, including picketing and civil disobedience such as sit-ins in government facilities. In 1968 an assertive American Indian Movement (AIM) was organized to address issues ranging from police brutality to housing and employment discrimination. In recent decades AIM and other Indian organizations have strongly protested the use of Indian names and sacred symbols by white-oriented sports teams. The highly stereotyped and racist use of sacred chants, face paint, headdresses, and drums for entertainment purposes has understandably outraged Native Americans and generated significant anti-racist framing and protests.[56] For Native Americans, traditional home-culture frames have been very important sources of support for everyday living under difficult circumstances, as well as for much anti-oppression counter-framing. Indeed, there is an unbroken line of transmission from early home-culture frames predating European invasions to such home-culture frames today. Russell Means, a very influential Indian leader, has emphasized the importance of spirituality and humanity in Native American home-culture frames and counter-frames, today as in the past:

Being is a spiritual proposition. Gaining is a material act. Traditionally, American Indians have always attempted to be the best people they could. Part of that spiritual process was and is to give away wealth, to discard wealth in order not to gain. Material gain is an indicator of false status among traditional people, while it is "proof that the system works" to Europeans.... The European materialist tradition of despiritualizing the universe is very similar to the mental process which goes into dehumanizing another person. And who seems most expert at dehumanizing other people? ... European culture itself is responsible.[57]

Native American counter-framing thus frequently includes a strong critique of the materialistic greed, lack of spirituality, or human insensitivity of much in European American culture and institutions. In this framing the white despiritualizing is linked to whites' dehumanizing of those not like them.

In a 1990s speech to Dine (Navajo) students Means developed another important aspect of the counter-frame in his critique of the untrustworthiness of U.S. government officials who made treaties with Native Americans:

They've admitted that they're nothing but liars, and I admit that, yes you are, and you lied about our treaty, and you lie about your Constitution. Therefore, I advocate that, under international law, constitutional law, our law, and anybody else's law, we revert back to our legal status before we signed the treaty. And guess what that legal status is? Free! We are free people. When one nation unilaterally admits they violated an international covenant, then that covenant no longer has legal force in a court of law, and you become a free people. . . . Wisdom, that's what our culture and our heritage is all about.[58]

Those operating out of this Native American counter-frame insist that the legal treaties that indigenous societies made with the U.S. government over centuries were the legal and moral grounds for relationships between Native Americans and the white-run government. Because the U.S. government has broken virtually all these treaties, Native Americans no longer have obligations to the U.S. government and are "free." Not surprisingly, thus, numerous Native American leaders like Means have cited their own cultural understandings and international law, and called for the return of Native American lands, reparations for land theft and genocide, and the right to control their areas and destinies without white interference.

Alex White Plume, president of the Oglala Lakota Nation, has asserted on behalf of his people a strong counter-framing in regard to the U.S. government and its treaties. He wrote a demanding letter to then President George W. Bush, asking on behalf of his Nation that the "United States fulfill its obligation to respect and protect the human rights of Indian peoples in this country." Discussing white violations of sacred Indian sites, he called on the federal government to honor treaty obligations. He added: "We are also calling on the United States to fulfill its legal and moral obligations to Indian peoples by voting to approve the Declaration on the Rights of Indigenous Peoples at the upcoming September session of the U.N. General Assembly."[59] However, the U.S. government voted against the widely accepted Declaration in 2007, one of only four governments that did so. Three of the latter soon changed their position to one of support, and the U.S. government under the direction of President Obama in 2010 was the *last* country to announce support of the Declaration. Significantly, Native American leaders had been part of the U.N. committee that wrote this important Declaration, one written from an indigenous counter-frame accenting the "restitution of the lands, territories and resources" and the enforcement of treaties with indigenous peoples.

In these statements and actions, we see some elements of a strong Native American counter-frame that are somewhat similar to those of the African American counter-frame. We observe an insistent critique of the white theft of Native American lands and destruction of Native American societies, a forceful countering of white stereotyping, a positive assertion of the humanity of Native Americans, and a strong accent on the importance of Native American traditions accenting freedom, justice, and respect for all human beings—doubtless the earliest liberty-and-justice framing in the Americas. Included in this too is a strong critique of Western materialism and lack of spirituality.

Asian Americans and Counter-Framing

At this stage in U.S. development, Native Americans and African Americans seem to be the groups of color that have managed, by means of collective memory and much effort now over fifteen generations of contacts with white Americans, to develop particularly strong counter-frames to the white racial frame. Research on other Americans of color, including Asian Americans and Latino Americans, suggests that most subgroups within these broad umbrella groups have at this point in time relatively less developed anti-racist counter-frames. They do, however, have strong home-culture frames that often contain elements of passive resistance, and some in these groups have begun to move toward well-developed, more aggressive counter-frames. One reason for the relative slowness of this development may be because today the majorities of people in most Asian American and Latino groups are immigrants and their children—that is, first or second generation Americans.

In one recent research study, interviews with forty-three middle class Asian Americans found that most did not have a well-developed anti-racist counter-frame. These Asian Americans often reported trying as individuals to gain control of their lives by constructing views of Asian Americans counter to dominant white stereotypes, but most had not engaged in, or benefited from, substantial collective efforts to develop an anti-racist counter-frame. Like African Americans and other Americans of color, these respondents indicated that being critical of white racism brought harsh criticism and rejection from white teachers, coworkers, or supervisors, as well as some family members and friends. As a result, many opted to conform more or less openly to significant elements of the white racial frame and to white folkways, and thus to stay invisible and under the white racial "radar" as much as they can. Many of these Asian American interviewees have come to view their values and needs as of necessity being close to those of whites. In this research only a modest number of the respondents had so far moved beyond individual grappling with everyday discrimination to actively engage in substantial collective efforts against anti-Asian oppression.[60]

Among the larger Asian American groups, the Japanese American group appears to have the most people with a substantial anti-racist counter-framing of U.S. society, perhaps because of their longer decades of residence as families in the United States and their World War II experience with discriminatory imprisonment in U.S. concentration camps discussed in Chapter 5. Japanese Americans have created the oldest Asian American civil rights organizations, organizations with significant anti-racist counter-framing. Moreover, during the 1960s–1970s era a small "yellow power" movement developed alongside the black power movement, mainly in West Coast cities. Asian American students constructed the term "Asian Americans" to counter racist terms like "Orientals," and they protested the lack of Asian American history courses on college campuses and for an end to anti-Asian discrimination in society. Since that era, the increase in pan-Asian organizations has helped to create a shared Asian American umbrella consciousness among college students and other Asian Americans seeking to combat the white racial framing of Asians and associated anti-Asian discrimination.[61]

In addition, numerous Asian American groups with relatively weak anti-racist counter-frames have a traditional home-culture frame on which to draw for often more subtle types of everyday resistance. For example, in several cities where there are large Asian American communities one finds organizational activity directed at asserting Asian cultural perspectives. In Houston, local Vietnamese and Chinese American organizations have been successful in putting up street signs in their home languages beneath English signs, and thereby asserting the significance of their home languages. There is also action accenting elements of this home-culture frame in building construction. In Asian American communities in Los Angeles and Houston, one finds new buildings built in a traditional Chinese or other Asian design. Alternative Asian cultural framing often provides options for positively accenting one's cultural background and a symbolic countering of white dominance in urban space even where there is less developed anti-racist framing. Moreover, in numerous cities some Asian American groups have created organizations with a partial counter-frame, such as organizations supporting Asian American political candidates supportive of the political and economic interests of Asian American communities— with varying degrees of electoral success.[62]

We should note, however, that drawing on the home-culture frame can create certain problems for Asian Americans and other Americans of color—between the first (immigrant) and later generations, with other groups of color, and with the white-dominated society. Sociologist Rosalind Chou has discussed how emphasizing aspects of the home-culture frame in countering messages from the white frame often creates tensions in Asian

American families, with the younger generations often trying hard to move away from their home-culture and substantially assimilate to much of the white racial framing. Accenting the home-culture especially has drawbacks in an anti-immigrant era like the present: "Major complaints and mythologies of immigrants in this anti-immigrant era are that they 'refuse to learn the language' and are not truly 'American.' Immigrants like Latinos and Asians have yet to be fully embraced as 'real Americans,' and their traditions, customs, and values can be targeted." In addition, a too-heavy accent on important home-culture elements may "prevent the formation of multiethnic and multiracial alliances."[63]

Latino Americans and Counter-Framing

Compared to the black and Native American counter-frames, which are nearly four centuries old and have widely accepted collective ideas critical of European Americans and racial oppression, the current Latino anti-racist counter-frame is more variable in shape, and the strong version of the counter-frame seems not so widely accepted. Some elements critical of white-run institutions are common to all versions of the Latino counter-frame, but like others this counter-frame runs across a continuum in emphasis and use. At one end there is a well-developed view deeply critical of U.S. racism that is similar to that of the African American counter-frame. Among Chicano activists, such as veteran political activist José Angel Gutiérrez and small groups of other Chicano activists, there is much critical analysis of a white-racist society and of anti-Latino racism, as well as open resistance to imposed white pressures for one-way assimilation to the dominant culture. This anti-racist counter-framing is conscious and overtly political. At the other end of the counter-frame continuum, as with other groups of color, there are some middle class and upper class Latinos who have adapted aggressively to white norms and folkways and accepted rather uncritically important aspects of the omnipresent white racial frame. The counter-framing of these Latinos appears to be relatively weak or nonexistent.[64]

Like some other Americans of color, many Latinos have accented an "ethnic persona" strategy in trying to avoid being viewed by whites as black or near-black, and thus being recipients of societal penalties that go with the bottom rungs of the U.S. racial hierarchy. Some Mexican Americans and other Latinos have intentionally suppressed the view of themselves as part of a racial group subordinated by whites and accented instead a white-Hispanic or Hispanic "ethnicity" in order to deal with whites and, they hope, to integrate more fully into white-run institutions. Even recent Latin American immigrants quickly learn that being identified as "not white" has seriously negative effects in U.S. society, and as a result many have tried to evade a racial classification by trying to accent their cultural and other similarities to whites. Indeed, some have joined the U.S. military to demonstrate their patriotism and "Americanness."[65]

Still, in most Latino communities some significant lessons about dealing with whites are taught. These range in degree of overtness and thoroughness depending on family traditions and parental choices. In discussing these issues with me, one savvy Latino professional has described well how this more subtle process worked in his early years:

> I do not remember explicit advice being given as "advice," but, yes, lots of stories shared across generations (my grandfather to me, for example) with implicit advice or ideas on how to deal with whites. My father would tell stories of working a mule almost to death when his white boss criticized him for working too slowly. My uncle told stories of throwing a water drinking tin cup into the air when whites did not want Mexicans to drink out of the same water barrel at a baseball game, stories of friends who did not back down from whites, like my father's friend who shot and killed a deputy sheriff in a gun fight years after the deputy had pistol-whipped him after handcuffing him for public intoxication. The implicit advice in all of these many, many stories is you should not back down from whites because we have to defend our dignity and if you back down the whites will do even worse things to you.[66]

The *implicit* advice in these narratives is framed as not backing down in confrontations with whites if possible, although there is no explicit counter-framing of whites as racial oppressors and little explicit language for dealing with that oppression, compared to the more explicit and direct dealing with such matters in the strong Chicano or African American counter-frames.

Nonetheless, traditional home-culture frames accenting family values and the Spanish language, among other features, are strong among Latino groups such as Mexican Americans, in part because many are first or second generation Americans with relatively close ties to home countries. Many make use of elements of a home-culture frame, frequently choosing certain traditional Latino cultural values and preferences over those pressed on them by the dominant U.S. culture. These values and preferences include those having to do with recurring choices in regard to language, food, music, and religion. In a recent study of Latino professionals by Maria Chávez, one lawyer pointedly underscored the importance of Latino home-culture:

I think that I've given it my best good effort trying to deal with all these white groups and I gave up! ... It's just uncomfortable and I don't like it. ... I play it because it's business. I have business things I gotta do and I can eat cheese and crackers like anybody else, a little wine. But I miss that Budweiser with carnitas. And I just want to go in do my thing and get the hell out of there ... I'm tired of that bullshit game where I have to be a white guy. Why don't they become Mexicans?[67]

This Mexican American lawyer makes clear that he has withdrawn a bit from the discomforts of the white-controlled business subculture, and in his moderate resistance strategies he makes use of elements of his home culture. His insights into the perils of conforming to whiteness in the business subculture are indeed moving in the direction of an aggressive counter-frame.

Given the high concentrations of Latinos in certain towns and cities, such as in large areas of San Antonio, Los Angeles, New York City, and Miami, many can often avoid much of the surrounding white culture and frequently accent in their lives traditional elements of a home-culture framing of community and society. This reality, which one sees in numerous Mexican American, Puerto Rican, and Cuban American communities, as well as those of smaller Latino groups, underscores a major weakness in much popular and scholarly conceptualization of immigration. Discussions of Latin American and other immigration often ignore the traditional home-culture framing that immigrants and their children regularly operate from. Latino immigrants may be incorporated to a significant degree in the white-run economic sphere, and even accept some white racist framing of U.S. racial groups, including some for their own group, yet often actively resist incorporation on certain home-culture dimensions—such as in regard to traditional family views, language, music, food, or religion. As we have seen for all groups of color, certain elements of home-cultures can provide an important basis for everyday life, including struggles against white cultural dominance. The home-culture frame also provides a base for some to periodically mount a more aggressive anti-racist counter-framing against white oppression.[68]

Internalizing the White Racial Frame

When it comes to racial matters faced in everyday life, Americans of color are usually multiframers. Much research suggests that they typically have elements of the white racial frame competing in their minds with traditional elements of the home-culture frame and/or with elements of an anti-racist counter-frame. Especially in the cases of African Americans and Native Americans this mental struggle between frames is often intense because members of both groups pick up aspects of the constantly imposed white racial frame while at the same time most hold to some elements of the anti-oppression frames that have been part of their communities for generations.

Maintaining the anti-racist counter-frame is difficult because of constant bombardment with the white racial frame in most major institutional settings. The white-controlled media play a central role in making the dominant racial framing widespread and apparently "normal." The subtle or overt goal of many whites with influence in the media, schools, and other white-controlled institutions is to reduce the resistance to persisting racial inequalities and discrimination by Americans of color, especially by getting them to internalize important elements of the dominant white racial framing. The insidious and persisting power of this dominant frame can be seen in its contemporary impact on those who are generally its main targets. For example, one research study using the Implicit Association Test, with its white and black photos, found that just over half of African Americans who took the tests rejected the implicit negative reaction to the black photos, but just under half (48 percent) did actually reveal a significant, implicit, pro-white or anti-black bias.[69]

Because they too are constantly bombarded with the white-framed negative images of themselves, Americans of color are also influenced by them, although variably. They too are under heavy pressure from whites to adopt the dominant white framing of racial matters, and when they do act to some degree out of that white frame, they help to reinforce this country's systemic racism and its continuing racialized advantages for whites.

For example, when an Asian or Latino American uses common racist epithets for African Americans, he or she is usually operating out of the age-old white racial frame. Similarly, when an African or Asian American uses common anti-Latino epithets and imaging, he or she is also usually operating out of the white racial frame. One can think of numerous other examples, across many groups. Given the omnipresence of the white racial frame, Americans of color frequently stereotype or characterize yet other Americans of color using the racialized language, stereotyping, imaging, or emotions of that white frame. Moreover, once one thinks out of that dominant white frame, even if a person of color, one may also discriminate against other people of color motivated by what has been taken from that frame. In this sense, then, the dominant frame pressures or inclines all people in whose heads it is imbedded to view and treat the frame's racialized others negatively. Only when there are substantial anti-racist counter-pressures, generally speaking, will there be strong tendencies to resist many of the racialized constructions and impulses that stem from the dominant racist frame. That white frame thus plays a significant role in alienating people in various racial groups from one another.

In addition, the pressures to conform to the white frame and white folkways are intense, and the rewards of conformity can be tempting. All too often, Americans of color are bought off with, as some critics have put it, "scraps from the master's table." Although full white symbolic, political, and socioeconomic capital is inaccessible to people of color, those who adapt vigorously to white framing, norms, and demands may be allowed by whites certain "scraps" of social, economic, or political capital, sometimes including controlled access to white networks. Some middle and upper class Americans of color, thus, may have enough socioeconomic resources to isolate themselves from some white discrimination and may be more likely to accept or assert aspects of the white frame, with counter-framing being less important for them. Those who internalize certain elements of the white racial frame well, and often operate openly out of it, are frequently rewarded by whites, sometimes dramatically so, as appears to be the case for key government figures like Clarence Thomas and Condoleezza Rice. In each historical era, some leaders from racially oppressed groups have been bought off by whites seeking to weaken their leadership and organization in communities of color. Such co-opted leaders, including academics of color, thus become important to the maintenance of this country's white-racist system.[70]

Conclusion

In recent decades, the counter-framing tradition of African Americans and other Americans of color, which accents institutional and ideological racism, has stimulated work on a renewed systemic and structural racism perspective in the social sciences, as well as new critical work on racial issues in legal scholarship. Since the mid-1970s, with a few exceptions such as Bob Blauner and this author, critical legal scholars ("critical race theorists") have often been ahead of social scientists in developing important aspects of this new structural paradigm.[71] Legal scholars of color such as Derrick Bell, Richard Delgado, and Patricia Williams, among others, have developed important and critical race analyses that accent the importance of racist ideology, white-supremacist legal institutions, and racialized power.[72]

We have noted previously the influential work of Derrick Bell, a founder of critical race theory, in regard to such ideas as "interest convergence," an idea that helps to explain how significant racial change occurs when it is in the interest of white America. Influenced by the black counter-framing tradition, Bell also argued that a major function of contemporary discrimination by whites is to protect "property rights in whiteness"—that is, "to facilitate the exploitation of black labor, to deny us access to benefits and opportunities that otherwise would be available, and to blame all the manifestations of exclusion-bred despair on the asserted inferiority of the victims."[73] Bell also argued for an older counter-framed view that he termed "racial realism"—that is, that "black people will never gain full equality in this country. Even those herculean efforts we hail as successful will produce no more than temporary 'peaks of progress,' short-lived victories that slide into irrelevance as racial patterns adapt in ways that maintain white dominance."[74]

As in the black counter-framing tradition, both critical race theorists in the legal field and structural and systemic racism analysts in social science have accented the importance of voicing the experiences and perspectives of Americans of color, critically analyzing racist U.S. institutions, and focusing on social justice solutions for institutional racism no matter what the difficulties may be.

CHAPTER 9

Toward a Truly Multiracial Democracy

Thinking and Acting Outside the White Frame

One great barrier to racial change in this country is the pervasive and deep-seated character of the white racial frame, with its extensive rationalizing elements and emotion-laden legitimation of white privilege and continuing discrimination. It is certainly possible for whites not to act out of that dominant frame, as many periodically do. Yet, most whites, at least much of the time, live their daily lives unreflectively out of some version of that white racial frame. Important elements of that frame control much societal interaction and communication, even for otherwise savvy whites, because these elements are omnipresent and considered "normal." Most whites do not even realize they routinely operate from some version of this dominant frame. Because of it, most have never committed to the comprehensive racial desegregation of major institutions, to aggressive enforcement of antidiscrimination laws, or to reparations to Americans of color for past and present racial oppression.

At a few points in history, many whites have accepted some significant change, but this has typically come under pressure from protest movements and with some white leaders moving to reduce racial discrimination because of the protests. Historically, periods of dismantling aspects of the racist system have lasted a decade or two, and then been followed by significant backtracking, retrenchment, and/or the slowing down of new racial change. This was true after the brief Reconstruction period following the Civil War in the nineteenth century, as well as for the contemporary period since the 1960s civil rights movements.

Today, we still live in a hierarchical society in racial, class, and gender terms, one where white men continue to make the lion's share of major decisions about our economic development, laws, and important public policies. As a nation, we have never come close to being a real democracy where a majority of ordinary Americans have many representatives like themselves in Congress and have substantial and regular input into most major public policy issues. The Constitution was made by fifty-five white men representing the upper 2 percent or so of the population in economic terms. Since that founding era powerful whites, mostly men, have ruled and run this country, for the most part in terms of their group interests and from an assertive version of the white racial frame. From the founding era to the present, most whites have had trouble giving up the racially framed notion that whites are distinctively "good" people and part of a superior European-origin civilization. One major problem with the dominant white frame is its arrogance about the superiority of U.S. institutions compared to those of other countries. This traditional arrogance has often led to oppressive results in the United States and overseas.

Americans of color had no role in making the Constitution or early amendments, nor have they had a significant role in most major judicial rulings since the Constitution's making. It is centuries past time for this to be changed. In this supposed democracy a mostly white, male, and well-off elite should not have the power to regularly tell the rest of the citizenry what to do, or what all major laws should be. In regard to many racial issues and other societal issues the viewpoints of Americans of color should be of at least equal importance to those of the white politicians, judges, media commentators, or public. When Americans of color are contacted in opinion surveys, they often make it clear they do not agree with the views of white elites and other whites on society's discriminatory structure and patterns today or, furthermore, on numerous other societal issues such as weak enforcement of civil rights laws.[1]

Our dominant social, economic, and political institutions do not imbed anything close to the rhetorical ideal of "liberty and justice for all." Indeed, the major carriers of a vital liberty-and-justice frame today are dispropor-tionately African Americans and other Americans of color, a frame often seen in their protests against discrimination. In view of the historical and contemporary evidence, it is time to rebuild our political and economic system so that it is a true democracy that lives up to rhetoric about liberty and justice. Revolutionary changes come but rarely in societies, and this country is long overdue for major changes in its deep foundation of racism.

Pressures and Possibilities for Societal Change

What can bring a significant change in the dominant racial hierarchy and its legitimating frame? Public intellectuals like Thomas Kuhn and Stephen Jay Gould have written about how changes come in society and, more generally, in life on the planet. Both noted that revolutionary shifts frequently come in starts and spurts, not all at once. In discussing paradigm shifts in science, Kuhn accented the important innovative role of new or younger thinkers less committed to prior scientific paradigms and who develop breakthrough ideas suggesting new ways of looking at the world. For Gould, life's evolution has involved long periods of stability punctuated by dramatic bursts of change. Small changes accumulate to force larger ones. Choice points emerge where the system can move in two or more important directions. Gould's "punctuated equilibrium" theory of change accents a deep structure, long periods of equilibrium, and periodic revolutionary bursts. In the U.S. case, racial oppression has a deep structure, long equilibrium periods, and occasional bursts of substantial change. Today, those concerned about significantly eradicating large-scale oppression in U.S. society need to press hard for new societal choice points and, then, to be prepared to act when those choice points come.[2]

In the United States, important societal choice points have begun to suggest themselves. Demographic data indicate the United States is becoming ever more diverse. Whites are less than half the populations of Hawaii, New Mexico, California, and Texas. They are a minority in half the 100 largest metropolitan areas. Over the next few decades they will become the statistical minority in all the most populous states, as well as in all major metropolitan areas. No later than 2050, demographers estimate, Americans of color will be more than half the population. Already, in the 2008 election the first American of color was elected president substantially because he got the overwhelming majority of votes of voters of color. A substantial majority of white voters, in contrast, voted for his white opponent. One significant question these demographic changes raise is how most whites— especially those in the powerful elites—will deal with this continuing increase in racial and ethnic diversity in the future United States.[3]

Many whites, leaders and ordinary citizens, frame these demographic changes as threatening. Numerous prominent white analysts like Patrick Buchanan, former Republican presidential candidate and media commentator, and Samuel Huntington, influential Harvard professor, have written and spoken from a white frame that accents the declining white percentage in the population as very negative for whites and the future of "Western civilization." In public comments they have revealed the old white frame in a fiercely stated version, as well as substantial ignorance about the actual social realities of this changing society.[4]

Evaluating Oppression: International Perspectives

Numerous issues examined in this book raise the general question of what standard to use in evaluating the highly unjust system of racial oppression and inequality in the United States. As we have noted, the white founders, and most whites since, have periodically accented a rhetorical liberty-and-justice frame. In breaking with the British, the U.S. founders often made use of liberty-and-justice language borrowed from philosophers like John Locke, yet it was a limited or rhetorical framing, one applied mainly to white men with property.[5] Since that time, however, many U.S. groups have pressed to get this idea of liberty and justice expanded to include them as individuals or groups.

As often expressed, the idea of "liberty and justice for all" seems vague, yet aspects of it are easy to articulate and are accepted across much of the globe. In the U.S. case most people seek the freedom to be themselves, speak freely, and have healthy environments for themselves and their families without oppressive barriers. This framing of their lives is generally in line with perspectives on civil rights in the U.S. Bill of Rights and the Universal Declaration of Human Rights of the United Nations. Article 1 of that Universal Declaration, an international human rights standard, updates the U.S. Declaration of Independence with the statement that "all human beings are born free and equal in dignity and rights." The Universal Declaration's Article 7 states that "all are equal before the law and are entitled without any discrimination to equal protection of the law." The Declaration continues in Article 25 with an assertion that human rights encompass more than political rights: "Everyone has the right to a standard of living adequate for the health and well-being of himself and his family, including food, clothing, housing." This international liberty-and-justice framing goes beyond the U.S. Constitution and its limited vision of civil rights to a broader view of full human economic, social, and political rights.[6]

Other United Nations conventions have been signed by the U.S. government and add to this larger human rights context, from which we can judge the oppressiveness of systemic racism in the United States. For example, the UN International Convention on the Elimination of All Forms of Racial Discrimination requires that all governments make illegal the dissemination of ideas of racial superiority and organizations that promote racial discrimination. The U.S. government came slowly to ratify this international convention, in 1994, although numerous nations had ratified long before. By signing, the U.S. government agreed to adopt "all necessary measures for speedily eliminating racial discrimination in all its forms and manifestations."[7] Yet, top U.S. officials have not undertaken to live up to this international obligation to speedily rid the United States of all "forms and manifestations" of racial discrimination.

One reason for this lack of action is how a majority of white Americans view ideals of justice and equality. These concepts have been important since the seventeenth century, yet a rhetorical framing and assertion of them have long helped whites to conceal for themselves the freedom-denying reality of this country's systemic racism and other oppressions. Today, as in the past, most whites assert ideals of liberty and justice, but a majority do not wish them to be aggressively applied in their own actions or by government—especially to the extensive racial discrimination and inequalities faced by Americans of color. Thus, white Americans and Americans of color frequently disagree over how well the country has done in regard to the liberty and justice ideals. For example, one national poll found that most whites surveyed thought that the U.S. was living up to the liberty-and-justice frame of the Pledge of Allegiance, while more than half the black respondents felt the country was not.[8]

At a time when the federal government and local governments are mostly not enforcing civil rights laws as aggressively as they should, and are not enacting numerous human rights provisions of United Nations treaties and conventions signed by the U.S. government, many innovators, activists, and ordinary citizens in other countries are accenting a renewed moral language of cosmopolitanism—the view that all human beings are citizens of one global moral community, have many human rights, and must be treated with dignity and fairness. This global perspective on human rights is certainly not new for people of the United States, for we hear it in the words of numerous civil rights leaders in the 1960s and since. For instance, near the end of his life in 1965, Malcolm X positioned the 1960s struggles as about *human rights* and viewed them in an international context:

> It is incorrect to classify the revolt of the Negro as simply a radical conflict of black against white or as a purely American problem. Rather, we are today seeing a global rebellion of the oppressed against the oppressor, the exploited against the exploiter.

A broad framing of human rights rejects the primacy of particular nation-states and accents instead the global citizenship of all. Numerous world crises, such as human-induced climate changes, are substantially matters of international human rights and needs. In many areas of the globe there is a renewed language of cosmopolitanism, ethical globalization, and global democracy. This cosmopolitan emphasis builds on the broad rights perspectives expressed in the Universal Declaration and other United Nations documents—which in turn drew not only on the best in European human rights traditions but also from human rights traditions and counter-frames of Native, African, Latino, and Asian Americans, as well as of other people of color across the globe.[9]

Unmistakably, continuing racial hostility, discrimination, and inequality directed against people of color destroy the possibility of authentic democracy for this society. To create the reality of real democracy with this broad array of human rights will ultimately require a substantial destruction of the persisting system of oppression, including its racial hierarchy and rationalizing racial frame.

Deframing and Reframing: Countering the White Racial Frame

The centuries-old white racial frame is a gestalt, a composite of elements and subframes fused into a whole. Countering it in white adults and children is difficult because it is so fundamental to the social, material, and ideological construction of U.S. society. This white frame severely limits what most white people believe, feel, say, and do in regard to racial matters. Indeed, most whites, privileged by definition, have great difficulty in relating to people who are the recurring victims of societal injustice. The dominant frame seems to be substantially responsible for this severe lack of empathy and cross-racial understandings. In U.S. society we generally do not teach people to be routinely critical thinkers, but encourage them to mostly follow the lead of economic, political, and media leaders on racial matters. This lack of critical thinking helps to perpetuate elements of the white racial frame.

Over decades of teaching experience with thousands of college students, I have found that, until most whites have accurate instruction in the history and contemporary reality of racial oppression, they reject many important understandings needed to be supportive of and sympathetic to major changes in racial oppression. It typically takes many hours of instruction and dialogue over months to get white youth or adults to begin to think critically about the array of racially stereotyped images, beliefs, emotions, and interpretations of the dominant racial frame, as well as about the racial hierarchy it legitimates and structures. Substantially changing that centuries-old framing will require much effort and innovation, and new educational strategies. Today, as in the past, very few Americans have had even a brief Stereotyping 101 or Racism 101 course at any point in their educations.

Deframing and reframing education in regard to racism should be an essential part of our regular educational efforts. *Deframing* involves consciously taking apart and critically analyzing elements of the white racial frame, while *reframing* means accepting or creating a new frame to replace that white frame. Whites, and many others, need to be made aware of the reality of the white frame imbedded deeply in their minds, and they should be taught the importance of deframing it, and then reframing away from that dominant frame to an authentic liberty-and-justice framing of society.[10]

In this regard, one important step is for whites and others to understand well the black anti-racist counter-frame. Recall central aspects of that counter-frame: a strong analysis and critique of white oppression; an aggressive countering of anti-black framing; and a positive assertion of the humanity of all people and their right to real freedom and justice. Each dimension challenges aspects of the white frame: its blatant, subtle, and covert support of racial oppression; its anti-black (and anti-other) racial mythologies; and its hypocritical support for "liberty and justice." Educators and others desiring to break down the white racial frame might start such an effort with workshops dealing centrally with important aspects of the black anti-racist frame, perhaps with some focus on important black thinkers and activists over the centuries. If done well, assertively teaching the experience-based understandings of anti-racist counter-frames can challenge the dominant white frame and have a destabilizing effect on the dominance of that frame in the minds of many. Such workshops are only a first step, and concerned educators and activists can build on them and develop more educational efforts, in an array of societal settings, that include assessing racist issues facing other Americans of color and digging ever deeper into aspects of systemic racism.

As we saw in research reviewed earlier, the dominant frame is so strongly imbedded in most white minds that people tend to reject new facts that contradict or challenge important elements of it. Entrenched frames tend to trump new facts unless the latter information is presented very well *and* as part of a clear and repeated counter-framing such as an authentic liberty-and-justice frame. Nonetheless, a savvy presentation of accurate facts about racism matters is necessary if whites and others are to change their traditional whitewashed perspective. When pressing for an anti-racist counter-frame, we should assess what are the important facts to communicate to people about U.S. racial matters and present them so they are relevant to and contradictory of the dominant racist framing. Research suggests that even modest steps in this direction can have an impact. In lab settings, just getting white subjects with a strong racist frame to observe members of the racially targeted groups in unstereotyped settings has been shown to weaken some implicit and explicit racial biases. As one review of the laboratory literature has put it, viewing a "black face with a church as a background, instead of a dilapidated street corner, considering familiar examples of admired blacks such as actor Denzel Washington and athlete Michael Jordan, and reading about Arab-Muslims' positive contributions to society all weaken people's implicit racial and ethnic biases."[11] Even modest changes in the presentation of relevant information can offer racially prejudiced people images countering their racist framing, and sometimes have modest positive effects on that framing.

In addition, some research suggests that an effective way to get people to change their framing of important issues is to induce them to seriously review information about a distinctively different view. In one study researchers conducted two similar experiments, one on social issues and another about personality impressions. Subjects were persuaded to reflect on a viewpoint opposite to their own in two different ways: "through explicit instructions to do so and through stimulus materials that made opposite possibilities more salient."[12] In both experiments getting the subjects to use a consider-the-opposite-view strategy had a more substantial impact on their thinking than just verbal instructions to be unbiased in reviewing the issue. Getting people to review countering information seriously was effective in getting them to alter judgments about important issues. The implications of this for getting whites (and others) to reframe away from the dominant racial frame may be to get them to think seriously, even for a short time, out of a meaningful and sincere version of the liberty-and-justice frame like that often expressed by major civil rights organizations.

Other Important Educational Strategies

Recent research on children shows that even modest educational efforts can bring a significant payoff in reframing. Providing new facts set in a more accurate interpretive framing of U.S. history can have an impact on the way that children think about racial matters. One southwestern project explored the impact of teaching white and black children about the racial discrimination faced by black historical figures. Researchers studied two groups of white and black children (both 6–11 years old) who had six twenty-minute daily history lessons providing biographical information on important white and black Americans, all taught by the same white teacher. Each group of students was divided between those who got black biographies with some reference to the racial discrimination faced by the person under consideration and those who got the same biographies without references to the discrimination. Before and after the biography lessons the researchers gave all children an evaluative scale designed to measure positive and negative views of black and white Americans. The white children who had the brief racial discrimination lessons had significantly more positive attitudes and less negative attitudes about black Americans than the white control group that had not gotten such lessons. They also indicated a stronger preference for racial fairness and, among those over age 7, indicated more racial guilt.[13]

The history presentations to the black children had less effect. Both the youngest black children (6–7) who were taught the black biographies with discrimination information and those who were taught the lessons without that information developed more positive (or less negative) views of black Americans. Children aged 8–9 became less negative toward black Americans, while the black children aged 10–11 did not change their views, probably because they were already familiar with some of these achievements. The researchers found, as with the white children, that those who had the lessons about discrimination reported a greater valuing of racial fairness than those in the control group. The black children's views of whites became more positive on some issues and more negative on other issues as a result of the biographical lessons about white and black historical figures, probably because the teacher accented positive and negative contributions of whites historically.[14] This study reveals that historical lessons about discrimination can have positive effects on the racial attitudes of white children. In addition, the same lessons can have positive effects on younger black children's views of their own group. That changes came with brief history lessons suggests how important even modest-length courses in Stereotyping 101 or Racism 101 might be for all Americans.

In their journal article these researchers note that they debriefed the children after the study: they offered explanations of their purpose and told children about contemporary white and black international figures who were "working to counter the effects of racism. Thus, all children were informed that, although some European Americans have discriminated against African Americans, other European Americans have fought against racial discrimination."[15] As in much other research on U.S. racial matters, the central centuries-old role of whites in creating and maintaining racial oppression was not explained, as "bad" whites are balanced with "good" whites who fought discrimination. While it is important to stress for children the reality of a few whites fighting aggressively against racism, this balancing effort plays down the fact that a substantial majority of whites have long perpetrated or colluded in continuing racial oppression. Historical and contemporary research reveals that relatively few whites have dissented strongly and publicly with racial oppression. In my view, anti-racist educational strategies should be candid about the past and present realities of white racial oppression, as well as the ability for people of all racial backgrounds to oppose oppression by challenging the dominant racial frame.[16]

There are yet other educational strategies for getting whites, both students and older adults, to analyze critically their imbedded racial framing. One is to have them keep diaries of racial conversations and events they engage in or encounter every day. Having them later discuss such diaries can bring racial hostility and discrimination into open and critical discussion, such as in educational settings. In one study noted previously, we had 626 white students at numerous colleges and universities keep journals of racial events for several weeks. In addition to recording about 7500 blatantly racist episodes and events, some students reported that this diary exercise had made them more conscious of the ways they and friends or relatives regularly engaged in racist language, discussions, and actions. In one journal entry, one white student concluded thus about her discussions with another journal writer:

> As we talked, we began discussing the contents of our journals and we both came to the conclusion that neither of us ever realized how many racial comments we hear everyday. Talking with my friend gave me a new perspective on just how much I am surrounded by racial issues and comments, and it made me realize how often I simply ignore or don't even notice certain comments that should bother me.

A white male student came to even stronger conclusions about the actions he needs to take in the future:

> I would like to express what I have gained out of this assignment. I watched my friends and companions with open eyes. I was seeing things that I didn't realize were actually there. By having a reason to pick out of the racial comments and actions I was made aware of what is really out there. Although I noticed that I wasn't partaking in any of the racist actions or comments, I did notice that I wasn't stopping them either. I am now in a position to where I can take a stand and try to intervene in many of the situations.[17]

Using such diary exercises can lead to consciousness raising about white participation in or resistance to everyday racism. This consciousness raising usually means bringing into the open half-conscious or unconscious racist beliefs, images, and emotions and raising them to the level of full consciousness for a thorough critical assessment.

Challenging Emotions: Listening to Americans of Color

One dilemma faced by those teaching deframing and anti-racist reframing is that the traditional white racial frame is usually deeply imbedded in an array of emotions that often trump overt reasoning and rational decision-making. When it comes to racial matters, most whites act on the basis of emotion-laden beliefs more than they do on careful reasoning and empirical facts. Educators and activists attempting to change whites' racial framing in fundamental ways run into problems because they view these whites as open to being convinced solely by overt and rational arguments. In such cases one strategy is to press people to examine critically their emotion-laden beliefs and other framing of racial matters. We cannot change the emotional dimension of being human, but we can make good use of certain *positive* emotions that run counter to negative emotions of the dominant racial frame. We can, for example, accent beliefs that link well to a liberty-

and-justice frame, such as the religion-generated belief of "love your neighbor as yourself," which is easily associated with the idea of fairness.

In doing anti-racist education we can make effective use of emotional connections between individuals—for instance, by relating well the personal stories of those who have suffered from oppression and fought it. Research shows that the best human communication often makes use of personal stories. Political candidates who tell strong personal stories about their lives in ways voters can relate to usually do better than those who do not.[18] We have previously noted the effectiveness of personal stories in the experiment that involved teaching biographies to white and black children. Biographies create personal connections. Effective transmission of anti-racist ideas can involve telling true stories about people dealing with racial hostility and discrimination.

One important aspect of systemic racism is that most whites, including major decisionmakers in the private and public sectors, have never listened seriously and regularly to the experienced and pained voices and racism-shaped narratives of Americans of color. Creating situations where whites can encounter these narratives is very important, for equal-status interracial interaction often forces some reframing. Social scientists Tiffany Hogan and Julie Netzer examined whether white women could relate to and understand the experiences of black women with racial discrimination. Conducting in-depth interviews with white women, they found that being female did not necessarily increase understanding of anti-black discrimination, although it sometimes did. However, those white women who were socially stigmatized in additional ways (for example, as lesbians) were better able than other white women to empathize with some accounts of discrimination faced by black women. These researchers suggested that white women can draw on their own experiences and understandings to relate to discrimination faced by black Americans in these ways: (1) by borrowed approximations, that is, by relying on the accounts that black friends or acquaintances give to make sense of discriminatory black experiences; (2) by global approximations, that is, by relying on general values of fairness to relate to accounts of anti-black discrimination; and (3) by overlapping approximations, that is, by relying on aspects of their own gendered oppression to make sense of black experiences with discrimination.[19]

The way in which borrowed approximations worked was illustrated in an interview with a white woman who had learned about anti-black discrimination from significant interpersonal experience with a black woman with whom she worked:

> I always thought that Sally was totally accepted at work, . . . and on the
> surface you don't see any problems. Everyone is friendly, everyone is

nice. And Sally is just about the nicest person you would ever hope to find. . . . I went to her hairdresser with her and I was the only white woman in the shop, and she was talking with her girlfriend about work and alluding to the fact that she just really had a lot of barriers there, and that some of the things that people said to her, not intentionally but the way that they said it, were really racist. . . . It did surprise me. . . . Here's a nice person [Sally] who is at work, and I figured that most of the other people, I thought that they would just feel like I do. When I look at her, I see her as a person, . . . and I just think of her as one of my coworkers and a friend, not as a black person. And I just assumed that everybody else felt the same way. I couldn't imagine that some of the people that she was working with, that I consider to be very nice people, too, would think of her first as black.

This woman, although still in need of much more reframing, was able to understand a bit better anti-black discrimination through borrowing understandings that come from the recounted experiences and counter-framing of a fellow employee.

Some empathy was essential in this white woman's gaining understanding across the color line. One of the harsh realities of racial oppression, in the past and present, lies in the many ways that oppression destroys empathy across racial lines. Recall from Chapter 6 this journal entry from an black student at a western college:

This is one of those sad and angry nights for me. Tonight marks the third time since the beginning of the school year that I've been called a nigger by a bunch of white students on a . . . weekend. . . . Sometimes it seems that if I am around all white people, then I become nothing more than a token Black "exhibit" for their amusement.[20]

Here we observe whites engaging in racist name-calling and other racialized practices with no thought for their impact on the black man. This recurring breakdown of whites' empathy, what might be termed social alexithymia, is commonplace in the many such accounts of mistreatment by whites that we got from several hundred students of color who kept brief journals for us at numerous colleges and universities. Recall too the national opinion survey noted in Chapter 1, in which only 5 percent of whites said that they often have both sympathy and admiration for black Americans. Clearly, thus, most whites need to learn to listen carefully, frequently, and well to the experienced voices of people of color such as this student.

In doing anti-racism education and bringing significant changes in systemic racism we need to understand better, and to activate more routinely, the deep-lying human propensity to interpersonal empathy, especially for white Americans. Without such empathetic understanding, human beings would never have survived over many millennia. A major difficulty lies in breaking down the major barriers that systemic racism regularly presents to generating cross-racial empathy.

Groups Engaging in Active Dissent

In everyday situations we need many more Americans, especially whites, to disrupt and counter millions of racist communications and other racist actions that daily take place. A barrier to racial change is the reluctance of most people, including those who know change is morally necessary, to take significant anti-racist action. Zygmunt Bauman has made this insightful comment about the Holocaust inflicted by German officials on Europe's Jews: "Evil can do its dirty work, hoping that most people most of the time will refrain from doing rash, reckless things—and resisting evil is rash and reckless."[21] Today, in the U.S. there are many whites who know the racist framing and hierarchy need to be systematically replaced, yet remain passive and do not object to even the more overt racist performances and other racist actions by whites around them.

Societal evils like the European Holocaust need not have happened if a significant number had acted to stop it. While most people put self-preservation above moral duty, this was not inevitable:

> Evil is not all powerful. It can be resisted. The testimony of the few who did resist shatters the authority of the logic of self-preservation. It shows it for what it is in the end—a choice. One wonders how many people must defy that logic for evil to be incapacitated. Is there a magic threshold of defiance beyond which the technology of evil grinds to a halt?[22]

Bauman raises a practical question about the number who need to dissent to bring change. During the 1960s civil rights movement only a small percentage of Americans participated in any civil rights protest, yet enough did to bring important changes. In the case of today's continuing racism, thus, we need to encourage many more people to defy the logic of self-preservation and disrupt racist performances that reinforce the white racist frame. With individual and collective efforts, we can reach this threshold of everyday defiance and begin the process of bringing down the system of racial oppression.

Today, numerous anti-racist groups across the U.S. have taken up the cause of informing, challenging, and bringing change to communities in regard to white privilege and racism. Let us briefly consider two important examples. In Duluth, Minnesota, dedicated activists organized what they called the *Un-Fair Campaign*. The main goal of this anti-racist campaign, as expressed in a mission statement, has been "to raise awareness about white privilege in our community, provide resources for understanding and action, and facilitate dialogue and partnership that result in fundamental, systemic change towards racial justice." The diverse group of activists have sought a local "community free of individual, systemic and institutionalized racism." As of mid-2012, they had secured important support for these anti-racist efforts from fifteen area organizations, including the City of Duluth, the NAACP, local colleges, and religious groups. The *Campaign* has sought to increase awareness of and to counter white privilege and racism in the Duluth area, which is about 90 percent white, by various tactical means. These activists have made good use of a website (www.unfaircampaign.org), Facebook, billboards and posters (with tag-lines "It's Hard to See Racism When You're White" and "Fair Skin is Not *Fair* Skin"), special community events, and the local media. They have crafted educational programs about white privilege and racism in schools and other community settings. The aggressive campaign and its candid messages have helped to reshape local public discourse about racism, generating both strong local support and hostile reactions. Undeterred, campaign activists have persisted in their important anti-racism efforts.[23]

Another important group effort by diverse activists in the Midwest examines the many ways the white racial frame shapes an array of social settings, including liberal white settings where openly racist thought is rejected. Based in Saint Paul, Minnesota, since 2004, this Antiracism Study Dialogue Circles Metamorphosis (ASDIC) program has used innovative dialogue and study groups to generate local change. ASDIC works on several areas of pedagogy and practice—such as empowering local voices to speak out on white racism and its history, increasing resistance practices aimed toward a just and democratic society, and exploring how the white frame regularly creates "raced" persons. Activists and others have worked to increase the emotional and spiritual dispositions necessary to confront white racism, to counter-frame the "origin" stories underlying white racism, and to provide resources and relationships necessary to create personal anti-racist efforts and healthy anti-racist communities.[24]

The ASDIC program provides a model for existing and future groups in other cities and regions. They have provided quality racial-equity curriculum materials for use by local groups, effective education and tools for people to deal with personal and institutional racism in everyday life, and much networking and other social capital among change agents working against white racism within and across midwestern communities. Over its relatively short life, the organization has facilitated about 90 workshops and dialogue circles, with a total of about 1500 participants. These important workshops and circles have included a diversity of community participants—teachers, students, nonprofit and government staff, and members of religious organizations. ASDIC has also worked with other midwestern organizations in hosting an annual Overcoming Racism Conference, with presentations and workshops designed to support local and regional anti-racism trainers and organizations.[25]

In their efforts anti-racism groups like ASDIC have underscored how widespread the contemporary white racial frame actually is. It significantly influences an array of people. For instance, while liberal and progressive whites are usually sincere about their commitments to racial justice, activists of color who work with them often describe problems these whites can create in trying to jointly build and maintain anti-racist movements. One white anti-racist researcher recently assessed this issue thus:

> Understanding institutional racism exacts very few psychic and emotional costs for a white progressive —because the blame can be placed on institutions, on other people, and this usually doesn't trigger typical white defensive reactions.... There is no personal emotional cost for most progressive whites in acknowledging these kinds of structural privileges. Deeply self-reflecting on one's personal investment, one's personal privilege, is something quite different. White anti-racists may assume their goodness, especially so because they are anti-racists.... The cost of imagining they personally act out their whiteness in any way, particularly in relationships with people of color, is much greater, much more difficult work, much more likely to trigger defenses. It's much more likely to make them "feel bad," and therefore, much less likely to happen. So this is what is likely to contaminate their relationships with people of color—their unexamined personal investment in whiteness.[26]

Many liberal whites assume that being liberal on racial matters means that they are well-meaning and unproblematic in interracial interactions. However, the traditional white framing of white virtue can contaminate interactions with people of color in collective efforts. Often a very difficult task for whites involved in anti-racist organizations is to be reflectively critical of their own white-framed racial views and emotions, and to listen, instead of trying to dominate, in anti-racist coalitions.

Multiracial coalitions are indeed part of the solution for future racial change in the United States. For decades numerous Americans of color have argued for more coalitions of people of color, as well as coalitions including whites truly committed to social justice. Black scholar and activist Angela Davis has accented this:

> I think in black communities today we need to encourage a lot more cross racial organizing. . . . I think it is important to recognize that there is a connection between the predicament of poor black people and the predicament of immigrants who come to this country in search of a better life. . . . I think we have to . . . seek to create coalitional strategies that go beyond racial lines. We need to bring black communities, Chicano communities, Puerto Rican communities, Asian American communities together.[27]

Individual Dissenting: Some Examples

Individual action is also necessary. Individual whites and white-oriented others, thus, need to go beyond deframing and replace major elements of the white frame with significant elements of the liberty-and-justice frame—and to act aggressively out of this latter frame. As part of anti-racist educational strategies, we can teach whites and others how to counter racist ideas and performances in backstage and frontstage settings of their daily lives. Consider these examples of how one might dissent. For instance, concerned whites and others can counter racist joking and similar racist performances by using barbed humor (e.g., "Did you learn that racist joke from the Klan?"), by feigning an ignorance that highlights the racist problem (e.g., "Can you please explain that racial comment?"), and by reframing racist conversations and other racist performances in terms of the important ideas of fair play, moral responsibility, justice, and inclusiveness associated with an active liberty-and-justice frame. Such active reframing thus imbeds not only new verbal-cognitive understandings but also important positive emotions.[28]

In regard to such counter-framing, consider this example of a racist event. At a campaign rally for his reelection, then Senator George Allen (R-Virginia) called out across the crowd to an Asian Indian man (S. R. Sidarth) whom he pointed out as a person working for his political opponent, Jim Webb. Senator Allen said this to Sidarth: "This fellow here, over here with the yellow shirt, macaca, or whatever his name is. He's with my opponent. He's following us around everywhere. . . . Let's give a welcome to macaca, here. Welcome to America and the real world of Virginia." Allen knew the young man's name, yet called him the derogatory "macaca," a racist epithet sometimes used for people of color.[29]

Reviewing this, Drew Westen, a neuroscientist and consultant, has made suggestions about how someone might have responded (Jim Webb did not respond) to this racist incident with a clear reframing of the event:

> I share with all Virginians a deep disgust for what we witnessed in our state today. Whatever your feelings about race, I do not think there's a decent, God-fearing Virginian who believes that publicly ridiculing a young man for the color of his skin is anything short of morally repugnant. . . . In ridiculing Mr. Sidarth today, and "welcoming him to America," Mr. Allen wasn't just attacking a fellow child of God, or a fellow American. He was attacking a fellow Virginian. In this country, and in this state, we don't care where your ancestors come from. If you're born in Fairfax, Virginia, where this young man was born, you're just as much of an American as Senator Allen, and you don't need him to welcome you here.[30]

Westen then suggests that the assertive reframing might have continued with an accent on Allen's previous racist actions, such as his opposing the creation of the Martin Luther King, Jr., holiday in Virginia.

Drawing on Westen's analysis and my research, I see three important ideas for how to dissent in social situations where whites take action that stems from racial stereotypes, images, or emotions of the conventional white racial frame. Responding to racist performances can usefully involve these strategies. (1) Remind whites in your audience of their better values, such as in this case their sense of fairness in the treatment of a young person of a different racial background. (2) If the audience is religious, accent the best moral ideas from their religious tradition (such as "Love thy neighbor as thyself"). (3) Emphasize that the attacked "they" in such racist performances is actually a "we"—that is, try to foster identification by audience members with those being racialized and attacked.[31] One can add to this a recognition that people who regularly engage in dissenting actions against racist performances will often pay some price in lost friends or other severed relationships. For that reason, a fourth major piece of advice for anti-racist dissenters should be to encourage them to join support groups of dissenters of all backgrounds who engage in disruptive interventions of white-racist performances.

Restoration and Reparations for Centuries of Trauma

Beyond reframing toward a more meaningful liberty-and-justice framing of this society, there is a great need for significant remedial and reparative action to restore groups unjustly oppressed for centuries to their rightful place in a just society. This involves providing them with socioeconomic and other resources they and their ancestors have rightfully earned but have lost over centuries of oppression. The critical Christian theologian Jennifer Harvey has argued that, if the creation and development of the United States is evaluated from the viewpoint of international human rights laws, the U.S. is today an illegitimate and immoral nation.[32] White crimes against humanity—such as the genocide inflicted on indigenous peoples and the enslavement and legal segregation inflicted on African Americans—have no statute of limitations. In her view there is much need, and still time, to deal responsibly and thoroughly with this great racialized immorality.

One deeply moral response is to provide extensive economic and other social reparations to compensate for centuries of extensive oppression. For centuries, to the present, white leaders and analysts, including numerous physical and social scientists, have seriously ignored or downplayed the longterm human costs of this systemic racism—and the substantial restoration and reparations needed to address those considerable costs. For example, recent human trauma studies have generated discussions of the ways individual and group traumas in U.S. history, such as the oppression faced by black Americans, are culturally constructed and altered in individual and collective memories over time. Reviewing black memories of slavery and Jim Crow, for example, some scholars have argued that these memories are mediated through the media and involve for black Americans a "meaning struggle" over the painful historical memories.[33] However, one major problem with this type of human trauma analysis is the emphasis on constructed memories of traumatic events among targeted black individuals and their descendants, rather than on the white group that created the horrific traumas and on how these damaging traumas persist not just because of ongoing meaning struggles but mainly because of the continuing structures of white discrimination and other oppression.

The discerning analyst of African colonialism, Frantz Fanon, underscored how Western medicine, including psychoanalysis, had cleverly shifted the concept of trauma from the material wounds and losses of Africans and others exploited by Europeans to an array of the exploited's psychological difficulties. Recently, Rebecca Saunders and Kamran Aghaie have argued that the psychological emphasis in much contemporary analysis of human trauma neglects these very issues of societal responsibility and redress:

> Concomitantly—and consequentially—the meaning of recovery increasingly shifted from a material notion of reparation, indemnification, or restitution to an immaterial conception of cure or restoration. Indeed, it is worth considering how slippage between these meanings of recovery may perform considerable ideological work—in

the context, for example, of truth commissions, tort law, or national memorializations. Have truth commissions [such as in South Africa] emphasized psychological healing over material indemnification?[34]

Their argument is that there is much need for both psychological assistance and material reparations and restoration in response to the severely traumatic and long-lasting character of societal oppression in the U.S. and elsewhere.

Undoubtedly, insightful psychological intervention is one important strategy for dealing with some traumatic impacts of the dominant racial frame and systemic discrimination. Americans of color often do absorb some of the white racist frame's negative racial stereotypes and images of people like themselves. Those internalized views—such as racial notions that their group is lacking in ability, effort, or intelligence—can have harmful effects on how they view themselves.

Children are especially vulnerable. When influential white adults, such as schoolteachers, subtly or overtly call up negative stereotypes of children's racial groups, that action can have significant effects on the performance of children of color under their authority. Today, there are practical solutions for this recurring discrimination by teachers in classrooms. For instance, such stereotype-threat actions by teachers need to be caught by other teachers and principals and stopped, and the teachers need to be educated about the damage done by conventional racial framing. Redress and support for children harmed by white teachers, and by whites generally, is also necessary. Researchers have found that teachers providing even modest positive enhancements for students of color can significantly improve school performance. One study undertook randomized experiments to see if researchers could lessen the psychological threat for students of color by having them accent in their minds a stronger sense of their personal abilities. They had black students do a brief in-class writing assignment asking them about their own positive values and how they applied those values to themselves. This modest exercise significantly improved grades achieved on subsequent tests by the students. Such exercises suggest that the achievement gap that often exists between white students and students of color could be significantly lessened with "timely and targeted" instructional innovations that enhance the self-esteem of students of color.[35]

Beyond such targeted innovations, we must aggressively and constantly educate white (and other) teachers about the white racial frame that they hold in their heads. There are numerous white narratives relevant to education that are still part of this contemporary frame—such as the racist narrative that asserts that many children of color are constitutionally, biologically, or culturally lacking in intellectual ability. In addition, conventional white framing does not contain important and progressive narratives about children of color. In contrast, there is a progressive narrative in the counter-frames of black Americans and other Americans of color about how students of color are eager to learn but have been barred by whites from moving up the mobility ladder by means of an array of racial barriers—a narrative that is known to but ignored by numerous white educators. Clearly, in regard to education, one redressive action should be to make this positive framing of students of color central and required for white teachers—and to press the latter to critically assess their racist framing and reframe their views in terms of an active fairness and justice perspective.

Material Reparations: Required by a Serious Liberty-and-Justice Frame

Psychological and instructional interventions are only a modest step forward and are far from sufficient to deal with past and present impacts of racial oppression inflicted on African Americans and other Americans of color. More substantial macro-level changes in the dominant racial hierarchy and its rationalizing frame require extensive material restorations and reparations. The voices and views of Americans of color, including those leading anti-racism struggles, frequently have made this crucial point about large-scale structural change. Consider this savvy commentary by Dr. Martin Luther King, Jr.:

> Justice for black people will not flow into society merely from court decisions nor from fountains of political oratory. Nor will a few token changes quell all the tempestuous yearnings of millions of disadvantaged black people. White America must recognize that *justice for black people cannot be achieved without radical changes in the structure of our society.*[36]

Most U.S. civil rights leaders have regularly linked social justice goals to major changes in the structures of contemporary racism. For example, César Chávez, the Latino founder of the United Farm Workers union, spoke frequently of social justice being the strength and goal of the farmworkers' rights movement, and indeed as being constantly on the side of those who struggle against societal oppressions.[37]

Without a doubt, anti-racism groups need to focus heavily on structural and material changes as part of their social justice goals, in addition to educational efforts previously discussed. Without significant changes in the power and resources hierarchy, in the socioeconomic privileges of those who are white and those who are not, the societal reality of oppression can change, at best, only modestly. The system of racial oppression has involved the great material power and racial framing power of whites exercised over groups of color for several centuries. White "superiority" has always been more than symbolic, for it has meant having political and economic power to restrict and reduce sharply the socioeconomic resources and life chances of many Americans of color.

Huge inequalities in wealth between white Americans and black Americans or other Americans of color continue to be documented in the media and numerous research studies by scholars. Numerous other racial inequalities, such as those of income and education, are regularly documented by the media and researchers. For example, in 2008 Institute for Policy Studies researcher Dedrick Muhammad summarized glaring U.S. racial inequalities in a report, *Forty Years Later: The Unrealized American Dream*. He showed then that the income gap between black and white Americans was closing extraordinarily slowly, for at the rate of change then black Americans would only gain income equality with white Americans in about 537 years. At the rate of change then, the wealth gap between black and white Americans would take 634 years to close. After his analysis, from 2009 to 2010, the income gap actually increased a little. In addition, the wealth gap has increased significantly over recent years.[38]

Symbolic and legal changes in racial patterns are important, but not nearly enough. Pressing just for interracial "colorblindness," as many people do, is very inadequate for a society that still has a strong racial hierarchy and huge racial inequalities. Preaching colorblindness and tolerance may be helpful in efforts at certain types of modest change, but pursued as the central goal it tends to operate as a deflecting tactic taking the emphasis off the very substantial efforts necessary to bring major changes in the still highly inegalitarian U.S. racial order.

The 1960s civil rights laws are thought by a majority of whites to have "solved the problem of race." In popular and mainstream social science analyses, discriminatory acts are often viewed as effectively countered by these laws. However, civil rights laws and especially their enforcement patterns have been greatly shaped by our white-framed and institutionally racist legal system. As noted previously, these laws were passed only when key members of the white elite saw them as being in their interest. Civil rights laws did help to improve the U.S. image globally. They brought an end to official segregation and opened up some new opportunities for Americans of color, yet today these laws have only a modest impact on persisting patterns of racial discrimination and other oppression in many sectors of society. These laws have mostly been enforced, and then often weakly, by white officials in government agencies and courts. These agencies and courts are mostly governed by white-generated laws and understandings that accent an individualistic approach to prejudice and discrimination.

Conventional white interpretations of prejudice and discrimination in recent decades have ignored the important institutional and societal context that maintain the deep structural reality of racial oppression. This societal structure still regularly generates and shapes millions of individual acts of discrimination rising out of the white frame. Yet, few of these white actions against Americans of color are significantly redressed by private or government remedies. Research on progress in civil rights, including the impact of civil rights laws, shows that, even when enforced well, government policies against discrimination do not represent significant compensation for past or present racial discrimination.[39]

Given the long history of economic theft from African Americans and other Americans of color by white Americans, and the trillions of dollars in costs that Americans of color have suffered over centuries, the idea of major reparations is not "radical," but necessarily flows from a moral doctrine of redressing longstanding conditions of unjust enrichment and unjust impoverishment. Indeed, if the U.S. government can find more than two trillion dollars to bail out private Wall Street financial and related institutions, as it did in 2008–2009, then it likely can find the substantial amounts of money needed to meet this country's moral obligations to oppressed Americans of color on whose ancestors' bodies, literally, this country was built. Well-planned and well-distributed reparations and other restoration efforts appear to be a much better government option than the limited remedial programs of the past, such as "affirmative action," which has involved mostly modest programs originally created by elite whites responding to the 1960s civil rights protests. Concrete economic reparations can be more easily seen, by all parties, as actual compensation for the great damages suffered at the hands of whites over centuries—and thus not as a "handout." In addition, whites and others need to be educated to understand this connection between major government reparative compensation and the huge historical damages of racial oppression. This too is essential if a program of reparations is ever to become an effective government policy.[40]

Especially necessary are restoration and reparations programs for the groups that have suffered at white hands for the longest period, Native Americans and African Americans. One important result of such steps for black Americans would be to begin the process of accenting the black counter-frame over the white racist frame, and greater black control over black lives. At a conference on reparations in Nigeria, the prominent Nigerian poet Dr. Chinweizu Ibekwe argued that

> More important than any monies to be received; more fundamental than any lands to be recovered, is the opportunity the reparations campaign offers us for the rehabilitation of Black people, by Black

people, for Black people; opportunities for the rehabilitation of our minds, our material condition, our collective reputation, our cultures, our memories, our self respect, our religions, our political traditions and our family institutions; but first and foremost for the rehabilitation of our minds.[41]

Broad Societal Benefits from Racial Change

What does U.S. society as a whole have to gain from a large-scale program ending racial oppression and generating reparations and restoration for Americans of color? Robert Browne has suggested that reparations for African Americans in the form of economic capital transfers would not involve a "loss of resources to the economy, but rather a redistribution away from heretofore favored classes."[42] Such transfers will likely boost the economy, and there will probably be a society-wide energy gain as African Americans come out from under the oppressiveness of racism and gain much new energy for seeking broader societal goals. At the same time, whites could abandon their unhealthy racial obsession with African Americans and their racist orientations to other people of color. Racist framing may not be a sign of severe mental illness, but it is *mentally unhealthy* to conform strongly to the contemporary white racist framing of society.[43] In addition, whites could abandon continuing patterns of racial discrimination and put much new energy into societal goals necessary for real equality and social justice.

A century ago, scholar-activist W. E. B. Du Bois made strong arguments for the societal benefits of ending racism and building real democracy. In his view, when a society's dominant group oppresses many other people, as it does in systemic racism, it suppresses vast stores of human wisdom. Oppressing a great many people has meant excluding much knowledge, understanding, and creativity from use in society generally. Ending racial oppression involves the kind of moral thinking and action that is in the long run good for a society's general health, and thus for all Americans. By fully bringing in the perspectives and understandings of formerly oppressed and excluded Americans the U.S. government and larger society can better meet the challenges of a likely difficult national and global future.[44]

Consider the benefits that have flowed to all Americans from the 1950s–1960s civil rights movements. Without these struggles against societal oppression, white Americans themselves would likely have fewer civil rights today. Undoubtedly, the civil rights movements liberated southern and border states, in fact the whole country, from the extreme political and social straitjackets of official segregation. Southern and border states developed fully modern economic and political systems only after the 1950s–1960s civil rights movements. Before those movements, and the important civil rights laws and presidential executive orders they helped to generate, not one major white-owned firm in the South had chosen to desegregate its skilled workforce. All major white employers there had acted irrationally from an economic viewpoint and accepted the economic costs of a worker recruitment pool severely limited and stratified by rigid segregation. The 1964 Civil Rights Act, banning workplace discrimination and allowing the federal government to cut off contracts to discriminating employers, brought major changes to southern and border state workplaces. Major manufacturing company executives finally employed significant numbers of black workers in formerly all-white jobs only as a result of the new civil rights laws, presidential executive orders, and federal court decisions. Moreover, research interviews with white and black southerners have shown that most feel that legal segregation would have continued for a long time without the civil rights movements and new civil rights laws. If there had been no civil rights movements against Jim Crow segregation, subsequently (perhaps to the present day) the United States would have been significantly less democratic.[45]

Clearly, too, there is a major moral gain from restoration and reparations programs for the United States, since for the first time in its history this country would make a real commitment to implementing a meaningful version of the rhetorical liberty-and-justice frame. Today, as in the past, the system of racial oppression requires that most whites contradict their commonly expressed moral precepts of liberty and justice by living lives that maintain actively, or collude in, discrimination against other racial groups. By regularly engaging in racial hostility and discrimination, and/or watching friends and relatives do so, a great many whites rob themselves of a strong claim to the morality they often assert.

White Isolation and the Price We All Pay

Yet another benefit from large-scale racial change is that it will move many whites out of social isolation and put them more directly in touch with more of this country's important social realities. For all their ability or education, most elite whites and most rank-and-file whites do not realize how socially isolated they really are. Living in substantially segregated neighborhoods, a majority of whites do not see or understand the reality of the country's great racial segregation, or the consequences of that for them and the society's future. Indeed, social science research has shown that most whites have no really deep and sustained equal-status relationships with Americans of color.[46]

Indeed, many Americans of color report that countless whites they encounter seem uncomfortable or disoriented when interacting with them.

One social science researcher, who is a man of color, noted to me that at his college he sometimes encounters intelligent whites who seem comfortable talking with other whites, even white strangers, yet have much difficulty in comfortably conversing with him. "It is like they do not know how to—as if men of color are somehow different from whites, as if we spoke a different language, or as if we are 'aliens.'"[47] Such whites pay a significant social price from years of societal segregation and isolation from meaningful relationships with people of color.

There is significant research that shows that the commonplace versions of the white racial frame can significantly interfere with whites having successful interactions with people of color. One research study of fifty white college students found that interracial interactions were especially difficult for those with strong prejudices about racial outgroups. Interactions with people of other racial groups resulted in whites who were very prejudiced being more likely than other whites to perform poorly on a Stroop color/word matching task: Whites with high levels of prejudice "who engaged in an interracial interaction had impaired performance on the Stroop task—a task requiring executive control—compared with both high-prejudice participants who interacted with a White person and low-prejudice participants."[48] These data add more evidence on the price of contemporary racism for whites. While that price is not nearly as high as for Americans of color targeted by racial discrimination, there is a significant and cumulative price to be paid by racism's white maintainers. The researchers here interpret their data using an energy model, what they term a "resource model of executive function." Engaging in an exercise involving significant self-control, such as in interacting with racial others viewed negatively, can have a temporary negative impact on one's ability to do a second important task. This is a substantial price to pay for holding strongly to a conventional white racist framing. Unmistakably, there are benefits for whites in abandoning elements of that racist framing.

In several opinion surveys a substantial proportion of white respondents have claimed that they have black friends or other friends of color. In one NORC survey, 42 percent said they had a close black friend. However, when asked for first names of their good friends, only 6 percent listed a black person. Moreover, in-depth interviews with whites, from working class people to top corporate executives, indicate that most have on average very few or fleeting equal-status contacts with African Americans (e.g., work acquaintances), and actually develop their views of African Americans mostly from racial framing gained from parents, peers, and the media. As a result, their views mostly reflect the conventional white frame's views of African Americans. If most whites who claim black friends did interact in a sustained way with them, or even if they read seriously important writings on racism matters by African Americans, they might come to understand that there is much important knowledge about how society operates in African American communities and that the conventional white frame is a distorted and destructive way of viewing society.[49]

Some optimistic analysts suggest that new communication technologies, such as those establishing the Internet and its social networking sites, will eventually break down major racial barriers and increase cross-racial interaction, especially for younger Americans. However, research by Eszter Hargittai and others shows that racial characteristics shape Internet use in much the same way as they do the rest of society. A person's racial group, together with parents' education, enabled Hargittai to predict the networking websites a person uses. New communication technologies do not necessarily bring major changes in persisting patterns of socio-racial segregation.[50]

White Isolation and International Incompetence

As the demographic worlds in which U.S. whites live become less white, the stubborn inability to look beyond the white racial frame and to really "see" and relate well and justly to people of color will likely become ever more costly for whites' everyday lives and for the political-economic decisions they, and especially white leaders, make about national and international matters.

Today, most elite and rank-and-file white Americans, as well as many other Americans, share much of the white racial frame's accent on an assertive U.S. nationalism and (white) Americanism, a perspective that often results in great ignorance of other countries and peoples across the globe. This exceptionalist framing views the United States as not only the "best country," but also as not having competition for that honor. Recall the national opinion poll that found nearly two thirds of those polled thought that "overall the U.S. is better than other nations."[51] Ironically, but certainly, white American dominance and privilege have personal and societal costs, which include a substantial cutting off of oneself and one's group from much of the world's population and the rich forms of knowledge that population holds. By operating out of some version of the white racial frame, most white leaders and analysts severely limit their understanding of and access to this world's great array of intellectual and cultural riches.

One major consequence for all people of most powerful whites' social and cultural isolation and ignorance is that the latter frequently make national and international political and economic decisions that shape the lives of many millions (even billions) of people about whom they know little or nothing. This leads many elite whites and the powerful organizations they control to habitually justify many of their momentous decisions with rationales and conceptual models in which other people are reduced to abstracted and dehumanized units, models with abstracting language like "supply and demand flows," "externalities," and "collateral damage." The most serious form of environmental destruction is, quite likely, that which destroys the human environments in which human beings can be fully creative, respectfully interactive, and making use of the full array of their knowledge and talents.

Interestingly, because of the global mass media, increasing numbers of people worldwide are becoming more aware of the huge inequalities of wealth and power across countries, and some are organizing to do something about it. They are beginning to challenge the Western accounts of their own histories, as well as of world history. They are demanding more economic and political power in international organizations and arrangements. In 2008–2009 the U.S. economic system went into the most substantial decline since the 1930s Depression, with a significant impact on the world economy. This major U.S.-generated economic crash led many of the world's leaders and influential analysts to openly discuss a possible decline in U.S. international dominance and question more openly U.S. (and European) control of major world institutions, such as the World Bank, which has always been headed by an American. With large-scale and recurring U.S. economic crises in the early twenty-first century, the world's political-economic reality began shifting to a much more multipolar world where the U.S. has increasingly been challenged economically and politically by other powerful countries.[52]

Conclusion: Taking Action for Change

Many Americans who are aware of the obligation to rebuild this society and eradicate systemic racism are pessimistic about a significant reduction in that racism because it is backed by so much white power and privilege. Considering that we face today the results of centuries of well-buttressed racial discrimination and other oppression, major social change will not come easily. Still, it can yet be accomplished. The good news about human oppressions is that they are not inevitable. What is created by human action can be dismantled by assertive human action where there is the will to bring significant change. We whites especially must take the responsibility for the centuries-old system of racial hostility and discrimination and work with those long oppressed in developing speedy and innovative ways to bring it down. "We the people," with all the people involved this time, need to foster and elect the societal leadership that will effectively coordinate efforts to substantially change the system of racial oppression and bring this society under real democratic control.

Where do we begin? Unquestionably, one place to start is with aggressive and effective enforcement of U.S. civil rights laws. To this day, and in spite of common beliefs to the contrary, we have never had an aggressive and persistent enforcement of major civil rights laws in all important institutional areas, such as housing and employment, usually because of large-scale white resistance. To get this very important civil rights enforcement, and to make other necessary changes that sharply reduce or eliminate racial inequalities, we need, among other things, to replace the current, mostly white, leaders in all major institutional sectors with a much more representative and democratic group of leaders who support serious racial change, reparations, and restoration. This is especially true for much of the leadership of the Congress. It is true for the (mostly white) conservative justices on the Supreme Court who have over the last few decades severely limited the reach of civil rights laws. They have, for example, rejected the legal relevance of institutional and systemic racism and narrowed the legal definition of discrimination to mostly cover incidents in which a defendant can prove that specific individuals discriminated because of intentional racial bias.[53]

Another critical effort should be directed at changing the structures of information presentation on racial matters, so that our mainstream media and our educational system, under more concerned and representative leadership, regularly incorporate significant and accurate information or instruction on issues of racist framing and other historical and contemporary white-imposed racism. In this way we can significantly challenge the dominance of the white-racist framing of society and press for its replacement with a sincere and fully implemented liberty-and-justice frame.

To get major structural changes in contemporary patterns of racial discrimination and inequality will likely take another large-scale movement of diverse Americans like that of the 1960s civil rights movement or the 1840s–1850s antislavery movement. This will happen only if enough Americans of all backgrounds, and especially white Americans, become much more knowledgeable about the continuing destructive operation and impacts of systemic racism, including the deep white racial frame and the strong racial hierarchy, and then become very strongly committed to establishing major organizations aimed at bringing major changes in our still racially oppressive structures. Systemic racism will eventually be replaced with a more humane and socially just political-economic system, or U.S. society will not likely survive in the longterm.

Suggestions for Further Reading

Books by Joe Feagin and his colleagues:

Systemic Racism: A Theory of Oppression. New York: Routledge, 2006.
Two-Faced Racism: Whites in the Backstage and Frontstage. New York: Routledge, 2007 (with L. H. Picca).
The Myth of the Model Minority: Asian Americans Facing Racism. Boulder, CO: Paradigm Books, 2008 (with R. Chou).
How the United States Racializes Latinos: At Home and Abroad. Boulder, CO: Paradigm Books, 2009 (edited, with J. Cobas, J. Duany).
Yes We Can: White Racial Framing and the 2008 Presidential Campaign. New York: Routledge, 2010 (with A. Harvey-Wingfield).
Racist America (revised edition). New York: Routledge, 2010.
White Party, White Government: Race, Class, and U.S. Politics. New York: Routledge, 2012.

Notes

Preface

1. "President-Elect Obama: The Voters Rebuke Republicans for Economic Failure," *Wall Street Journal*, November 5, 2008, http://online.wsj.com/article/SB122586244657 800863.html (retrieved December 28, 2008).
2. Ibid.
3. Seth Stephens-Davidowitz, "The Effects of Racial Animus on a Black Presidential Candidate: Using Google Search Data to Find What Surveys Miss," unpublished research paper, Harvard University, November 2011; and Seth Stephens-Davidowitz, "How Racist Are We? Ask Google," *New York Times*, June 10, 2012, http://search.proquest.com.lib-ezproxy.tamu.edu:2048/docview/1019461946 (retrieved July 21, 2012).
4. The CNN exit poll data were posted at Slate's website, "2008 Presidential Candidates Share of White Vote by State," http://www.slate.com/id/2204464/sidebar/2204528 (retrieved December 12, 2008).
5. Bill Bishop, "No, We Didn't: America Hasn't Changed as Much as Tuesday's Results Would Indicate," November 10, 2008, http://www.slate.com/blogs/blogs/bigsort/default.aspx (retrieved December 17, 2008); see also Paul Taylor and Richard Morin. "Americans Claim to Like Diverse Communities but Do They Really?" Pew Research Center, December 2, 2008, http://pewresearch.org/pubs/1045/americans-claim-to-like-diverse-communities-but-do-they-really (retrieved December 17, 2008).
6. Louwanda Evans, "Facing Racism at 30,000 Feet: African American Pilots, Flight Attendants, and Emotional Labor," Ph.D. dissertation, Texas A&M University, College Station, Texas, 2012. Used by permission.

Chapter 1

1. The first survey is in Richard Morin, "Misperceptions Cloud Whites' View of Blacks," *Washington Post*, July 11, 2001, p. A01; for countering data, see Joe R. Feagin and Clairece B. Feagin, *Racial And Ethnic Relations* (eighth edition; Upper Saddle River, NJ: Prentice-Hall, 2008), pp. 178–189. The second survey is in Lawrence Bobo, "Inequalities

that Endure? Racial Ideology, American Politics, and the Peculiar Role of the Social Sciences," paper presented at conference on "The Changing Terrain of Race and Ethnicity," University of Illinois, Chicago, Illinois, October 26, 2001.

2. Thomas Kuhn, *The Structure of Scientific Revolutions* (third edition; Chicago: University of Chicago Press, 1996).

3. J. M. Blaut, *The Colonizer's Model of the World: Geographical Diffusionism and Eurocentric History* (New York: Guilford Press, 1993), p. 38.

4. Robert E. Park, *Race and Culture* (Glencoe, IL: Free Press, 1950); Milton M. Gordon, *Assimilation in American Life* (New York: Oxford University Press, 1964); Gunnar Myrdal, *An American Dilemma* (New York: McGraw-Hill, 1964). For discussions of mainstream scholars, see Feagin and Feagin, *Racial and Ethnic Relations*, pp. 28–42.

5. See, for example, Geoffrey R. Stone, Louis M. Seidman, Cass R. Sunstein, and Mark Tushnet, *Constitutional Law* (third edition; Boston: Little, Brown, and Co., 1996).

6. Another common approach is to consider individuals' racial characteristics ("race") as they record such on a questionnaire/interview form as a statistical "variable." See Tukufu Zuberi and Eduardo Bonilla-Silva, eds., *White Logic, White Methods* (Lanham, MD: Rowman & Littlefield, 2008).

7. J. M. Blaut, *The Colonizer's Model of the World: Geographical Diffusionism and Eurocentric History* (New York: Guilford Press, 1993), pp. 64, 102–103.

8. Edward W. Said, *Orientalism* (New York: Vintage Books, 1979).

9. See, for example, Talcott Parsons, "Full Citizenship for the Negro American? A Sociological Problem," in *The Negro American*, ed. Talcott Parsons and Kenneth B. Clark (Boston: Houghton Mifflin, 1965–1966), p. 740ff.

10. Anthony Giddens and Christopher Pierson, *Conversations with Anthony Giddens: Making Sense of Modernity* (Palo Alto, CA: Stanford University Press, 1998), p. 94.

11. See Lera Boroditsky, "How Language Shapes Thought: The Languages We Speak Affect our Perceptions of the World," *Scientific American*, February 2011, http://scientificamerican.com (retrieved July 3, 2012). I am indebted here to scholarly discussions with Glenn Bracey.

12. Henry Wiencek, *An Imperfect God: George Washington, His Slaves, and the Creation of America* (New York: Farrar, Straus and Giroux, 2003), p. 7; also see pp. 356–357.

13. Winthrop D. Jordan, *White over Black: American Attitudes Toward the Negro, 1550–1812* (Chapel Hill: University of North Carolina Press, 1968), p. 137.

14. See, for instance, Drew Westen, *The Political Brain: The Role of Emotion in Deciding the Fate of the Nation* (New York: Public Affairs, 2007), p. 238.

15. See, for example, Patricia Hill Collins, *Black Feminist Thought: Knowledge, Consciousness, and the Politics of Empowerment* (Boston: Unwin Hyman, 1990); Joe Feagin and Hernán Vera, *White Racism: The Basics* (New York: Routledge, 1995); Eduardo Bonilla-Silva, "Rethinking Racism: Toward a Structural Interpretation," *American Sociological Review* 62 (June 1997): 465–480; the numerous legal scholars in Richard Delgado and Jean Stefancic, eds., *White Studies: Looking Behind the Mirror* (Philadelphia: Temple University Press, 1997); and Joe R. Feagin, *Systemic Racism: A Theory of Oppression* (New York: Routledge, 2006).

16. See George Lakoff, *Don't Think of an Elephant: Know Your Values and Frame the Debate* (White River Junction, VT: Chelsea Green Publishing, 2004), pp. 16–25; David A. Snow, E. Burke Rochford, Steven K. Worden, and Robert D. Benford, "Frame Alignment and Mobilization," *American Sociological Review* 51 (1986): 464–481; K. Fisher, "Locating Frames in the Discursive Universe," *Sociological Research Online* 2 (1997), http://www.socresonline.org.uk/socresonline/2/3/4.ht (retrieved October 30, 2007); and Robert M. Entman and Andrew Rojecki, *The Black Image in the White Mind: Media and Race in America* (Chicago: University of Chicago Press, 2001).

17. Leslie Houts Picca and Joe R. Feagin, *Two-Faced Racism: Whites in the Backstage and Frontstage* (New York: Routledge, 2007), pp. 5–6.

18. Erving Goffman, *Frame Analysis: An Essay on the Organization of Experience* (Boston: Northeastern University Press, 1974), pp. 1–20. I am also influenced here by G. Todd Gitlin, *The Whole World is Watching* (Berkeley, CA: University of California Press, 1980), pp. 10–12.
19. I draw here on George Lakoff, *The Political Mind: Why You Can't Understand 21st-Century American Politics with an 18th-Century Brain* (New York: Viking, 2008), pp. 24–33, 240, 250.
20. See Joe R. Feagin and Eileen O'Brien, *White Men on Race: Power, Privilege and the Shaping of Cultural Consciousness* (Boston: Beacon, 2003); Feagin, *Systemic Racism*; and Joe R. Feagin and Clairece B. Feagin, *Racial And Ethnic Relations* (eighth edition; Upper Saddle River, NJ: Prentice-Hall, 2008).
21. Lakoff, *The Political Mind*, pp. 27–30, 42.
22. William James, *The Principles of Psychology* (New York: Dover, 1950 [1890]), Vol. 1, pp. 111–112, 125–126. See also Pierre Bourdieu and Loïc J. D. Wacquant, *An Invitation to Reflexive Sociology* (Chicago: University of Chicago Press, 1992), pp. 18–19, and Eduardo Bonilla-Silva, *Racism Without Racists: Color-Blind Racism and the Persistence of Racial Inequality in the United States* (New York: Rowman & Littlefield, 2006), p. 104.
23. On scripts, see William H. Sewell, Jr., "A Theory of Structure: Duality, Agency, and Transformation," *American Journal of Sociology* 98 (1992): 14–22.
24. Maurice Halbwachs, *On Collective Memory*, ed. and trans. L. Coser (Chicago, IL: University of Chicago Press, 1992), pp. 38, 52. I build here on ideas introduced in Picca and Feagin, *Two-Faced Racism*, especially Chapter 1.
25. D. J. Howard, "Familiar Phrases as Peripheral Persuasion Cues," *Journal of Experimental Social Psychology* 33 (1997): 231–243; T. L. Chartrand and J. A. Bargh, "The Chameleon Effect: The Perception-Behavior Link and Social Interaction," *Journal of Personality and Social Psychology* 76 (1999): 893–910; and Henry Plotkin, *Evolution in Mind: An Introduction to Evolutionary Psychology* (revised edition; Cambridge, MA: Harvard University Press, 2000), pp. 159, 252–253.
26. Paul Connerton, *How Societies Remember* (Cambridge: Cambridge University Press, 1989), pp. 2–3; Gary Alan Fine and Terence McDonnell, "Erasing the Brown Scare: Referential Afterlife and the Power of Memory Templates," *Social Problems* 54 (2007): 183.
27. Kristen M. Lavelle, "'Our Generation Had Nothing to Do with Discrimination': White Southern Memory of Jim Crow and Civil Rights," Ph.D. dissertation, Texas A&M University, College Station, 2011.
28. Ibid. I draw interpretive quotes from Lavelle in a May 2012 email.
29. Fareed Zakaria, *The Post-American World* (New York: W. W. Norton, 2008), p. 65. See also pp. 68–74.
30. Joe R. Feagin, Hernán Vera, and Nikitah Imani, *The Agony of Education: Black Students in White Colleges and Universities* (New York: Routledge, 1996), p. 18; see also Connerton, *How Societies Remember*.

Chapter 2

1. See Timothy Mitchell, "The Stage of Modernity," *Questions of Modernity*, ed. Timothy Mitchell (Minneapolis: University of Minnesota Press, 2000), pp. 1–34.
2. Karl Marx, *Capital*, trans. Ben Fowkes (New York: Vintage Books, 1977), Vol. I, pp. 915, 926; I am influenced here by Karl Kersplebedeb's review of Sylvia Federici, *Caliban and the Witch: Women the Body and Primitive Accumulation* (New York: Autonomedia, 2004), at http://www.kersplebedeb.com/caliban/caliban_review.html #t3 (retrieved February 1, 2008).
3. Letter from Marx to Pavel Vasilyevich Annenkov, in *Letters of Marx and Engels 1846, Marx–Engels Collected Works* (New York: International Publishers, 1975), Vol. 38, p. 95.

4. Tom Keefer, "Constructs of Capitalism: Slavery and the Development of Racism," http://newsocialist.org/old_mag/magazine/39/article03.html (retrieved December 13, 2007).

5. On racial formation, see Michael Omi and Howard Winant, *Racial Formation in the United States* (New York: Routledge, 1994); on history, see Eric Williams, *Capitalism and Slavery* (Chapel Hill: University of North Carolina Press, 1994 [1944]), pp. 106–121; and Joe R. Feagin, *Racist America: Roots, Current Realities, and Future Reparations* (New York: Routledge, 2000), Chapters 1–2.

6. J. Sakai, *Settlers: Mythology of the White Proletariat* (Chicago: Morningstar Press, 1989), pp. 8–9.

7. Edmund S. Morgan, *American Slavery, American Freedom: The Ordeal of Virginia* (New York: Norton, 1975), p. 5.

8. Walter J. Ong, *Orality and Literacy: The Technologizing of the Word* (New York: Methuen, 1988), pp. 75–77. I am indebted to discussions with Shari Valentine here.

9. Charles Mills, *The Racial Contract* (Ithaca: Cornell University Press, 1997), p. 93; on the men at the convention, see Feagin, *Racist America*, pp. 9–12.

10. Donald E. Lively, *The Constitution and Race* (New York: Praeger, 1992), pp. 4–5; see also Joe R. Feagin, *Systemic Racism: A Theory of Racial Oppression* (New York: Routledge, 2006), pp. 21–55.

11. Lawrence Goldstone, *Slavery, Profits, and the Struggle for the Constitution* (New York: Walker and Company, 2005), pp. 115–117.

12. Garry Wills, *"Negro President": Jefferson and the Slave Power* (Boston: Houghton Mifflin, 2003), pp. 5–9; and Irene Diggs, "The Biological and Cultural Impact of Blacks on the United States," *Phylon* 41 (1980): 160.

13. Robert Caro, *The Years of Lyndon Johnson: Master of the Senate* (New York: Knopf, 2002), pp. 9–11, 90–94. Madison is quoted on p. 9.

14. Richard Kluger, *Simple Justice: The History of Brown v. Board of Education and Black America's Struggle for Equality* (New York: Knopf, 1975), Vol. 1, p. 65.

15. *Dred Scott v. Sandford*, 60 U.S. 393, 408 (1856).

16. Robin Einhorn, *American Taxation, American Slavery* (Chicago: University of Chicago Press, 2006), pp. 7–8, 250.

17. Gautham Rao, "The Federal Posse Comitatus Doctrine: Slavery, Compulsion, and Statecraft in Mid-Nineteenth Century America," *Law and History Review* (Spring 2008), http:// www.press.uillinois.edu/journals/lhr/rao26_1.pdf (retrieved February 1, 2008).

18. Vincent Harding, *There is a River: The Black Struggle for Freedom in America* (New York: Harvest/HBJ Books, 1993), p. xxv. Italics added.

19. Wills, "Negro President," p. 8.

20. Diggs, "The Biological and Cultural Impact of Blacks on the United States," p. 160.

21. Harriet Beecher Stowe, *A Key to Uncle Tom's Cabin* (Boston: John P. Jewett, 1853), p. 39.

22. Ibid., p. 31; on New England, see Joanne Pope Melish, *Disowning Slavery: Gradual Emancipation and "Race" in New England* (Ithaca, NY: Cornell University Press, 1998), pp. 165–167.

23. Quoted in Kenneth O'Reilly, *Nixon's Piano: Presidents and Racial Politics from Washington to Clinton* (New York: Free Press, 1995), p. 45.

24. I draw on the summary of change ideas, especially of Michael L. Tushman and Elaine Romanelli, in Connie G. Gersick, "Revolutionary Change Theories: A Multilevel Exploration of the Punctuated Equilibrium Paradigm," *Academy of Management Review* 16 (1991): 13–19.

Chapter 3

1. Deborah L. Madsen, *American Exceptionalism* (Jackson: University Press of Mississippi, 1998), p. 1.

2. George Lakoff and Mark Turner, *More than Cool Reason* (Chicago: University of Chicago Press, 1989), pp. 210–212.
3. Arthur O. Lovejoy, *The Great Chain of Being: A Study of the History of an Idea* (Cambridge: Harvard University Press, 1973 [1936]), p. 59; see also W. Michael Byrd and Linda A. Clayton, *An American Health Dilemma* (New York: Routledge, 2000), Vol. 1, pp. 54–55.
4. I draw on a review of Robert Bucholz and Newton Key, *Early Modern England 1485–1714: A Narrative History* (Oxford: Blackwell Publishing, 2004), at http:// www.h-net. org/reviews/showrev.cgi?path=242801123091235 (retrieved December 12, 2007); on Gordon J. Schochet, *The Authoritarian Family and Political Attitudes in 17th Century England* (New Brunswick, NJ: Transaction Books, 1998), pp. xiii–xiv, 5–90; and on George Lakoff and Mark Johnson, *Philosophy in the Flesh: The Embodied Mind and Its Challenge to Western Thought* (New York: Basic Books, 1999), pp. 292–310.
5. See Helena Woodard, *African-British Writings in the Eighteenth Century* (Westport, CT: Greenwood Press, 1999), pp. xv–xviii.
6. Michael Guasco, "To 'Doe Some Good Upon Their Countrymen': The Paradox of Indian Slavery in Early Anglo-America," *Journal of Social History* 41 (Winter 2007): 253–282; and Peter Silver, *Our Savage Neighbors: How Indian War Transformed Early America* (New York: W. W. Norton, 2008), p. xxi.
7. See Winthrop D. Jordan, *White Over Black: American Attitudes Toward the Negro, 1550–1812* (Chapel Hill: University of North Carolina Press, 1968), pp. 40–43; and Richard Drinnon, *Facing West: The Metaphysics of Indian-Hating and Empire-Building* (Norman, OK: University of Oklahoma Press, 1997 [1980]), p. 51 and passim.
8. In non-English-speaking parts of Europe and in North Africa, some elements of a protoracial framing of people of African descent can be seen earlier in the writings of Ibn Khaldun (1332–1406) and Jean Bodin (1530–1596).
9. David E. Stannard, *American Holocaust: Columbus and the Conquest of the New World* (New York: Oxford University Press, 1992), p. 247.
10. Robert F. Berkhofer, Jr., *The White Man's Indian: Images of the American Indian from Columbus to the Present* (New York: Knopf, 1978), p. 4.
11. Both are quoted in Stannard, *American Holocaust*, p. 227.
12. Berkhofer, *The White Man's Indian*, p. 16.
13. All are quoted in ibid., pp. 19–22.
14. Drinnon, *Facing West*, pp. 52–53.
15. Ibid., p. 53.
16. Quoted in ibid., p. 19.
17. George Rawick, as quoted in David R. Roediger, *The Wages of Whiteness: Race and the Making of the American Working Class* (London: Verso, 1991), p. 95; see also Ronald T. Takaki, *Iron Cages: Race and Culture in 19th Century America* (New York: Oxford University Press, 1990), pp. 12–15.
18. Roy Harvey Pearce, as quoted in Drinnon, *Facing West*, p. 102.
19. Jordan, *White Over Black*, pp. 12–39.
20. Ibid., p. 80.
21. The quote and interpretation are from A. Leon Higginbotham, Jr., *Shades of Freedom: Racial Politics and the Presumptions of the American Legal Process* (New York: Oxford University Press, 1996), pp. 19–20; see also Jordan, *White Over Black*, pp. 73–74.
22. The cases are discussed in Higginbotham, *Shades of Freedom*, pp. 21–22; see also Joe R. Feagin, *Racist America: Roots, Current Realities, and Future Reparations* (New York: Routledge, 2000), pp. 39–42.
23. Quoted in Jordan, *White Over Black*, p. 110.
24. Higginbotham, *Shades of Freedom*, p. 25.
25. Ibid., pp. 30–38; see also James Walvin, *Questioning Slavery* (New York: Routledge, 1996).
26. Quoted in Jordan, *White Over Black*, p. 97.
27. Quoted in ibid., p. 275.

28. Quoted in ibid., pp. 96–97.
29. Higginbotham, *Shades of Freedom*, p. 32.
30. Roediger, *The Wages of Whiteness*, p. 21; and Manning Marable, *Black American Politics* (London: New Left Books, 1985), p. 5.
31. Quoted in A. Leon Higginbotham, Jr., *In the Matter of Color* (New York: Oxford University Press, 1978), p. 44.
32. W. E. B. Du Bois, *Darkwater* (New York: Humanity Books, 2003), p. 56; for a contemporary analyst, see Ron Eyerman, *Cultural Trauma: Slavery and the Formation of African American Identity* (Cambridge, UK: Cambridge University Press, 2001), p. 17.
33. Audrey Smedley, *Race in North America* (Boulder, CO: Westview Press, 1993), p. 38.
34. Woodard, *African-British Writings in the Eighteenth Century*, p. 28; and Bradd Shore, "Human Diversity and Human Nature," in *Being Humans: Anthropological Universality and Particularity in Transdisciplinary Perspectives*, ed. Neil Roughley (Berlin: Walter de Gruyter, 2000), p. 87. I have changed the text to modern spelling.
35. Quoted in Shore, "Human Diversity and Human Nature," p. 87. I have changed the text to modern spelling.
36. Bureau d'adresse et de rencontre, "Another Collection of Philosophical Conferences of the French Virtuosi upon Questions of All Sorts for the Improving of Natural Knowledge Made in the Assembly of the Beaux Esprits at Paris by the Most Ingenious Persons of That Nation," render'd into English by G. Havers and J. Davies (London: Printed for Thomas Dring and John Starkey, 1665), pp. 377–379), at http://eebo.chadwyck.com. ezproxy.tamu.edu:2048/search/fulltext?ACTION=ByID&ID=D00000127257250000 &SOURCE=var_spell.cfg&WARN=N&FILE=../session/1198083025_22267 (retrieved June 8, 2007).
37. Samuel Sewall, *The Selling of Joseph, A Memorial* (Boston: Bartholomew Green and John, 1700), as reprinted at http://www.pbs.org/wgbh/aia/part1/1h301t.html (retrieved May 11, 2008); see also Mason I. Lowance, Jr., ed., *A House Divided: The Antebellum Slavery Debates in America, 1776–1865* (Princeton University Press, 2003).
38. John Saffin, "A Brief, Candid Answer to a Late Printed Sheet, Entitled, 'The Selling of Joseph,'" in Lowance, *A House Divided*, at http://press.princeton.edu/chapters/ s7553. html (retrieved May 11, 2008).
39. Cotton Mather, *The Negro Christianized An Essay to Excite and Assist the Good Work, The Instruction of Negro-Servants in Christianity* (Boston: B. Green, 1706), p. 15.
40. Ibid., p. 5. See also Anthony S. Parent, Jr., *Foul Means: The Formation of a Slave Society in Virginia, 1660–1740* (Chapel Hill: University of North Carolina Press, 2003), p. 200.
41. Edward Long, *The History of Jamaica* (London, 1714), Vol. 2, pp. 65, 353, 371.
42. Higginbotham, *In the Matter of Color*, p. 309.
43. Quoted in Walvin, *Questioning Slavery*, p. 80.
44. See Ellis Cose, *Color-Blind: Seeing Beyond Race in a Race-Obsessed World* (New York: HarperCollins, 1997); on prototypes, see George Lakoff, *Women, Fire, and Dangerous Things: What Categories Reveal about the Mind* (Chicago: University of Chicago Press, 1987), pp. 8–86.
45. Smedley, *Race in North America*, p. 27.

Chapter 4

1. A. Leon Higginbotham, Jr., *Shades of Freedom: Racial Politics and the Presumptions of the American Legal Process* (New York: Oxford University Press, 1996), p. 38.
2. Winthrop D. Jordan, *White Over Black: American Attitudes Toward the Negro, 1550–1812* (Chapel Hill: University of North Carolina Press, 1968), p. 91.
3. Peter Silver, *Our Savage Neighbors: How Indian War Transformed Early America* (New York: W. W. Norton, 2008), pp. 132, 282; see also pp. xx–xxv, and appendix.
4. Gregory T. Knouff, *Soldiers' Revolution: Pennsylvanians in Arms and the Forging of Early American Identity* (University Park: Pennsylvania State University Press, 2003),

pp. 158–174, 285–286; Silver, *Our Savage Neighbors*, p. 87ff; and Edmund S. Morgan, *American Slavery, American Freedom: The Ordeal of Colonial Virginia* (New York: Norton, 1975).

5. B. L. Rayner, *Life of Thomas Jefferson* (Boston: Lilly, Wait, Colman, & Holden, 1834), http://etext.virginia.edu/jefferson/biog/lj08.htm (retrieved May 14, 2008).

6. Richard Drinnon, *Facing West: The Metaphysics of Indian-Hating and Empire-Building* (Norman: University of Oklahoma Press, 1997 [1980]), p. 98.

7. Thomas Jefferson, *Notes on the State of Virginia*, ed. Frank Shuffelton (New York: Penguin Books, 1999 [1785]), p. 147.

8. Joseph J. Ellis, *Founding Brothers: The Revolutionary Generation* (New York: Vintage Books, 2000), p. 159.

9. "The Letters of Thomas Jefferson: 1743–1826," Arts Faculty, University of Gröningen, http://www.let.rug.nl/usa/P/tj3/writings/brf/jefl224.htm (retrieved May 14, 2008).

10. Quoted in A. Leon Higginbotham, Jr., *In the Matter of Color* (New York: Oxford University Press, 1978), p. 59.

11. Ronald T. Takaki, *Iron Cages: Race and Culture in 19th Century America* (New York: Oxford University Press, 1990), p. 83.

12. Frederick Jackson Turner, *The Frontier in American History* (New York: Henry Holt and Company, 1935).

13. Drinnon, *Facing West*, pp. 355–356.

14. William H. Tucker, *The Science and Politics of Racial Research* (Urbana: University of Illinois Press, 1994), p. 8; George Mosse, *Toward the Final Solution: A History of European Racism* (London: Dent & Son, 1978), p. 20.

15. See, for example, the Wikipedia article on "Enlightenment," http://en.wikipedia.org/wiki/Age_of_Enlightenment.

16. Milton Cantor, "The Image of the Negro in Colonial Literature," *New England Quarterly* 36 (December 1963), p. 468; Bernard Romans, *A Concise History of East and West Florida* (New York, 1773), p. 105.

17. Quoted in Jordan, *White Over Black*, p. 146; see also p. 158.

18. Anthony Benezet, *Short Account of that Part of Africa Inhabited by the Negroes* (Philadelphia, 1762), p. 31.

19. Quoted in Cantor, "The Image of the Negro in Colonial Literature," pp. 453, 455.

20. Benjamin Franklin, *Observations Concerning the Increase of Mankind, Peopling of Countries, Etc.* (1751), as quoted in *Benjamin Franklin: A Biography in His Own Words*, ed. Thomas Fleming (New York: Harper and Row, 1972), pp. 105–106. I have changed this to modern capitalization. See also Claude-Anne Lopez and Eugenia W. Herbert, *The Private Franklin: The Man and His Family* (New York: Norton, 1975), pp. 194–195.

21. See Joe R. Feagin, *Systemic Racism: A Theory of Oppression* (New York: Routledge, 2006), Chapter 2.

22. F. Nwabueze Okoye, "Chattel Slavery as the Nightmare of the American Revolutionaries," *William and Mary Quarterly* 37 (January 1980): 13.

23. Quoted in "A Rhetoric of Rights: The Arguments Used in the 'American Conversation' in the Era of the Revolution," http://assumption.edu/ahc/1770s/coreargs.html (retrieved November 1, 2004).

24. Patrick Henry, "Liberty or Death Speech," www.historyplace.com/speeches/henry.htm (retrieved June 26, 2008).

25. Hume and Kant are quoted in Emmanuel C. Eze, *Race and the Enlightenment* (Cambridge, MA: Blackwell, 1997), pp. 33, 118.

26. Tucker, *The Science and Politics of Racial Research*, p. 9; Ivan Hannaford, *Race: The History of an Idea in the West* (Baltimore: Johns Hopkins University Press, 1996), pp. 205–207.

27. John C. Calhoun, "Slavery A Positive Good," http://teachingamericanhistory.org/library/index.asp?document=71 (retrieved May 5, 2007).

28. Sander L. Gilman, *Difference and Pathology: Stereotypes of Sexuality, Race, and Stereotypes* (Ithaca, NY: Cornell University Press, 1985) p. 137.

29. Alexis de Tocqueville, *Democracy in America* (New York: Random House/Vintage Books, 1945), Vol. 1, pp. 344–345. The second quote is on p. 372.
30. Frederick Douglass, "The United States Cannot Remain Half-Slave and Half-Free," in *Frederick Douglass: Selected Speeches and Writings*, eds. P. S. Foner and Y. Taylor (Chicago: Lawrence Hall Books, 1999), pp. 657–658.
31. J. Gerald Kennedy and Liliane Weissberg, eds., *Romancing the Shadow: Poe and Race* (revised edition; New York: Oxford University Press, 2001), p. 196; Elise Lemire, *"Miscegenation": Making Race in America* (Philadelphia: University of Pennsylvania Press, 2002).
32. Stetson Kennedy, *Jim Crow Guide: The Way It Was* (Boca Raton: Florida Atlantic University Press, 1990 [1959]), p. 47.
33. Martha Hodes, *White Women, Black Men: Illicit Sex in the Nineteenth-Century South* (New Haven, CT: Yale University Press, 1997), pp. 1–2; and Joel Kovel, *White Racism: A Psychohistory* (New York: Columbia University Press, 1984).
34. David R. Roediger, *The Wages of Whiteness: Race and the Making of the American Working Class* (London: Verso, 1991), pp. 106–120; and M. M. Manring, *Slave in a Box: The Strange Career of Aunt Jemima* (Charlottesville, VA: University Press of Virginia, 1998), pp. 6–8.
35. Lerone Bennett, *Forced into Glory: Abraham Lincoln's White Dream* (Chicago: Johnson Publishing Co., 1999), pp. 90–150, 610–615; and Joe R. Feagin, "Foreword," in Sharon Rush, *Huck Finn's Hidden Lessons: Teaching and Learning Across the Color Line* (Lanham, MD: Rowman & Littlefield, 2006), pp. i–viii.
36. William G. Allen, *The American Prejudice Against Color: An Authentic Narrative, Showing How Easily the Nation Got Into an Uproar* (London: W. and F. G. Cash, 1853), and passim (no pagination).
37. Harriet Beecher Stowe, *A Key to Uncle Tom's Cabin* (Boston: John P. Jewett, 1853), p. 27.
38. Martin R. Delany, *The Condition, Elevation, Emigration, and Destiny of the Colored People of the United States* (1852) (no publisher or pagination), http:// www.gutenberg. org/ebooks/17154 (retrieved May 12, 2008). Italics added.
39. Arnoldo De León, "Initial Contacts: Niggers, Redskins, and Greasers," in *The Latino/a Condition: A Critical Reader*, ed. Richard Delgado and Jean Stefancic (New York: New York University Press, 1998), p. 161.
40. John C. Calhoun, "Conquest of Mexico," http://teachingamericanhistory.org/library/ index.asp?document=478 (retrieved December 13, 2007). Italics added.
41. Quoted in Takaki, *Iron Cages*, p. 177.
42. Laura E. Gómez, *Manifest Destinies* (New York: New York University Press), pp. 10–149.
43. Ibid., p. 149.
44. I draw here on Joe R. Feagin and Clairece B. Feagin, *Racial and Ethnic Relations* (Upper Saddle River, NJ: Prentice-Hall, 2008), pp. 279–360.
45. Ibid.
46. Rudyard Kipling, "The White Man's Burden: The United States and the Philippine Islands," *McClure's Magazine* 12 (February 1899), http://www.fordham.edu/halsall/ mod/ Kipling.html (retrieved May 22, 2008).
47. Theodore W. Allen, *The Invention of the White Race* (New York: Verso, 1994), pp. 21–50, 184; David R. Roediger, *The Wages of Whiteness: Race and the Making of the American Working Class* (London: Verso, 1991), p. 127. I draw here on Joe R. Feagin, *Racist America: Roots, Current Realities, and Future Reparations* (New York: Routledge, 2000), pp. 14–74.
48. Gilman, *Difference and Pathology*, p. 138.
49. Ibid., pp. 87–90.
50. Audrey Smedley, *Race in North America* (Boulder, CO: Westview Press, 1993), p. 26.
51. Quoted in George Frederickson, *The Black Image in the White Mind* (Hanover, NH: Wesleyan University Press, 1971), p. 230.
52. See Frederick L. Hoffman, "Vital Statistics of the Negro," *Arena* 5 (April, 1892): 542, as cited in Frederickson, *The Black Image in the White Mind*, pp. 250–251; see also George

Fitzhugh, *Sociology for the South; or, the Failure of Free Society* (Richmond, 1854); and Henry Hughes, *Treatise on Sociology, Theoretical and Practical* (Negro Universities Press, 1968 [1854]).

53. Ralph Ellison, *Shadow and Act* (New York: Random House, 1964), p. 305.
54. Tucker, *The Science and Politics of Racial Research*, p. 35.
55. Carl C. Brigham, *A Study of American Intelligence* (Princeton, NJ: Princeton University Press, 1923), pp. 124–125, 177–210.
56. Lothrop Stoddard, *The Rising Tide of Color: Against White World-Supremacy* (New York: Scribner's, 1920), p. 3.
57. Tucker, *The Science and Politics of Racial Research*, p. 93. I draw generally on Theodore Cross, *Black Power Imperative: Racial Inequality and the Politics of Nonviolence* (New York: Faulkner, 1984), pp. 93, 157.
58. *Plessy v. Ferguson*, 163 U.S. 537 (1896).
59. Ibid, pp. 556, 552. Italics added.
60. *Missouri ex rel. Gaines v. Canada*, 305 U.S. 337 (1938); and *Brown et al. v. Board of 228 Education of Topeka et al.* 347 U.S. 491 (1954). See Robert A. Pratt, "*Brown v. Board of Education Revisited*," *Reviews in American History* 30 (2002): 141–144.
61. *Brown v. Board of Education*, 349 U.S. 301 (1955). Italics added.
62. Congressional Record, *84th Congress Second Session*. Vol. 102, part 4 (March 12, 1956) (Washington, DC: Governmental Printing Office, 1956), pp. 4459–4460.
63. Ibid.
64. James J. Kilpatrick, *The Southern Case for School Segregation* (New York: Crowell-Collier Press, 1962), pp. 20–21.
65. Robert Caro, *The Years of Lyndon Johnson: Master of the Senate* (New York: Random House Vintage Books, 2002), p. 778.

Chapter 5

1. See, for example, Howard Schuman, Charlotte Steeh, and Lawrence Bobo, *Racial Attitudes in America: Trends and Interpretations* (Cambridge: Harvard University Press, 1985), pp. 71–162; Dinesh D'Souza, *The End of Racism: Principles for a Multiracial Society* (New York: Free Press, 1995).
2. Andrew Scott Baron and Mahzarin R. Banaji, "The Development of Implicit Attitudes: Evidence of Race Evaluations From Ages 6 and 10 and Adulthood," *Psychological Science* 17 (2006): 52–53; John F. Dovidio, John C. Brigham, Blair T. Johnson, and Samuel L. Gaertner, "Stereotyping, Prejudice, and Discrimination: Another Look," in *Stereotypes and Stereotyping*, ed. C. Neil Macrae, Miles Hewstone, and Charles Stangor (New York: Guilford, 1995), pp. 276–319; and Sonja M. B. Givens and Jennifer L. Monahan, "Priming Mammies, Jezebels, and Other Controlling Images: An Examination of the Influence of Mediated Stereotypes on Perceptions of an African American Woman," *Media Psychology* 7 (2005): 102–103.
3. Eduardo Bonilla-Silva and Tyrone A. Forman, " 'I Am Not A Racist But . . .': Mapping White College Students' Racial Ideology in the U.S.A.," *Discourse and Society* 11 (2000): 51–86.
4. Debra Van Ausdale and Joe R. Feagin, *The First R: How Children Learn Race and Racism* (Lanham, MD: Rowman & Littlefield, 2001), p. 1.
5. See D. J. Howard, "Familiar Phrases as Peripheral Persuasion Cues," *Journal of Experimental Social Psychology* 33 (1997): 231–243; T. L. Chartrand and J. A. Bargh, "The Chameleon Effect: The Perception-Behavior Link and Social Interaction," *Journal of Personality and Social Psychology* 76 (1999): 893–910. See also Henry Plotkin, *Evolution in Mind: An Introduction to Evolutionary Psychology* (revised edition; Cambridge, MA: Harvard University Press, 2000), pp. 159, 252–253.
6. Nina Eliasoph, " 'Everyday Racism' in a Culture of Political Avoidance: Civil Society, Speech, and Taboo," *Social Problems* 46 (1999): 484. On homogeneous networks, see

Miller McPherson, Lynn Smith-Lovin, and James M. Cook, "Birds of a Feather: Homophily in Social Networks," *Annual Review of Sociology* 27 (2001): 415–444.

7. Joe R. Feagin and Hernan Vera, *White Racism: The Basics* (New York: Routledge, 1995), p. 159.

8. The quote is from a research summary by Siri Carpenter, "Buried Prejudice: The Bigot in Your Brain," *Scientific American* (May 2008), http://www.sciam.com/article. cfm?id=buried-prejudice-the-bigot-in-your-brain (retrieved June 1, 2008). See also L. S. Vygotsky, *Mind in Society: The Development of Higher Psychological Processes*, ed. M. Cole, V. John-Steiner, S. Scribner, and E. Souberman (Cambridge, MA: Harvard University Press, 1978); and Steven Shaffer, "Resurrecting the Linguistic Relativity Hypothesis," http://www.scshaffer.com/files/scsshaffer-lrh.pdf (retrieved February 6, 2006), pp. 2–17.

9. Baron and Banaji, "The Development of Implicit Attitudes," pp. 52–53.

10. Thierry Devos and Mahzarin R. Banaji, "American =White?" *Journal of Personality and Social Psychology* 88 (2005): 447–466. I am influenced here and later by George Lakoff and Mark Turner, *More than Cool Reason* (Chicago: University of Chicago Press, 1989), pp. 167, 208–210.

11. I am indebted here to discussions of these issues with Sean Chaplin.

12. Peter J. Richardson, Robert T. Boyd, and Joseph Henrich, "Cultural Evolution of Human Cooperation," in *Genetic and Cultural Evolution of Cooperation*, ed. P. Hammerstein (Cambridge: MIT Press, 2003), pp. 372–381.

13. Leslie Houts Picca and Joe R. Feagin, *Two-Faced Racism: Whites in the Backstage and Frontstage* (New York: Routledge, 2007).

14. Jacqueline Soteropoulos, "Skeptics Put Cops on Trial: The American Public isn't Giving Government or Police Officers the Blind Trust it Once Did," *Tampa Tribune*, April 17, 1995, p. A1; and Nick Mrozinske, "Derivational Thinking and Racism," unpublished research paper, University of Florida, Fall 1998.

15. On the 2008 and 2012 campaigns, see expert posts at www.racismreview.com.

16. "Tea Party Supporters: Who They Are and What They Believe," *CBS News*, April 14, 2010, http://www.cbsnews.com/8301-503544_162-20002529-503544.html (retrieved April 15, 2011); and Lydia Saad, "Tea Partiers Are Fairly Mainstream in Their Demographics," Gallup, http://www.gallup.com/poll/127181/tea-partiers-fairly-mainstream-demographics.aspx (retrieved May 5, 2011). I summarize more detailed analyses in Joe R. Feagin, *White Party, White Government: Race, Class, and U.S. Politics* (New York: Routledge, 2012).

17. Devin Burghart, Leonard Zeskind, and the Institute for Research & Education on Human Rights, *Tea Party Nationalism*, August 2010, http://www.irehr.org/issue-areas/ tea-party-nationalism (retrieved April 15, 2011); and Kate Zernike, *Boiling Mad: Inside Tea Party America* (New York: Henry Holt Times Books, 2010), passim.

18. Devin Burghart, "Tea Party Nation Warns of White Anglo-Saxon Protestant 'Extinction,'" IREHR, March 29, 2011, http://www.irehr.org/issue-areas/tea-parties/ 19-news/76-tea-party-nation-warns-of-white-anglo-saxon-protestant-extinction (retrieved April 15, 2011).

19. Eduardo Bonilla-Silva, *Racism without Racists* (second edition; Lanham, MD: Rowman & Littlefield, 2006); see also Leslie Carr, *"Color-Blind" Racism* (Thousand Oaks: Sage, 1997).

20. Leslie Houts Picca, "Is Backstage Racism a White Thing? Examining the Frontstage and Backstage for Students of Color," unpublished research paper, University of Dayton, Ohio, 2012. Used by permission.

21. Seth Stephens-Davidowitz, "The Effects of Racial Animus on a Black Presidential Candidate: Using Google Search Data to Find What Surveys Miss," unpublished research paper, Harvard University, November 2011.

22. Cheryl Harris, "Whiteness as Property," in *Critical Race Theory: The Key Writings that Formed the Movement* (New York: The New Press, 1995), p. 282.

23. Irene Diggs, "The Biological and Cultural Impact of Blacks on the United States," *Phylon* 41 (1980): 166.

24. Toni Morrison, *Playing in the Dark: Whiteness and the Literary Imagination* (New York: Vintage Books, 1992), p. 65.
25. Ralph Ellison, *Shadow and Act* (New York: Random House, 1964), p. 304.
26. Quoted in Dan T. Carter, *The Politics of Rage: George Wallace, The Origins of the New Conservatism, and the Transformation of American Politics* (second edition; Baton Rouge: Louisiana State University Press, 2000), p. 237.
27. See Charles Gallagher, "Miscounting Race: Explaining Whites' Misperceptions of Racial Group Size," *Sociological Perspectives* 46 (2003): 381–396.
28. Nilanjana Dasgupta, Debbie E. McGhee, and Anthony G. Greenwald, and Mahzarin R. Banaji, "Automatic Preference for White Americans: Eliminating the Familiarity Explanation," *Journal of Experimental Social Psychology* 36 (2000): 316–328; see also Shankar Vedantam, "Many Americans Believe They Are Not Prejudiced. Now a New Test Provides Powerful Evidence that a Majority of Us Really Are," *Washington Post Magazine*, January 23, 2005, p. W12.
29. The research is summarized in Vedantam, "Many Americans Believe They Are Not Prejudiced. Now a New Test Provides Powerful Evidence that a Majority of Us Really Are," p. W12; and Associated Press, "Racism Studies Find Rational Part of Brain Can Override Prejudice," http://www.beliefnet.com/story/156/story_15664_1.html (retrieved November 28, 2004).
30. See Ruth Frankenberg, *White Women, Race Matters* (Minneapolis: University of Minnesota Press, 1993), pp. 12–50; and Joe R. Feagin, Hernán Vera, and Pinar Batur, *White Racism: The Basics* (second edition; New York: Routledge, 2001), pp. 186–253.
31. See "Stereotypes and Prejudice: Their Automatic and Controlled Components," pp. 5–18.
32. Thomas Jefferson, *Notes on the State of Virginia*, ed. Frank Shuffelton (New York: Penguin Books, 1999 [1785]). A quick Internet search turns up many white supremacist websites.
33. "Orange County GOP official refuses to resign over racist email," Los Angeles Wave, Wire services, April 16, 2011, http://www.wavenewspapers.com/news/orange-county-racist-ape-chimp-email-gop-republican-obama-davenport-119993794.html (retrieved February 10, 2012).
34. Claudio E. Cabrera, "Judge Admits Sending Racist Email About Obama," *The Root*, March 1, 2012, http://www.theroot.com/racist-obama-emails-judge-richard-cebull (retrieved March 2, 2012).
35. J. L Eberhardt, P. A Goff, V. J Purdie, and P. G. Davies, "Seeing Black: Race, Crime, and Visual Processing," *Journal of Personality and Social Psychology* 87 (2004): 876–893.
36. Ibid.
37. "Bennett Under Fire for Remarks on Black Crime," CNN.com, September 30, 2005, 230 http://www.cnn.com/2005/POLITICS/09/30/bennett.comments/index.html (retrieved January 20, 2009).
38. See P. R. Klite, R. A. Bardwell, and J. Salzman, "Local TV News: Getting Away with Murder," *Press/Politics* 2 (1997): 102–112; Franklin D. Gilliam, Jr., and Shanto Iyengar, "Prime Suspects: The Effects of Local News on the Viewing Public," unpublished research paper, University of California (Los Angeles, n.d); Robert M. Entman, "Violence on Television: News and Reality Programming in Chicago," *Report for the Chicago Council on Urban Affairs*, May 9, 1994; Daniel Romer, Kathleen H. Jamieson, and Nicole J. de Coteau, "The Treatment of Persons of Color in Local Television News," *Communication Research* 25 (June 1998): 286–290.
39. Givens and Monahan, "Priming Mammies, Jezebels, and Other Controlling Images," pp. 87–106.
40. "Imus Called Women's Basketball Team 'Nappy-headed Hostility'," MediaMatters, April 7, 2007, http://mediamatters.org/items/200704040011 (retrieved November 7, 2008).
41. Benjamin Franklin, "Observations Concerning the Increase of Mankind, Peopling of Countries, Etc." (1751), as quoted in *Benjamin Franklin: A Biography in His Own*

Words, ed. Thomas Fleming (New York: Harper and Row, 1972), pp. 105–106. I use modern capitalization.

42. Yanick St. Jean and Joe R. Feagin, *Double Burden: Black Women and Everyday Racism* (New York: M. E. Sharpe, 1998), pp. 90–91.

43. Sophie Trawalter, Andrew R. Todd, Abigail A. Baird, and Jennifer A. Richeson, "Attending to Threat: Race-based Patterns of Selective Attention," *Journal of Experimental Social Psychology* 44 (2008): 1322–1327.

44. Sut Jhally and Justin Lewis, *Enlightened Racism* (Boulder: Westview Press, 1992), pp. 95–110.

45. W. E. B. Du Bois, *Dusk of Dawn* (New Brunswick, NJ: Transaction, 1984 [1940]), p. 6.

46. Joel Kovel, *White Racism: A Psychohistory* (New York: Columbia University Press, 1984), p. xl.

47. Ibid., pp. xli–xlvii. See also Feagin, Vera, and Batur, *White Racism*, pp. 1–33.

48. See the website www.stormfront.org.

49. Thierry Devos, Brian A. Nosek, and Mahzarin R. Banaji, "Aliens in their Own Land? Implicit and Explicit Ascriptions of National Identity to Native Americans and White Americans," research paper presented at the SPSP Groups and Intergroup Relations Pre-Conference, Memphis, Tennessee, January 2007.

50. "Bob and the Showgram," http://en.wikipedia.org/wiki/Bob_and_the_Showgram# Native_Americans (retrieved July 8, 2008). I am indebted to Kristen Lavelle for the transcript and comments.

51. For a detailed discussion see Joe Feagin and Clairece B. Feagin, *Racial and Ethnic Relations* (eighth edition; Upper Saddle River, NJ: Prentice Hall, 2008), pp. 141–164.

52. See Laurel R. Davis, "Protest Against the Use of Native American Mascots: A Challenge to Traditional American Identity," *Journal of Sport and Social Issues* 17 (April 1993): 9–22; Randi Hicks Rowe, "NCAA Decides; New Policy Prohibits Usage of Racially Abusive Names By College Teams," *American Indian Report* 21 (2005): 8–9; C. Richard King and Charles Fruehling Springwood, "Introduction," in *Team Spirits: The Native American Mascots Controversy,* ed. C. Richard King and Charles Fruehling Springwood (Lincoln: University of Nebraska Press, 2001). Several chapters in the King and Fruehling book detail various mascot controversies.

53. Robert G. Lee, *Orientals: Asian Americans in Popular Culture* (Philadelphia, PA: Temple University Press, 1999), p. 8.

54. Jacobus tenBroek, Edward N. Barnhart, and Floyd W. Matson, *Prejudice, War, and the Constitution* (Berkeley, CA: University of California Press, 1968), p. 31. In this section I am generally influenced by Rosalind S. Chou and Joe R. Feagin, *The Myth of the Model Minority: Asian Americans Facing Racism* (Boulder, CO: Paradigm Books, 2008), pp. 3–23, and by Feagin and Feagin, *Racial and Ethnic Relations*, pp. 284–318.

55. The quote is in Dennis M. Ogawa, *From Japs to Japanese* (Berkeley, CA: McCutchan, 1971), pp. 11–12. See also Carey McWilliams, *Brothers Under the Skin* (revised edition; Boston: Little, Brown, 1964), pp. 148–149; and Stanley Sue and Harry H. L. Kitano, "Stereotypes as a Measure of Success," *Journal of Social Issues* 29 (1973): 83–98.

56. "Daphne Kwok, Organization of Chinese Americans, and John O'Sullivan, *National Review*, Discuss Recent Cover Story for That Magazine That Asian Americans Are Saying is Offensive and Racist," NBC News Transcripts, March 21, 1997; Mae M. Cheng, "Magazine Cover Ripped; Coalition Calls National Review Illustration Racist," *Newsday*, April 11, 1997, p. A4.

57. Doris Lin, "The Death of (Icebox.com's) Mr. Wong," USAsians.net, http://us_asians. tripod.com/articles-mrwong.html (retrieved December 14, 2006).

58. Jennifer Fang, "Team America: Racism, Idiocy, and Two Men's Pursuit to Piss Off as Many People as Possible," Asian Media Watch, October 28, 2004, http:// www. asianmediawatch.net/teamamerica/review.html (retrieved December 17, 2006).

59. Helen Zia, *Asian American Dreams: The Emergence of an American People* (New York: Farrar, Straus, and Giroux, 2000), p. 134ff.

60. Steven A. Chin, "KFRC Deejay Draws Suspension for On-Air Derogatory Remarks," *San Francisco Examiner*, December 6, 1994, p. A2; "Current Affairs," JACL News, http://www.jacl.org/index.php (retrieved December 19, 2006); Media Action Network for Asian Americans, "Latest Headline News," http://www.manaa.org (retrieved December 18, 2006).

61. Rosina Lippi-Green, *English with an Accent* (New York: Routledge, 1997), pp. 238–239.

62. William Petersen, "Success Story, Japanese-American Style," *New York Times*, January 9, 1966, p. 21.

63. "Success Story of One Minority Group in the U.S.," *U.S. News & World Report*, December 26, 1966, pp. 73–76.

64. Long Le, "The Dark Side of the Asian American 'Model Student,' " August 2, 2006, http://news.newamericamedia.org/news (retrieved January 5, 2007); for examples of white mocking, see Picca and Feagin, *Two-Faced Racism*.

65. Quoted in Gilberto Cardenas, "United States Immigration Policy toward Mexico," *Chicano Law Review* 2 (summer 1975), pp. 70–71; see also Ralph Guzmán, "The Function of Anglo-American Racism in the Political Development of Chicanos," in *La Causa Politica*, ed. F. Chris Garcia (South Bend, IN: University of Notre Dame Press, 1974), p. 22.

66. Quoted in Otto Santa Ana, " 'Like an Animal I was Treated': Anti-Immigrant Metaphor in U.S. Public Discourse," *Discourse & Society* 10 (1994): 220.

67. Samuel P. Huntington, *Who Are We? The Challenges to America's National Identity* (New York: Simon & Schuster, 2004).

68. Santa Ana, " 'Like an Animal I was Treated'," pp. 194–220; see also Otto Santa Ana, *Brown Tide Rising: Metaphors of Latinos in Contemporary American Public Discourse* (Austin: University of Texas Press, 2002).

69. Carey McWilliams, *North from Mexico* (New York: Greenwood Press, 1968), p. 213; see also Feagin and Feagin, *Racial And Ethnic Relations*, pp. 213–220.

70. Quoted in George A. Martinez, "Mexican Americans and Whiteness," in *The Latino/a Condition: A Critical Reader*, ed. Richard Delgado and Jean Stefancic (New York: New York University Press, 1998), p. 178.

71. Linda A. Jackson, "Stereotypes, Emotions, Behavior, and Overall Attitudes Toward Hispanics by Anglos," Research Report 10, Julian Samora Research Institute, Michigan State University, January 1995, http://www.jsri.msu/RandS/research/irr/rr10.htm (retrieved June 9, 2001).

72. National Conference of Christians and Jews, *Taking America's Pulse: The National Conference Survey on Inter-Group Relations* (New York: National Conference, 1994).

73. Hilario Molina II, "Racializing the Migration Process: An Ethnographic Analysis of Undocumented Immigrants in the United States," Ph.D. dissertation, College Station, Texas, Texas A&M University, 2012.

74. Maria Chávez, *Everyday Injustice: Latino Professionals and Racism* (Lanham, MD: Rowman & Littlefield, 2011), pp. 1–2.

75. See, for example, Ann V. Millard and Jorge Chapa, *Apple Pie and Enchiladas: Latino Newcomers in the Rural Midwest* (Austin: University of Texas Press, 2004).

76. Jane H. Hill, *The Everyday Language of White Racism* (New York: Wiley-Blackwell, 2008), pp. 134–157; and Jane H. Hill, "Mock Spanish: A Site for the Indexical Reproduction of Racism in American English," unpublished research paper, University of Arizona, 1995.

77. I am indebted to scholarly discussions with Nestor Rodriguez.

78. See José Cobas and Joe R. Feagin, "Latinos/as and the White Racial Frame," *Sociological Inquiry* 78 (February 2008): 39–53.

79. Chou and Feagin, *The Myth of the Model Minority*, pp. 138–180; and Cobas and Feagin, "Latinos/as and the White Racial Frame," pp. 39–53.

80. Joan M. Herbers, "Watch Your Language! Racially Loaded Metaphors in Scientific Research," *BioScience* 57 (February 2007): 104.

81. Richard J. Herrnstein and Charles Murray, *The Bell Curve: Intelligence and Class Structure in American Life* (New York: Free Press, 1994), pp. 295–316.

82. "Nobel Winner in 'Racist' Claim Row," CNN.com, October 18, 2007, http://edition. cnn.com/2007/TECH/science/10/18/science.race/index.html?iref=mpstoryview (retrieved January 20, 2009).

83. Dorothy Roberts, *Fatal Invention* (New York: The New Press, 2011), Kindle loc. 5589-96.

84. See, for example, Jiannbin Lee Shiao, Thomas Bode, Amber Beyer, and Daniel Selvig, "The Genomic Challenge to the Social Construction of Race," *Sociological Theory* 30 (June 2012): 67–70. For a sustained critique, see Troy Duster, *Backdoor to Eugenics* (second edition; New York: Routledge, 2003).

85. Dorothy Nelkin and M. Susan Lindee, *The DNA Mystique: The Gene as a Cultural Icon* (New York: W. H. Freeman and Company, 1995), p. 129.

86. Jay S. Kaufman and Susan A. Hall, "The Slavery Hypertension Hypothesis: Dissemination and Appeal of a Modern Race Theory," *Epidemiology* 14 (2003): 116; see also 111–118. I am indebted to comments from Jessie Daniels. See Jessie Daniels and Amy J. Schultz, "Whiteness and the Construction of Health Disparities," in *Gender, Race, Class, and Health*, ed. Leith Mullings and Amy J. Schulz (San Francisco, CA: Jossey-Bass, 2006), pp. 89–127.

Chapter 6

1. Leslie Houts Picca, "Is Backstage Racism a White Thing? Examining the Frontstage and Backstage for Students of Color," unpublished research paper, University of Dayton, Dayton, Ohio, 2012. Used by permission.

2. R. H. Fazio, J. R. Jackson, B. C. Dunton, and C. J. Williams, "Variability in Automatic Activation as an Unobtrusive Measure of Racial Attitudes: A Bona Fide Pipeline?" *Journal of Personality and Social Psychology* 69 (1995): 1013–1027; and, generally, Debra Van Ausdale and Joe R. Feagin, *The First R: How Children Learn Race and Racism* (Lanham, MD: Rowman & Littlefield, 2001).

3. Laurie A. Rudman and Richard D. Ashmore, "Discrimination and the Implicit Association Test," *Group Processes and Intergroup Relations* 10 (2007): 359–372.

4. Leslie Houts Picca and Joe R. Feagin, *Two-Faced Racism: Whites in the Backstage and Frontstage* (New York: Routledge, 2007), p. 101. I have reworked my ideas here, but draw generally on our joint analysis of diaries.

5. Ibid., pp. 17–18.

6. Nina Eliasoph, " 'Everyday Racism' in a Culture of Political Avoidance: Civil Society, Speech, and Taboo," *Social Problems* 46 (1999): 479–495.

7. Picca and Feagin, *Two-Faced Racism*, p. 124.

8. C. Richard King and David J. Leonard, "The Rise of the Ghetto-Fabulous Party," *Colorlines Magazine*, October 5, 2007, http://www.diverseeducation.com/artman/ publish/article_9687.shtml (retrieved May 22, 2009).

9. Jennifer C. Mueller, Danielle Dirks, and Leslie Houts Picca, "Unmasking Racism: Halloween Costuming and Engagement of the Racial Other," *Qualitative Sociology* 30 (2007): 315–335.

10. Rosalind Chou, "Racist Frame is Still Firmly in the Minds of Educated Whites," http:// www.racismreview.com (retrieved May 22, 2009); and Jennifer C. Mueller and Joe Feagin, "Pulling Back the 'Post-Racial' Curtain: Critical Pedagogical Lessons from Both Sides of the Desk," in *Teaching Anti-Racism in Contemporary America*, ed. Kristin Haltinner, Ron Aminzade, and David Pellow (New York: Springer, forthcoming).

11. Brendesha M. Tynes and Suzanne L. Markoe, "The Role of Color-Blind Racial Attitudes in Reactions to Racial Discrimination on Social Networking Sites," *Journal of Diversity in Higher Education* 3 (2010): 1–13; and Jessie Daniels, "Race and Racism in Internet Studies: A Review and Critique," unpublished research paper, New York, Hunter College, 2012.

12. Hernán Vera and Andrew Gordon, *Screen Saviors: Hollywood Fictions of Whiteness* (Lanham, MD: Rowman & Littlefield, 2003).
13. Julio Cammarota, "Blindsided by the Avatar: White Saviors and Allies Out of Hollywood and in Education," *Review of Education, Pedagogy, and Cultural Studies* 33 (2011): 242–259. I am indebted in this section to insights on movies offered by Shari Valentine, Louwanda Evans, and Jennifer Mueller in 2012 email exchanges.
14. Jessie Daniels and N. Lalone, "Racism in Video Gaming: Connecting Extremist and Mainstream Expressions of White Supremacy," in *Race, Gender, Class in Video Gaming*, ed. David Embrick and András Lukács (Lanham, MD: Lexington Press, 2012), p. 86; see also pp. 83–97.
15. Ibid., p. 93; see also p. 89.
16. Ibid. I am indebted to discussions with Jessie Daniels.
17. I am indebted to Todd Couch for viewing information and to him and Jennifer Mueller for insights about *The Cleveland Show*. See these online sources: http://www.imdb.com/title/tt1195935/fullcredits; http://www.nytimes.com/2009/08/30/arts/television/30itzk.html?_r=4&pagewanted=2; http://www.clevelandshowepisodes.tv/cleveland-show-season-1-episode-1-pilot.html; http://www.fox.com/cleveland/full-episodes/13295197/the-men-in-me (retrieved July 23, 2012).
18. See Joe R. Feagin and Melvin P. Sikes, *Living with Racism: The Black Middle Class Experience* (Boston: Beacon, 1995); and Joe R. Feagin, *Racist America: Roots, Current Realities, and Future Reparations* (New York: Routledge, 2000).
19. Pew Research Center, "Blacks See Growing Values Gap Between Poor and Middle Class: Optimism about Black Progress Declines," November 13, 2007, http://pewsocialtrends.org/pubs/700/black-public-opinion (retrieved May 5, 2008). The survey was done with National Public Radio.
20. Thomas Jefferson, *Notes on the State of Virginia*, ed. Frank Shuffelton (New York: Penguin Books, 1999 [1785]), p. 146.
21. Leslie Houts Picca and Joe R. Feagin, "Experiences of Students of Color," University of Dayton, unpublished research, 2008.
22. Daren Briscoe and Evan Thomas, "Hate on Campus," *Newsweek*, November 28, 2005, p. 41.
23. Quoted in Roxanna Harlow, "Teaching as Emotional Labor: The Effects of Professors' Race and Gender on the Emotional Demands of the Undergraduate College Classroom," Ph.D. dissertation, Indiana University, Bloomington, Indiana, 2002.
24. Jefferson, *Notes on the State of Virginia*, p. 146.
25. James F. Bonilla, "'Are You Here to Move the Piano?' A Latino Reflects on Twenty Years in the Academy," in *Faculty of Color: Teaching in Predominantly White Colleges and Universities*, ed. Christine A. Stanley (Bolton, MA: Anker Publishing Company, 2007), p. 70.
26. See Rosalind S. Chou and Joe R. Feagin, *The Myth of the Model Minority: Asian Americans Facing Racism* (Boulder, CO: Paradigm Books, 2008); and José Cobas and Joe R. Feagin, "Latinos/as and the White Racial Frame," *Sociological Inquiry* 78 (February 2008): 39–53.
27. African American professional, email communication, May 27, 2008. Used by permission.
28. W. E. B. Du Bois, *Dusk of Dawn: An Essay Toward an Autobiography of a Race Concept* (New Brunswick, NJ: Transaction Books, 1984 [1940]), p. 131.
29. Joe R. Feagin, "Documenting the Costs of Slavery, Segregation, and Contemporary Discrimination: Are Reparations in Order for African Americans?" *Harvard BlackLetter Law Journal*, 20 (2004): 49–80.
30. I am indebted here to scholarly discussions with Nestor Rodriguez.
31. Joe R. Feagin and Eileen O'Brien, *White Men on Race* (Boston: Beacon, 2003); Wendy Moore, *Reproducing Racism* (Lanham, MD: Rowman & Littlefield, 2008).

Chapter 7

1. Gilles Fauconnier and Mark Turner, *The Way We Think* (New York: Basic Books, 2003), pp. 17–73; and Gilles Fauconnier, "Tip of Iceberg," http://www.cogsci.ucsd. edu/~faucon/151/Tip%20of%20iceberg.pdf (retrieved November 7, 2007).
2. See, for example, Tiffany Chaparro, "America Celebrates Constitution Day," http:// teacher.scholastic.com/scholasticnews/indepth/constitution_day/constitution_day/ index.asp?article=constitutionday (retrieved December 21, 2007); and Weldon Havins, "Overview of the Legal System," http://whavins.com/nnlh1.htm (retrieved December 21, 2007).
3. Derrick Bell, "Brown and the Interest-Convergence Dilemma," in *Shades of Brown: New Perspectives on School Desegregation*, ed. Derrick Bell (New York: Columbia University Press, 1980), p. 97.
4. See Herbert Aptheker, *Early Years of the Republic and the Constitution: 1783–1793* (New York: International Publishers, 1976).
5. Robert Caro, *The Years of Lyndon Johnson: Master of the Senate* (New York: Random House Vintage Books, 2002), p. 104.
6. Marjorie R. Hershey, *Party Politics in America* (New York: Longman, 2011), pp. 131–132.
7. Paul Krugman, *The Conscience of a Liberal* (New York: Norton, 2007), p. 181.
8. Paul Jenkins, "The GOP's White Supremacy," *Huffington Post*, December 28, 2008, http://www.huffingtonpost.com/paul-jenkins/the-gops-white-supremacy_b_153823. html (retrieved December 29, 2008); and James Wright, "Black Republicans Ponder Their Future," *Afro Newspapers*, November 24, 2008, http://news.newamericamedia. org/news/view_article.html?article_id= (retrieved December 18, 2008).
9. See Joe R. Feagin, "Smearing Dr. Wright," http://www.racismreview.com/blog/ 2008/11/02/smearing-dr-wright-white-fear-and-republican-leaders-again (retrieved November 3, 2008).
10. *Matthew* 25: 29. See Robert K. Merton, *The Sociology of Science* (Chicago: University of Chicago Press, 1973), pp. 439–458.
11. Virginia Valian, *Why So Slow? The Advancement of Women* (Cambridge, MA: MIT Press, 1998), p. 4; see also pp. 3–5, 144.
12. R. F. Martell, D. Lane, and C. Emrich, "Male-Female Differences: A Computer Simulation," *American Psychologist* 51 (1996): 157–158. I draw on the summary in Valian, *Why So Slow*, p. 3.
13. See Feagin and O'Brien, *White Men on Race*; Ken Bolton and Joe Feagin, *Black in Blue: Black Police Officers in White Departments* (New York: Routledge, 2004); and Feagin and Sikes, *Living with Racism*.
14. Anne L. Schneider and Helen M. Ingram, *Policy Design for Democracy* (Manhattan: University Press of Kansas, 1997), p. 104. I am indebted here to suggestions from Maria Chávez.
15. See Samuel P. Huntington, "The Erosion of American National Interests," *Foreign Affairs* (September/October 1997): 28–29.
16. Susan González Baker and Frank Bean, "The Legalization Programs of the 1986 Immigration Reform and Control Act," in *In Defense of the Alien*, ed. Lydio F. Tomasi (New York: Center for Migration Studies, 1990), pp. 3–11; Susan González Baker, *The Cautious Welcome: The Legalization Programs of the Immigration Reform and Control Act* (Washington, DC: Urban Institute, 1990); Jose A. Pagan and Alberto Davila, "On-the-Job Training, Immigration Reform, and the True Wages of Native Male Workers," *Industrial Relations* 35 (January 1996): 45–58.
17. "5,100 Crosses at Mexico Border Mark Migrant Deaths," press release, Associated Press, October 30, 2009; "Major Provisions of 'The Secure Fence Act of 2006,'" Justice for Immigrants, Press Release, www.justiceforimmigrants.org/HR6061.html (retrieved October 22, 2006). On impact issues, see Rakesh Kochhar, "Latino Labor Report," research report, Pew Hispanic Center, Washington, DC, June 4, 2008; and Elizabeth

Chesler, "Notes: Denying Undocumented Immigrants Access to Medicaid: A Denial of Their Equal Protection Rights?" *Public Interest Law Journal* 17 (June 2008): 255–258.

18. Joe R. Feagin, *Racist America: Roots, Current Realities, and Future Reparations* (second edition; New York: Routledge, 2010), pp. 246–248; National Fair Housing Advocate, "Farmworkers Represented by CRLA and the County of Riverside Settle Major Fair Housing Case," http://www.fairhousing.com/news_archive/releases/crla5-23-00. html (retrieved March 1, 2001); Dan Rozek, "Elgin Denies Housing Bias against Hispanics," *Chicago Sun-Times*, October 3, 2000, p. 32; and "Center Calls for the Rejection of Anti-Immigrant Ordinances," Southern Poverty Law Center Report, September, 2006, p. 3.

19. Southern Poverty Law Center, *Under Siege: Life for Low-Income Latinos in the South* (Montgomery, AL: SPLC, 2009), p. 5.

20. Ibid., p. 4.

21. Feagin, *Racist America*, second edition, pp. 186–187. Bullard is quoted in Cynthia Gordy, "Troubled Waters," *Essence* (July 2007): 146–176. The data here are from this article.

22. Paul Mohai and Robin Saha, "Racial Inequality in the Distribution of Hazardous Waste: A National-Level Reassessment," *Social Problems* 54 (August 2007): 343–370.

23. Institute of Medicine, *Unequal Treatment: Confronting Racial and Ethnic Disparities in Health Care* (Washington, DC: National Academies Press, 2002); see also M. H. Chin, A. E. Walters, S. C. Cook, and E. S. Huang, "Interventions to Reduce Racial and Ethnic Disparities in Health Care," *Medical Care Research and Review* 64 (2007): 7S–28S; and Sheryl Gay Stolberg, "Race Gap Seen in Health Care of Equally Insured Patients," *New York Times*, March 21, 2002, p. A1.

24. "Racial Disparities in Medical Care," *New England Journal of Medicine* 344(19) (May 10, 2001): 1471–1473.

25. See Joe R. Feagin and Karyn McKinney, *The Many Costs of Racism* (Lanham, MD: Rowman & Littlefield, 2003); John Hoberman, *Black and Blue: The Origins and Consequences of Medical Racism* (Berkeley: University of California Press, 2012).

26. "Doctors' Different Perceptions on Racism in Health Care," *Race Relations Reporter*, June 15, 2002, p. 1. See also Feagin and McKinney, *The Many Costs of Racism*, passim.

27. Jo C. Phelan and Bruce G. Link, "Controlling Disease and Creating Disparities: A Fundamental Cause Perspective," *Journals of Gerontology* 60 (Series B., 2005): 29.

28. Michelle Alexander, *The New Jim Crow: Mass Incarceration in the Age of Colorblindness* (New York: New Press, 2010), pp. 110–111; and Joe R. Feagin, *White Party, White Government: Race, Class, and U.S. Politics* (New York: Routledge, 2012), pp. 100–117.

29. Alexander, *The New Jim Crow*, p. 49; and Naomi Murakawa, "The Origins of the Carceral Crisis: Racial Order as 'Law and Order' in Postwar American Politics," in *Race and American Political Development*, ed. Joseph Lowndes, Julie Novkov, and Dorian Warren (New York: Routledge, 2008), pp. 236–248.

30. Alexander, *The New Jim Crow*, pp. 49, 186; and Feagin, *White Party, White Government*, pp. 100–115.

31. Alexander, *The New Jim Crow*, pp. 53, 186; and Verna M. Weaver, "Frontlash: Race and the Development of Punitive Crime Policy," *Studies in American Political Development* 21 (Fall 2007): 242–243.

32. W. E. B. Du Bois, *The World and Africa* (New York: International Publishers, 1965 [1946]), p. 23.

33. Ibid., pp. 23–99; Robert J. C. Young, *Post-Colonialism* (Oxford: Oxford University Press, 2003); and John Willinsky, *Learning to Divide the World: Education at Empire's End* (Minneapolis: University of Minnesota Press, 1998).

34. Young, *Post-Colonialism*; and Willinsky, *Learning to Divide the World*.

35. See James Fulcher, *Capitalism: A Very Short Introduction* (Oxford: Oxford University Press, 2004), pp. 82–115; and Fareed Zakaria, *The Post-American World* (New York: W. W. Norton, 2008).

36. See Zakaria, *The Post-American World*.

37. Irene Diggs, "The Biological and Cultural Impact of Blacks on the United States," *Phylon* 41 (1980): 161.
38. William Henry III, *In Defense of Elitism* (New York: Doubleday, 1994). On the military-industrial complex and issues of colonialism, see Joe R. Feagin, Clairece B. Feagin, and David V. Baker, *Social Problems: A Critical Power-Conflict Perspective* (sixth edition: Upper Saddle River, NJ: Prentice-Hall, 2005), pp. 440–446 and passim.
39. See, for example, "World Conference Against Racism," http://en.wikipedia.org (retrieved June 11, 2008).
40. Harris Interactive and the Bradley Project, "E Pluribus Unum: A Study of Americans' Views on National Identity," May 13, 2008, http://www.bradleyproject.org/EPUReportFinal.pdf (retrieved November 3, 2008).
41. Zakaria, *The Post-American World*, p. 46. The data on the survey and on Western historians are on p. 34.
42. Feagin, Feagin, and Baker, *Social Problems*, pp. 459–499; Richard J. Barnet and John Cavanagh, *Global Dreams: Imperial Corporations and the New World Order* (New York: Touchstone, 1994), p. 138; Joe R. Feagin and Pinar Batur-Vanderlippe, "The Globalization of Racism and Antiracism: France, South Africa and the United States," University of Florida, unpublished manuscript, 1996; and Robert W. McChesney, "The New Global Media: It's a Small World of Big Conglomerates," *The Nation*, November 29, 1999, http://www.hartfordwp.com/archives/29/053.html (retrieved July 3, 2008).
43. Hsia-Chuan Hsia, "Imported Racism and Indigenous Biases: The Impacts of the U.S. Media on Taiwanese Images of African Americans," presented at Annual Meeting of American Sociological Association, August 1994, Los Angeles; and Nestor Rodriguez, personal communication, March 1996.
44. McChesney, "The New Global Media," n.p.

Chapter 8

1. John Locke, *Two Treatises of Government*, ed. Peter Laslett (Cambridge: Cambridge University Press, 1988), p. 170. Some scholars have argued with substantial evidence that some ideas on equality and justice of certain framers, especially Thomas Jefferson and Ben Franklin, were shaped by the thought of Native American societies.
2. See Scott L. Pratt, *Native Pragmatism: Rethinking the Roots of American Philosophy* (Bloomington: Indiana University Press, 2002); and "Pragmatism," http://en.wikipedia.org/wiki/Pragmatism#Central_pragmatist_tenets (retrieved June 20, 2008).
3. Quoted in Winthrop D. Jordan, *White Over Black: American Attitudes Toward the Negro, 1550–1812* (Chapel Hill: University of North Carolina Press, 1968), pp. 273–274. I use modern capitalization here.
4. "PBS Interview with James O. Horton," http://www.pbs.org/race/000_About/002_04background-02-04.htm (retrieved: December 19, 2003).
5. John Woolman, as quoted in *A House Divided: The Antebellum Slavery Debates in America, 1776–1865*, ed. Mason I. Lowance, Jr. (Princeton: Princeton University Press, 2003), http://press.princeton.edu/chapters/s7553.html (retrieved November 3, 2008).
6. Sterling Stuckey, *Slave Culture* (New York: Oxford University Press, 1987), pp. 25–45; and Bonnie L. Mitchell and Joe R. Feagin, "America's Racial-Ethnic Cultures: Opposition within a Mythical Melting Pot," in *Toward the Multicultural University*, ed. Benjamin Bowser, Terry Jones, and Gale Auletta-Young (Westport, CT: Praeger, 1995), pp. 65–86. I am indebted here to the scholarly comments of Louwanda Evans.
7. See, for instance, Nat Turner, http://en.wikipedia.org/wiki/Nat_Turner (retrieved June 6, 2008); Stuckey, *Slave Culture*, pp. 27–43; and Joe R. Feagin and Clairece B. Feagin, *Racial and Ethnic Relations* (Upper Saddle River, NJ: Prentice-Hall, 2008), pp. 197–198.
8. Feagin and Feagin, *Racial and Ethnic Relations*, pp. 197–199.
9. Quoted in Jordan, *White Over Black*, p. 111.

10. See Jessica McElrath, "David Walker," About.com, http://afroamhistory.about.com/od/davidwalker/a/bio_walker_d.htm (retrieved January 11, 2009).

11. David Walker, *Appeal to the Coloured Citizens of the World*, ed. Charles M. Wiltse (New York: Hill and Wang, 1965), pp. 7, 16, and 56.

12. Ibid., p. 75. His punctuation.

13. Thomas Tryon, *Advice to the Gentlemen Planters of the East and West Indies* (London, 1684), p. 115.

14. Henry Highland Garnet, "An Address to the Slaves of the United States of America," Buffalo, New York, Electronic Texts in American Studies, University of Nebraska, 2007 [1848]), Lincoln, NE, pp. 2, 4, 7, 9.

15. Martin R. Delany, *The Condition, Elevation, Emigration, and Destiny of the Colored People of the United States* (1852), no pagination (ebook).

16. Ibid.

17. W. E. B. Du Bois, *John Brown* (New York: International Publishers, 1962), pp. 263–264.

18. *John Washington's Civil War*, ed. Crandall Shifflett (Baton Rouge: Louisiana State University Press, 2008), p. 49. Some capitalization has been removed, and two words have been clarified.

19. Quoted in David W. Blight, *A Slave No More: Two Men Who Escaped to Freedom* (Orlando, FL: Harcourt, Inc, 2007), p. 257.

20. Quoted in *Bartlett's Familiar Quotations*, ed. Emily M. Beck (fifteenth edition; Boston, MA: Little, Brown, 1980), p. 556.

21. Frederick Douglass, "The United States Cannot Remain Half-Slave and Half-Free," in *Frederick Douglass: Selected Speeches and Writings*, ed. P. S. Foner and Y. Taylor (Chicago, IL: Lawrence Hall Books, 1999), pp. 657–658.

22. Anna Julia Cooper, *The Voice of Anna Julia Cooper*, ed. Charles Lemert and Esme Bhan (Lanham, MD: Rowman & Littlefield, 1998); and Ida B. Wells-Barnett, *A Red Record* (Chicago, IL: Donohue and Henneberry, 1895).

23. W. E. B. Du Bois, *The Souls of Black Folk* (New York: Bantam Books, 1989 [1903]), p. 3.

24. W. E. B. Du Bois, "The Future of Africa," *Advocate of Peace* 81 (January 1919): 12; Manning Marable, *W. E. B. Du Bois: Black Radical Democrat* (Boston: Twayne, 1986).

25. Oliver C. Cox, *Caste, Class, and Race* (Garden City, NY: Doubleday, 1948), pp. 332–333.

26. *Brown et al. v. Board of Education of Topeka et al.* 347 U.S. 491 (1954); and Nathan Newman, "Remembering the Popular Will for Civil Rights: Robert Caro's Master of the Senate," *Progressive Populist*, June 15, 2002, http://nathannewman.org/populist/06.15.02pop.html (retrieved September 9, 2003).

27. Richard Kluger, *Simple Justice: The History of* Brown v. Board of Education *and Black America's Struggle for Equality* (New York: Knopf, 1975), Vol. 2, p. 945.

28. Joe R. Feagin, "School Desegregation: A Political-Economic Perspective," in *School Desegregation: Past, Present, and Future*, ed. Walter Stephan and Joe R. Feagin (New York: Plenum Press, 1980), pp. 25, 29–35; W. E. B. Du Bois, "What is the Meaning of 'All Deliberate Speed'," in *W. E. B. Du Bois: A Reader*, ed. David L. Lewis (New York: Henry Holt, 1995), pp. 419, 422; and Philip A. Klinkner and Rogers M. Smith, *The Unsteady March: The Rise and Decline of Racial Equality in America* (Chicago, IL: University of Chicago Press, 1999), pp. 3–4.

29. Stokely Carmichael (Kwame Ture) and Charles V. Hamilton, *Black Power* (New York: Vintage, 1967).

30. See James M. Washington, ed., *A Testament of Hope: The Essential Writings and Speeches of Martin Luther King* (New York: HarperCollins, 1991), p. 314ff.

31. Coretta Scott King, ed., *The Words of Martin Luther King, Jr.* (New York: Newmarket Press, 1996), p. 52.

32. Lyndon B. Johnson, "To Fulfill These Rights" June 4, 1965, http://www.lbjlib.utexas.edu/johnson/archives.hom/speeches.hom/650604.asp (retrieved July 9, 2008). See also

George Lakoff, *Thinking Points: Communicating Our American Values and Vision* (New York: Farrar, Straus and Giroux, 2006), pp. 92–94.

33. Marimba Ani, *Yurugu: An African-Centered Critique of European Cultural Thought and Behavior* (Trenton, NJ: Africa World Press, 1994), pp 567, 570. See Molefi Kete Asante, *Afrocentricity* (Trenton, NJ: Africa World Press, 1988).

34. Louwanda Evans, "Facing Racism at 30,000 Feet: African American Pilots, Flight Attendants, and Emotional Labor," Ph.D. dissertation, Texas A&M University, College Station, Texas, 2012. Used by permission.

35. Ken Bolton and Joe Feagin, *Black in Blue: Black Police Officers in White Departments* (New York: Routledge, 2004), p. 94.

36. Ibid., p. 64.

37. Yanick St. Jean and Joe R. Feagin, *Double Burden: Black Women and Everyday Racism* (Armonk, NY: M. E. Sharpe, 1998), pp. 83–84.

38. Angela Davis, "Reflections on the Black Woman's Role in the Community of Slaves," *Black Scholar* 3 (December 1971): 2–15; Philomena Essed, *Understanding Everyday Racism* (Newbury Park, CA: Sage, 1991); Patricia Hill Collins, *Black Feminist Thought: Knowledge, Consciousness, and the Politics of Empowerment* (Boston, MA: Unwin Hyman, 1990); Elizabeth Higginbotham, *Too Much to Ask: Black Women in the Era of Integration* (University of North Carolina Press, 2001); and Yanick St. Jean and Joe R. Feagin, *Double Burden: Black Women and Everyday Racism* (New York: M. E. Sharpe, 1998). see note 47 for work of Adia Harvey Wingfield.

39. Jeremiah Wright, "National Press Club Address," April 28, 2008, http://www.americanrhetoric.com/speeches/jeremiahwrightntlpressclub.htm (retrieved November 7, 2008).

40. Jeremiah Wright, "Confusing God and Government," http://en.wikipedia.org/wiki/Jeremiah_Wright_controversy#cite_note-22 (retrieved January 29, 2009).

41. For detailed discussion, see Joe Feagin, "Dr. Wright is Still Right on Racism: Check the Research Data," http://www.racismreview.com/blog/2008/04/28/dr-wright-is-still-right-on-racism-check-the-research-data (retrieved November 9, 2008); and Adia Harvey Wingfield and Joe R. Feagin, *Yes We Can? White Racial Framing and the 2008 Presidential Campaign* (New York: Routledge, 2010).

42. On black commentators using white framing, see Joe R. Feagin, "Senator Obama's Critique of Black Fathers: Playing to the White Frame?" http://www.racismreview.com/blog/2008/06/15/senator-obamas-critique-of-black-fathersplaying-to-the-white-frame (retrieved November 9, 2008).

43. See Robert B. Hill, with Andrew Billingsley et al., *Research on the African American Family: A Holistic Perspective* (Westport, CT: Auburn House, 1993); and Yanick St. Jean and Joe R. Feagin, *Double Burden: Black Women and Everyday Racism* (New York: M. E. Sharpe, 1998). See note 47 for more of Adia Harvey Wingfield.

44. Feagin and Sikes, *Living with Racism*, pp. 311–318; and St. Jean and Feagin, *Double Burden: Black Women and Everyday Racism*, pp. 2–100. I am indebted to Sean Chaplin, Yanick St. Jean, and Adia Harvey Wingfield for scholarly comments here.

45. Debra Van Ausdale and Joe R. Feagin, *The First R: How Children Learn Race and Racism* (Lanham, MD: Rowman & Littlefield), pp. 190–196; Feagin and Sikes, *Living with Racism*, pp. 311–314; and St. Jean and Feagin, *Double Burden: Black Women and Everyday Racism*, passim. I am indebted here to scholarly comments by Brittany Slatton, Louwanda Evans, and Adia Harvey Wingfield.

46. William E. Sedlacek, *Beyond the Big Test* (San Francisco, California: Jossey-Bass, 2004), pp. 43–44; and Julie M. Hughes, Rebecca S. Bigler, and Sheri R. Levy, "Consequences of Learning About Historical Racism Among European American and African American Children," *Child Development* 78 (November/December 2007): 1689–1705.

47. Adia Harvey Wingfield, *Doing Business with Beauty: Black Women, Hair Salons, and the Racial Enclave Economy* (Lanham, MD: Rowman & Littlefield, 2008), pp. 83–84.

48. Ibid., p. 92.

49. Ibid., pp. 2–92.

50. Reuben A. B. May, *Talking at Trena's: Everyday Conversations at an African American Tavern* (New York: New York University Press, 2001), pp. 164.
51. Elijah Anderson, "The Cosmopolitan Canopy," *Annals of the American Academy of Political and Social Science* 595 (2004): 14–31.
52. Barack Obama, *The Audacity of Hope* (New York: Three Rivers Press, 2006), pp. 232–233.
53. For detailed discussion, see Wingfield and Feagin, *Yes We Can?*, Chapters 1–4.
54. I draw here on ibid., Chapter 8.
55. Feagin and Feagin, *Racial and Ethnic Relations*, pp. 143–152, 158–164.
56. Ibid.
57. Russell Means, "For America to Live, Europe Must Die!" Black Hills International Survival Gathering, Black Hills, South Dakota, July 1980, http://www.russellmeans.com (retrieved September 19, 2008).
58. Russell Means, "Free to be Responsible," Navajo Community College, Fall 1995, http://www.russellmeans.com (retrieved September 19, 2008).
59. White Plume, "An Open Letter to President George W. Bush," *Indian Country Today*, August 31, 2006, http://www.indiancountry.com/content.cfm?id=1096413572 (retrieved September 12, 2006).
60. Rosalind Chou and Joe R. Feagin, *The Myth of the Model Minority: Asian Americans Facing Racism* (Boulder, CO: Paradigm Books, 2008).
61. Roger Daniels, *Asian America: Chinese and Japanese in the United States Since 1850* (Seattle: University of Washington Press, 1988), p. 113; Min Zhou and James V. Gatewood, "Introduction: Revisiting Contemporary Asian America," in *Contemporary Asian America: A Multidisciplinary Reader*, ed. Min Zhou and James V. Gatewood (New York: New York University Press, 2000), pp. 27–35.
62. Helpful insights on Houston were provided by Nestor Rodriguez.
63. Rosalind S. Chou, *Asian American Sexual Politics: The Construction of Race, Gender, and Sexuality* (Lanham, MD: Rowman & Littlefield, 2012), pp. 143, 181; see also p. 58.
64. I am indebted in this section to comments from Hernán Vera, Nestor Rodriguez, and José Cobas. See José Cobas and Joe R. Feagin, "Latinos/as and the White Racial Frame," *Sociological Inquiry* 78 (February 2008): 39–53.
65. Brenda Gayle, ed., *Window on Freedom: Race, Civil Rights, and Foreign Affairs, 1945–1988* (Chapel Hill: University of North Carolina Press, 2007).
66. Anonymous Latino professional, communication, Spring 2008. Used by permission.
67. Maria Chávez, *Everyday Injustice: Latino Professionals and Racism* (Lanham, MD: Rowman & Littlefield, 2011), p. 43.
68. Marcelo M. Suárez-Orozco and Mariela M. Páez, eds., *Latinos: Remaking America* (Berkeley: University of California Press, 2002).
69. Nilanjana Dasgupta, Debbie E. McGhee, Anthony G. Greenwald, and Mahzarin R. Banaji, "Automatic Preference for White Americans: Eliminating the Familiarity Explanation," *Journal of Experimental Social Psychology* 36 (2000): 316–328; and Shankar Vedantam, "Many Americans Believe They are Not Prejudiced; Now a New Test Provides Powerful Evidence That a Majority of us Really Are," *Washington Post Magazine*, January 23, 2005, p. W12.
70. I am indebted here to scholarly discussions with Sean Chaplin and Adia Harvey Wingfield.
71. See Bob Blauner, *Racial Oppression in America* (New York: Harper and Row, 1972); Joe R. Feagin and Clairece Y. Feagin, *Discrimination American Style: Institutional Racism and Sexism* (Englewood Cliffs, NJ: Prentice-Hall, 1978); and Louis Knowles and Kenneth Prewitt, eds., *Institutional Racism in America* (Englewood Cliffs, NJ: Prentice-Hall, 1969).
72. For example, Derrick Bell, *Faces at the Bottom of the Well* (New York: Basic Books, 1992); Richard Delgado, *The Coming Race War?* (New York: New York University Press, 1996); Patricia J. Williams, *The Alchemy of Race and Rights* (Cambridge, MA: Harvard University Press, 1991).

73. Derrick Bell, "Property Rights in Whiteness—Their Legal Legacy, Their Economic Costs," in *Critical Race Theory: The Cutting Edge*, ed. Richard Delgado (Philadelphia: Temple University Press, 1995), p. 75.
74. Bell, *Faces at the Bottom of the Well*, p. 12. Italics omitted.

Chapter 9

1. See, for example, Richard Morin, "Misperceptions Cloud Whites' View of Blacks," *Washington Post*, July 11, 2001, p. A01; and Jon Cohen and Jennifer Agiesta, "3 in 10 Americans Admit to Race Bias," *Washington Post*, June 22, 2008, p. A01.
2. Thomas Kuhn, *The Structure of Scientific Revolutions* (Chicago: University of Chicago Press, 1962); Niles Eldredge and Stephen. J. Gould, "Punctuated Equilibria: An Alternative to Phyletic Gradualism," in T. J. M. Schopf, ed., *Models in Paleobiology* 238 (San Francisco: Freeman, Cooper and Company, 1972), pp. 82–115. I draw in part on summaries in Connie G. Gersick, "Revolutionary Change Theories: A Multilevel Exploration of the Punctuated Equilibrium Paradigm," *Academy of Management Review* 16 (1991), p. 13.
3. See Joe R. Feagin and Clairece B. Feagin, *Racial and Ethnic Relations* (Upper Saddle River, NJ: Prentice-Hall, 2008), pp. 363–365.
4. Patrick Buchanan, *State of Emergency: The Third World Invasion and Conquest of America* (New York: St. Martin's Griffin, 2007); and Samuel P. Huntington, "The Erosion of American National Interests," *Foreign Affairs* (September/October 1997): 28ff.
5. See John Locke, *Two Treatises of Government*, ed. Peter Laslett (Cambridge: Cambridge University Press, 1988), p. 170, "First Treatise," Chapter. 4, sec. 42.
6. United Nations, "Universal Declaration of Human Rights," in *The United Nations and Human Rights, 1945–1995* (New York: United Nations Department of Public Information, 1995), pp. 153–155.
7. United Nations, "International Convention on the Elimination of All Forms of Racial discrimination," in *The United Nations and Human Rights, 1945–1995* (New York: United Nations Department of Public Information, 1995), pp. 219–225.
8. Rasmussen Reports, "What They Told Us: Reviewing Last Week's Key Polls," http://www.rasmussenreports.com/public_content/lifestyle/general_lifestyle/82_say_u_s_is_best_place_to_live_41_say_u_s_lacks_liberty_and_justice_for_all (retrieved July 6, 2008).
9. Malcolm X, "Columbia University Speech," *Columbia Daily Spectator*, February 19, 1965, p. 3. I am influenced here by the summary at "Cosmopolitanism," http://en.wikipedia.org/wiki/Cosmopolitanism (retrieved November 4, 2008).
10. For a useful discussion of deframing M. L. J. Karskens et al., "Framing Conflict in Society," http://72.14.205.104/search?q=cache:WG1ZQ1LkLsUJ:www.nwo.nl/files.nsf/pages/NWOA_7GJHQ3/%24file/NWO%2520Framing%2520Conflict%2520in%2520 Society.pdf+deframing+lakoff+reframing&hl=en&ct=clnk&cd=2&gl=us&client= firefox-a (retrieved October 2, 2008).
11. Siri Carpenter, "Buried Prejudice: The Bigot in Your Brain," *Scientific American*, May 2008, http://www.sciam.com/article.cfm?id=buried-prejudice-the-bigot-in-your-brain (retrieved June 1, 2008).
12. Charles G. Lord, Mark R. Lepper, and Elizabeth Preston, "Considering the Opposite: A Corrective Strategy for Social Judgment," *Journal of Personality and Social Psychology* 47 (1984): 1231–1243.
13. Julie M. Hughes, Rebecca S. Bigler, and Sheri R. Levy, "Consequences of Learning About Historical Racism Among European American and African American Children," *Child Development* 78 (November/December 2007): 1689–1705. The quote is on p. 1695.
14. Ibid., pp. 1700–1701.
15. Ibid., p. 1693.

16. See Joe R. Feagin, *Systemic Racism: A Theory of Oppression* (New York: Routledge, 2006); and Leslie Houts Picca and Joe R. Feagin, *Two-Faced Racism: Whites in the Backstage and Frontstage* (New York: Routledge, 2007).
17. Picca and Feagin, *Two-Faced Racism*, p. 275.
18. See Drew Westen, *The Political Brain: The Role of Emotion in Deciding the Fate of the Nation* (New York: PublicAffairs, 2007).
19. Tiffany Hogan and Julie Netzer, "Knowing the Other," unpublished research paper, American Sociological Association, Miami Beach, Florida, 1993, as summarized in Joe R. Feagin, Hernan Vera, and Pinar Batur, *White Racism: The Basics* (second edition; New York: Routledge, 2001), pp. 231–233.
20. Leslie Houts Picca and Joe R. Feagin, "Experiences of Students of Color," University of Dayton, unpublished research, 2008.
21. Zygmunt Bauman, *Modernity and the Holocaust* (Ithaca, NY: Cornell University Press, 1989), p. 206.
22. Ibid., p. 207.
23. I am indebted to Lyn Clark Pegg and Margery Otto for information and insights on Duluth area efforts, including the mission statement, in Spring 2012 emails.
24. I draw on Spring 2012 emails and notes prepared by Herb Perkins and Bundy Trinz, and from insights on these groups from them, Margery Otto, and Tim Johnson.
25. I am indebted here to Herb Perkins, Bundy Trinz, Margery Otto, and Tim Johnson.
26. Jennifer Mueller, email communication, May 24, 2012. Used by permission.
27. Angela Davis, interview, PBS Frontline, http://www.pbs.org/wgbh/pages/frontline/shows/race/interviews/davis.html (retrieved July 30, 2012).
28. See countering strategies discussed at http://www.ouchthatstereotypehurts.com and at http://www.stirfryseminars.com.
29. Tim Craig and Michael D. Shear, "Allen Quip Provokes Outrage, Apology Name Insults Webb Volunteer," http://www.washingtonpost.com/wp-dyn/content/article/2006/08/14/AR2006081400589.html (retrieved October 6, 2008).
30. Drew Westen, *The Political Brain: The Role of Emotion in Deciding the Fate of the Nation* (New York: PublicAffairs, 2007), pp. 222–223.
31. Ibid., pp. 222–223.
32. Jennifer Harvey, *Whiteness and Morality* (New York: Palgrave Macmillan, 2007), pp. 148–160.
33. See Rebecca Saunders and Kamran Aghaie, "Introduction: Mourning and Memory," *Comparative Studies of South Asia, Africa and the Middle East* 25 (2005): 18. See also Christopher Lane, ed., *The Psychoanalysis of Race* (New York: Columbia University Press, 1998).
34. Saunders and Aghaie, "Introduction," p. 19. See Frantz Fanon, *Black Skin, White Masks*, trans. Charles Markmann (New York: Grove Press, 1967 [1952]).
35. Geoffrey L. Cohen, Julio Garcia, Nancy Apfel, and Allison Master, "Reducing the Racial Achievement Gap: A Social-Psychological Intervention," *Science* 313 (September 2006): 1307–1310.
36. James M. Washington, ed., *A Testament of Hope: The Essential Writings and Speeches of Martin Luther King* (New York: HarperCollins, 1991), p. 314. Italics added.
37. See "Education of the Heart: César E. Chávez in His Own Words," César Chávez Foundation, 1965.
38. Dedrick Muhammad, *Forty Years Later: The Unrealized American Dream* (Washington, DC: Institute for Policy Studies, 2008), pp. 5–6. More recent data are in Mazher Ali, Jeannette Huezo, Brian Miller, Wanjiku Mwangi, and Mike Prokosch, *State of the Dream 2011: Austerity for Whom?* (Boston: United for a Fair Economy, 2011).
39. On discrimination patterns, see Joe R. Feagin, *Racist America: Roots, Current Realities, and Future Reparations* (New York: Routledge, 2000); and Feagin, *Systemic Racism*. On redress issues, see Joe R. Feagin, "Documenting the Costs of Slavery, Segregation, and Contemporary Discrimination: Are Reparations in Order For African Americans?" *Harvard BlackLetter Law Journal*, 20 (2004): 49–80. On the failure of the legal system

to deal with systemic racism, see Wendy Moore, *Reproducing Racism* (Lanham, MD: Rowman & Littlefield, 2008).

40. Feagin, "Documenting The Costs of Slavery, Segregation, and Contemporary Discrimination," pp. 50–79.

41. Chinweizu Ibekwe, "Reparations and a New Global Order: A Comparative Overview," speech given to Second Plenary Session, Pan-African Conference on Reparations, Abuja, Nigeria, April 27, 1993.

42. Robert S. Browne, "Achieving Parity through Reparations," in *The Wealth of Races: The Present Value of Benefits from Past Injustices*, ed. Richard F. America (New York: Greenwood Press, 1990), p. 205.

43. See Thomas F. Pettigrew, "Racism and the Mental Health of White Americans: A Social Psychological View," in *Racism and Mental Health: Essays*, ed. Charles V. Willie, Bernard M. Kramer, and Bertram S. Brown (Pittsburgh: University of Pittsburgh Press, 1973), pp. 269–298.

44. W. E. B. Du Bois, "On the Ruling of Men," in *The Oxford W. E. B. Du Bois Reader*, ed. Eric J. Sundquist (New York: Oxford University Press, 1996), pp. 555–557.

45. See James J. Heckman and Bruce Payner, "The Impact of the Economy and the State on the Economies Status of Blacks: A Study of South Carolina," *American Economic Review* 79 (1989): 138–177; Stanley Greenberg, *Race and State in Capitalist Development* (New Haven: Yale University Press, 1980), pp. 231–233; and Gavin Wright, "The Economics of Civil rights," unpublished paper prepared for the Citadel Conference on the Civil Rights Movement in South Carolina, March 5–8, 2003, p. 5.

46. See Joe R. Feagin and Eileen O'Brien, *White Men on Race* (Boston: Beacon, 2003); and Leslie Houts Picca and Joe R. Feagin, *Two-Faced Racism: Whites in the Backstage and Frontstage* (New York: Routledge, 2007).

47. From a scholarly discussion with a professional of color, spring 2008. Used by permission.

48. Jennifer A. Richeson and J. Nicole Shelton, "When Prejudice Does Not Pay: Effects of Interracial Contact on Executive Function," *Psychological Science* 14 (May 2003): 287–290. The measure of racial bias was relatively unconscious, the Implicit Association Test (IAT).

49. The NORC survey is discussed in Tom W. Smith, "Measuring Inter-Racial Friendships: Experimental Comparisons," *GSS Methodological Report 91*, National Opinion Research Center, University of Chicago, (1999). On weak white contacts, see Feagin and O'Brien, *White Men on Race*; and Picca and Feagin, *Two-Faced Racism*.

50. Eszter Hargittai, "Whose Space: Differences Among Users and Non-Users of Social Network Sites," *Journal of Computer-Mediated Communication* 13 (2007), http://jcmc.indiana.edu/vol13/issue1/hargittai.html (retrieved November 6, 2008).

51. Harris Interactive and the Bradley Project, "E Pluribus Unum: A Study of Americans' Views on National Identity," research report, May 13, 2008.

52. Fareed Zakaria, *The Post-American World* (New York: W. W. Norton, 2008), p. 46.

53. See Barbara J. Flagg, "'Was Blind But Now I See': White Race Consciousness and the Requirement of Discriminatory Intent," *Michigan Law Review* 91 (1993): 953; and Moore, *Reproducing Racism*.

Index

moral order 40
moral stereotyping 52, 55–6, 62, 82–3, 94, 111
Morgan, Edmund 28
Morrison, Toni 99
Morton, Thomas 44
movies i, xii–xiii, 109, 111–12, 115, 129–30, 140, 159–60
Mr. Wong cartoon 112
Muhammad, Dedrick 219
multiframers 9, 20, 163, 195
multinational corporations 155
Murray, Charles 118
Myrdal, Gunnar 4
mythologizing 13, 17, 19, 34, 74, 96, 193, 205

naming processes 47–8
narratives: racial i, xi, 3, 10, 13–15, 17, 34, 91, 94, 97, 99, 122, 138, 140, 150, 209, 217–18; *see also* biographies
nation-states 7, 24–5, 29, 155–6; *see also* nationalism
National Association for the Advancement of Colored People (NAACP) 85, 174–5, 212
National Congress of American Indians 188
national identity 41, 97
National Negro Convention (1843) 171
National Review 112
nationalism 224; pan-African 174; white 94, 158
Native Americans x–xi, xiii, 26, 29, 34–5, 56, 68, 70, 77, 101, 130, 165, 193, 196; assimilation of 63; counter-frames 21, 188–; early framing of xii, 21, 41–5, 54–5, 57, 111, 113; exclusion of 34, 62; expulsion of 65; genocide 17, 19, 21, 24, 26, 64–5, 142; home-culture frames 188–9, 190–1; invisibility of 108; labor theft; land, seizure by colonists ix, xii, 19, 24–5, 27, 39, 65, 110, 190–1; paternalism towards 63–4; physical characteristics 64; positive framing of 59, 63–4, 190; reparations programs 220; resistance 59–60, 109–10, 188; rights 190; spirituality 191; stereotyping of 60, 64–5, 79, 108–9, 111, 116; Trail of Tears march 64; treaties with US government 190; wars against 27, 29, 60, 188
natural law 164
natural selection 82
Negroes' Character (Saffin), The 53
neo-colonialism 154–5

Netzer, Julie 209
New England 35, 51–4, 152, 165
New England Canaan (Morton) 44
New York Times 113
newspapers vii, 35, 54–5, 61, 66, 70, 74–5, 77, 79, 91, 104–5, 114, 159
Nicaragua 157
Nixon, Richard 144
nonverbal gestures 16, 91, 136–7
Northern elite 175
Northern racism 35, 80, 85
Notes on the State of Virginia (Jefferson) 62–3, 67, 133, 170

Obama, Barack 107, 190; election as president vii–viii, 21, 96, 145, 181–2, 187; racial identity 96–7, 102–3; understanding of anti-black discrimination 187–8; The Audacity of Hope 187
O'Donnell, Rosie 112
office holding 59
Oglala Lakota Nation 190
Omi, Michael 26
one drop of blood rule 48
O'Neill, Eugene 23
Ong, Walter 30
oppression, *see* anti-racist/oppression counter-frames; discrimination; segregation; slavery; systemic racism
oral cultures 30
ordinary whites: and slavery 23, 27, 36, 55; *see also* middle class; working class
Orientalism 6, 154
Othello (Shakespeare) 45
'other,' framing of the 39, 44–5, 57, 94, 107, 139

Pan-African Congress 174
parental influences 15–16, 91–2, 194, 196, 223; African American 128, 180, 184
Park, Robert E. 4
Parsons, Talcott 6
paternalism 59, 63–4, 75–6, 133, 158
patriarchy 14, 32, 40, 106
Pennsylvania 54, 67
Petersen, William 113
Petty, Sir William 50, 67
Pew Research Center 132–3
Philippines 80, 157
physical characteristics, *see* biological/physical characteristics
Picca, Leslie Houts 123
Plessy v. Ferguson (1896) 79, 84
policing 27, 104, 139, 150, 160, 184

THE SOCIAL ISSUES
COLLECTION™